A map of the first-century locations where Acts took place.

"René strips away 21 centuries of accumulated debris—myths and traditions and legends—for a fresh glimpse of the original Jesus movement that changed the world.

As he travels to the original locations in the Book of Acts, René discovers fresh insights through the latest expert research. He shows how Acts is the ultimate story of how unlikely people make a massive impact when they allow God to use them.

If the church ever needed to look like the one in the book of Acts, it's today—I'm thankful that René shows us the way. I highly recommend it."

CHIP INGRAM, Senior Pastor at Venture Christian Church and author of *The Real God: How He Longs for You to See Him*

"I LOVE this book. It's filled with awesome information, touches of humor, humanity, and hope. I've always wanted to go on a trip to Bible lands and René's book has given me an opportunity to go along for the ride."

KAREN O'CONNOR, author of *When God Answers Your Prayers: Inspiring Stories of How God Comes Through in the Nick of Time,*

"Once again René brings us right into a multi-dimensional view of the Bible. This book captures the adventure of the early church in such a way that it feels like you are stepping into the action yourself. I didn't want it to end! It made me not just appreciate the early church and their passion to let others know about Jesus, but it caused me to want to then continue that adventure of sharing about Jesus in today's world."

DAN KIMBALL, teaching and mission leader at Vintage Faith Church, and author of *They Like Jesus But Not The Church*

"What's the recipe for a book that reads like a sumptuous feast? Start with a good foundation—like the story uncovered in the New Testament book of Acts. Sprinkle in generous portions of Bill Bryson-like humor and Max Lucado-esque insights. Mix together and have it served up by Master Chef René Schlaepfer and you have a dish you will not be able to stop eating. I dare you to push away from this table!"

BILL BUTTERWORTH, speaker and author of *The Short List*

ACTS ODYSSEY

ON THE TRAIL OF THE APOSTLES

BY RENÉ SCHLAEPFER

"ACTS ODYSSEY: On the trail of the apostles"

© 2016 René Schlaepfer

ISBN 978-0-692-76991-1

1st printing: 2016

Unless otherwise indicated, Scripture quotations are from:
THE HOLY BIBLE, NEW INTERNATIONAL VERSION®, NIV®
Copyright © 1973, 1978, 1984, 2011 by Biblica, Inc.™
Used by permission. All rights reserved worldwide.

Scripture quotations marked NLT are taken from the *Holy Bible, New Living Translation*,
copyright © 1996, 2004, 2007 by Tyndale House Foundation. Used by permission of
Tyndale House Publishers, Inc., Carol Stream, Illinois 60188. All rights reserved.

Scripture quotations marked ESV are from *The Holy Bible, English Standard Version®*
(ESV®), copyright © 2001 by Crossway, a publishing ministry of Good News Publishers.
Used by permission. All rights reserved.

Scripture quotations marked NET are from the NET Bible® copyright ©1996–2016 by
Biblical Studies Press, L.L.C. http://netbible.com Quoted by permission. All rights reserved.

Unless otherwise indicated, all photographs are by Jamie Rom or René Schlaepfer.

Printed locally with vegetable-based inks at Community Printers, Santa Cruz, California, USA.

If you would like to reproduce or distribute any part of this publication, please contact:

Twin Lakes Church, 2701 Cabrillo College Drive, Aptos, CA 95003–3103, USA
or email info@tlc.org

CONTENTS

8. GROUP DISCUSSION RESOURCES

PART ONE

THE PROMISE & THE POWER

ACTS ODYSSEY

1
DETOUR

I look up at the ceiling. Dusty spider webs wave lazily in the breeze. The rusty blades of an ancient fan turn slowly. Someone at a manual typewriter clicks and clacks... one... letter... at... a time.

The detective jabbing the keys is interrogating me, asking the same questions he asked an hour ago. And an hour before that.

And I ask him the same questions I've been asking. Because I can't get any answers. "Can I call my wife? How long will I be here?"

He shrugs his shoulders. Relights his cigarette. And gets back to typing. Click. Clack.

Not the experience most tourists get to enjoy here in Greece.

How did I wind up detained indefinitely at an Athens police station, with no money, no passport, and no wallet, when I've done nothing wrong?

It all started with one little idea a few years earlier. I've always loved the Book of Acts in the Bible. So why not retrace the story by traveling through its original locations?

Seemed like such a good idea at the time.

Acts is a travel epic, like the *Lord of the Rings* or *Homer's Odyssey*. It breathlessly recounts the wild journeys of the very first generation of Jesus followers, from Jerusalem to Rome, on Imperial highways and Aegean sailboats. They encountered sorcerers and serpents and assassins and I experienced some surprises too, as I retraced their steps.

3

Acts is also an origin story. How did Christianity go from a few dozen men and women in Jerusalem to a world changing force in only about 30 years, and then go on to become the largest religion the world has ever seen? Acts is the astonishing story of the eruption of this brand-new faith.

And it's an inspirational story. If you love dramatic epics of the little guy surviving doubts, daunting odds, and determined enemies to win big, you'll love Acts. And if you're attracted to the idea of a loving, Jesus-following community — but often frustrated with what church has become — a study of Acts will give you the fresh enthusiasm for what a group of believers can be!

There's so much to recommend Acts that I've always wondered why many Christians skip from the gospels right to the epistles when between those books is this amazing, suspenseful story.

So an idea took shape: "Why not travel through the same country-side, and over the same seas, as the apostles did in Acts?" I asked myself. "As I go, I'll interview experts, learn the latest historical discoveries." And so I did.

It took me seven trips over several years, but I finally reached nearly every major location in Acts. I hope to describe the discoveries I made in a way that conveys my own delight — and sometimes downright shock.

CRAZY TRIP
Including this, maybe the biggest shock of all. After weeks of travel through Israel, Turkey, and Greece tracing Paul's footsteps, I'm finally in Athens.

What a trip. Along the way my traveling group and I observed a riot from our hotel window. We slipped into ancient ruins closed to the public. I stumbled onto a nest of snakes. You'll read all about those adventures in these pages.

And now I'm feeling a sense of relief. The most difficult part of the journey is over.

Or so I think. I put down my backpack and ask my teenage son David to take my picture at Mars Hill, the famous rocky outcrop near the Athens Acropolis where Paul preached in Acts 17.

And the instant we look away, someone swoops in and grabs my bag from between David's feet. I'd noticed a shifty-looking guy eyeing us earlier, and suddenly he was gone, and so was my pack. In it: my passport, my money, and the trip diary, *including all my notes for the book you're reading right now.*

Instantly I go into hyper-search mode with my son and run all around the Acropolis at top speed looking for our suspect. A man who works there sees my frantic hunt, asks, "What's wrong?" and when I tell him, he joins our pursuit.

We see the culprit walking up from a ravine, and I shout, "That's him!" The man helping me races ahead, grabs the suspect by the collar, and, to my surprise, starts slugging him in the mouth after every word as he yells, "Where? Is? This? Guy's? Bag?"

The thief (an Algerian ex-con drug dealer, I was later to discover) shrugs his shoulders and the Greek man shouts to me, "They usually throw the stuff they steal down this ravine to their partners. Let's go!" He commands my son, "Watch him!" And as 15-year-old David uneasily guards this bloodied ex-con, my new friend and I leap over a fence down into the wooded gully below the Acropolis.

So now I'm in the middle of what's starting to feel like a spy movie. I'm jumping over fences in a foreign capital, people are getting punched out, Jason Bourne drops out of the trees and incapacitates someone with a pencil. Well, that last part's not true. But at the moment? Would not have surprised me.

We sprint down a spooky trail and find, at the bottom of the canyon — my pack! The contents are dumped everywhere, but I recover almost everything, except my wallet and passport.

We trudge back up the hill. By now five or six police officers are there handcuffing the suspect. And I think it's all over — when suddenly a cop grabs me, and pushes both of us into the back of a squad car. He explains through gestures and broken English, "You... punch... him." I quickly correct, "Wait, I didn't slug him, it was..." and I look around for my avenging friend—who has disappeared. It's like those old stories about the vanishing rapture-predicting angel. Only apparently I had a fugitive-punching angel.

Off we speed to who knows where! All they'd heard was "Disturbance at the Acropolis," and it seems they're going to sort it all out back at the station.

Which, as I said, it's like something out of a film noir movie set. Those slow ceiling fans turning. Hard-bitten detectives smoking. Not a soul speaks English. My phone won't work, so I can't even tell my wife where I am.

I'm wondering: what happens now? How do I get out of here? Will I ever finish my project? How do I continue my travels if I don't have a passport?

Back to my Athens adventure a little later in this book. But what I experienced there, a little trouble with the authorities, detention, inconvenience, changed travel plans, was like a small taste of the constant adventure facing the apostles in this very part of the world in Acts.

But the hero of the book is not any of the apostles. It's the Holy Spirit, powerfully helping them through each obstacle.

And it can happen again. Acts is not just an *origin* story. It's a *continuing* story. Of how God works through you no matter what inconveniences or obstacles you face. It's not just about what happened "once upon a time." It's about what can happen "again in this time."

TRAVELING THE BIBLE

Here's the format of this book. Before each chapter you'll see the reference from the part of Acts I'm exploring. I encourage you to read those passages first.

DETOUR

You can also go online to watch the videos we filmed on location at WWW.TLC.ORG/ACTS. At the end of this book you'll find discussion questions for each video designed to tie into your personal or group study.

This book is divided into 49 short chapters, so if you read one a day, you can finish in seven weeks.

My goal? To get you to read through Acts like you'd read a novel. All the way through. It's much easier to understand Acts if you read it *as a book,* experiencing all its drama and power.

But sometimes it is hard to understand. That's why I describe many fascinating facts I unearthed in these exotic places during my travels. As I discovered, modern archaeology is revealing more every day about the world the Bible writers lived in.

THE MYSTERY OF ACTS

And while you're reading, here's a mission for you. Try to find clues that will help you puzzle out the reason Luke even wrote this book. No one knows for sure. It's an ancient mystery. But there are clues. So read Acts like a detective. What motifs do you see recurring? What arguments are being supported? I'll let you know what I think, later.

Now let's go on a journey.

> PRAYER FOR THE JOURNEY: Lord, as I prepare to go on a trip through Acts, prepare my heart. Change me. May the bold faith of the first disciples become mine.

TRAVEL IN THE ROMAN WORLD

Acts is a book of travel. So I wondered, what exactly did first-century travel look like? I got answers from an expert. We toured Turkey with Tulu Gökkadar, a Turkish graduate student in Classical Archaeology. Her specialty: travel in the first-century Roman world. Tulu even presented a paper all about it at the annual meeting of European Archaeologists in September 2014. She filled me in on details researchers are only now learning. If you imagine Roman travel as crude and primitive, you're way off the mark. In many ways travel wouldn't reach this level of sophistication again until the twentieth century.

Here's just one example. When not traveling by foot, the disciples could have rented stagecoaches, very much like covered wagons of the American West. The wagon rentals came with a driver, an animal team, and often a guide.

There were several types. The uncomfortable but affordable open-air *rheda* had seats for up to six people on open-air benches, plus room for luggage. The *carruca* was sort of a luxury *rheda*, enclosed like a stagecoach, often with space to rest (sleeping carriages were called *dormitoriae*). The *essedum* was a two-seater convertible built for speed, much like a chariot. Wagons could cover 50 miles a day, though 25 was average. In the heat of summer, Romans often preferred to travel at night.[1]

Romans universally complained about wagons. The thundering, squealing noise of their metal-rimmed wooden wheels grinding against the pavement was nerve-wracking. The sound of the Roman Empire was not a calm, quiet, murmur punctuated only by tweeting birds and rustling leaves. The grating shriek of iron on stone was everywhere. In an early example of a well-intentioned law having unintended consequences, Rome banned wagons from city limits during the workday because of the noise. So the wagon drivers worked all night instead. Roman poetry is filled with entertaining rants against the resulting cacophony.

Roman tomb decoration depicting travel to the afterlife in a stagecoach. This is a rare representation of the kinds of covered wagons available for rent in the first century AD. (Photo credit: Peter Robert Binter, 2005)

2
VIRAL

It's a few months before I start my first trip to the land of Acts. Many thousands of miles away from the Mediterranean world of the Bible, I'm face down in the dust of Chennai, India, as I crawl over a narrow ledge and into the Cave of Saint Thomas. The relative cool of the dark cavern is the first place I've found to escape the oppressive Indian heat.

According to local tradition, this is where the disciple Thomas was killed by a mob after preaching the gospel. I lay down on the floor of the cave, imagining the crowd calling for his death.

Wait, you're thinking. Thomas? In India?

A lot of very smart people think so. The local Christians have always taught it was Thomas who brought the gospel here. Trading ships traveled from the Roman Empire to India in the first century. And I'll share more intriguing clues pointing to Thomas' Indian presence later in this book.

One thing's for sure. Within about a generation after Christ, the young Jesus movement traveled to India — and nearly every other part of the known world. How did it go from a few frightened followers huddled together in an upper room in Jerusalem to a fearless, international, barrier-busting phenomenon?

As I ponder what happened in that cave, what turned Thomas from doubter to world-changer, the excitement I'm feeling for my first trip to the Mediterranean builds. He went from a man who shrank from any assertion that Christ was alive, a man of pragmatic reserve, to a man of fearless courage. He helped change the world. Could it happen again? To me? Could my heart get excited by investigating the story he and the other disciples lived out, in the places they lived them?

Little Mount in Chennai, Tamil Nadu, India, where the Apostle Thomas is said to have hidden from his persecutors. (Photo credit: Mega Rajan, 2006)

BACK TO THE BEGINNING

A few months later I peer out the window of an El Al 747, holding my breath as the coast of Israel slides into view and we begin our descent into Tel Aviv. I see ruins dotting the modern landscape. This is where it all began.

In the first-century Roman world, Judea, the land of the Jews, had crucial strategic importance. If Romans wanted access to Africa or Arabia, they needed to pass right through this narrow strip of hospitable land between the sea and the desert. The Empire survived on grain imported from the fertile Nile Delta in Egypt. So they exercised tight control over this area.

But to the Jews there was another reason this land was important. The Temple. Every year millions of Jews from around the world made pilgrimages to Jerusalem for one of the Temple feasts, then returned to their far-flung homes.

As Acts opens we're reminded that at the last major Jewish feast, Passover, Jesus was killed. And now, fifty days later, the next major holiday, Pentecost, is about to begin.

POWER TO GO ON

At this point almost every follower of Jesus has drifted away. Looks like his movement has been snuffed out. It's over. Extinguished by the authorities.

But little do those authorities know the risen Jesus has been spending time with this small band of believers for forty days. And then, just before he ascends to heaven, Jesus gives them a purpose and a promise that serve as fuel for a historic rocket launch.

The purpose: *You will be my witnesses.* (Acts 1:8)

Now think about the "you" in that sentence. Imagine the people he is saying this to. Peter. Mary Magdalene. John. Thomas. And the other surviving scruffy disciples. As Max Lucado puts it, "*You* hillbillies will be my witnesses. *You* uneducated simple folks will be my witnesses. *You* temperamental, parochial net casters and tax collectors. *You* will be my witnesses. You will spearhead a movement that will explode like a just-opened fire hydrant out of Jerusalem and spill into the ends of the earth…"[2]

And here's the point. If he used them, he can use you. No matter how small or unqualified you feel.

Also notice that Jesus doesn't say, "You will be my defense attorneys." He doesn't say "You will be my prosecutors." Or "You will be my judges," You don't have to defend God. You don't have to judge for God. You don't have to prosecute others for him. All God wants you to do is be a *witness*.

What's a witness? Simple. Someone who tells what they have seen. That's your mission. Be honest about what you see happening in your life. What God's doing. Be willing to share it winsomely and openly. When you and I do that, it spreads. Our stories are repeated. All across the world.

THE CHAIN OF WITNESSES

When our son Jonathan was four, I read him this verse and he responded with delight. "So Jesus told them, and they told some other people, and those people told other people, and that person told someone else, and that person told you, and now you are telling me. And now I get to tell other people, and it all goes all the way back to Jesus!"

I laughed and said, "You have it exactly right."

It's the greatest privilege you're ever given, to be part of a movement that goes all the way back to this commission from Christ.

If you feel you're too simple, too underqualified, have too much of a past and too little of a future to be used by God, think of these first few followers. God used them then. And he uses the same kind of regular folks today.

How? With the purpose comes the power. Look at the first half of Acts 1:8: "You will receive *power* when the *Holy Spirit* comes upon you…"

WHO IS THE HOLY SPIRIT?

What kind of power is this? That's important to clarify. The Holy Spirit is not an *it*. The Holy Spirit is not a *force*. The Holy Spirit is a *person*, the third person of the Trinity: God the Father, God the Son, and God the Holy Spirit. The Holy Spirit is not impersonal power, like electricity. He is personal, like a bodyguard or coach or guide.

Sometimes people call the Holy Spirit "The Comforter." That word goes back to one of the very first English translations of the Bible by John Wycliffe in the 14th century. But in Wycliffe's time, the word "comforter" had a different meaning than now. It comes from the Latin *fortis*, which means *brave*. The Comforter is the one who *fortifies*, who fills people with courage!

Jesus promises this power to his disciples. Including *you*. *You* will be *fortified* to do whatever God wants you to do.

How do you get this power? There's no formula for that in the pages of Acts. Remember, the Holy Spirit is a person. And you don't need a formula for a personal relationship. You hang out. Like the disciples did. Get to know your friend. Luke says they stayed and prayed.

> They all met together continually for prayer, along with Mary the mother of Jesus, several other women, and the brothers of Jesus. (Acts 1:14)

Prayer opens your life to the Spirit's influence. See, if you're a believer, God's Spirit is already inside you; the Bible says once you believe, you too are "sealed with the Holy Spirit" (Ephesians 1:13). Then you make daily choices to stay under his influence. Focused. Surrendered.

PERSONAL POWER

On my trip to India I met a man named Satish. Raised in the part of India associated with Thomas, he became a believer in Jesus after years of protesting that he would never convert. I asked him, "What made the switch turn on for you?"

He instantly responded, "Simple. Someone explained the Holy Spirit. The idea that there was only one God, who gives us his Spirit personally to guide and empower us, was something new and irresistible for me. I was raised believing the gods and lesser spirits were unreliable and impersonal. To think that God wants not to trick me but personally empower me — what a difference!"

Satish is now a Christian pastor in India. He even holds outreach meetings in the same region Thomas visited nearly 2,000 years ago.

VIRAL

Because he knows. The call of Christ was not just for those original disciples. The call is for him. And for you and me too.

> PRAYER FOR THE JOURNEY: *Heavenly Father, thank you that despite my past and despite my failings, you choose me to be your witness. Not your judge. Nor your prosecutor. Your witness. I need to be spiritually fortified for that today. Fill me with your Spirit, Lord. Amen.*

WHO WAS LUKE?

Although he's never actually mentioned by name, from the very earliest days of Christianity, Luke was thought to be the writer of Acts.

Luke is only mentioned by name in three Bible verses: Colossians 4:14, Philemon 24, and 2 Timothy 4:11. But from these verses we learn a lot:

- Luke was a medical doctor

The two books attributed to Luke have a lot of medical terminology. For example, when Luke describes Jesus' saying about a camel going through the eye of a needle, he doesn't use the normal word for needle Matthew and Mark employ. Instead he uses a Greek word for a surgeon's needle.

First-century Roman medical instruments found in Pompeii.
(Photo credit: Giorgio Sommer, 1914)

- Luke was a Gentile. Colossians 4:11 includes a list of greetings from believers who are "of the circumcision," that is, Jews. Verse 12 begins a new list, this time apparently Gentiles or non-Jews. Luke's name is in this second list.

- Luke was one of Paul's best friends and assistants.

- Luke is the only Gentile author of a book of the Bible.

This fourteenth-century painting of Luke by Italian artist Simone Martini was stolen by Nazis during World War II and hidden in the salt mines of Altaussee. It was recovered by the famous "Monuments Men" Allied task force on May 8, 1945. (Photo credit: Google Cultural Institute).

3
THE GEOGRAPHY OF FAITH

ACTS 1:8-26

I'm finally here. I arrive in Jerusalem in the late afternoon and look at the landscape of the Old City in the golden glow of twilight. Silhouetted steeples, minarets, and domes rise above crenellated medieval walls. More modern high-rises stab the sky around the ancient settlement. But beyond the city limits, there are no vast fields or ports or lakes. Only rugged wilderness.

And I realize how isolated this strange city is.

Jerusalem has never been on a major trade route. It's not on a harbor or river. The fertile fields of Israel lie in valleys to the north. Near Jerusalem there's only desert and the lifeless waters of the Dead Sea.

So how did this city become so cherished that when ancient maps were designed, Jerusalem was sometimes portrayed as the very center of the world?

One word: Faith.

About a thousand years before Christ, Solomon built the first temple here. It was destroyed and rebuilt before King Herod completed a spectacular renovation during the life of Christ. That became a major center of religious pilgrimage before the Romans destroyed it in 70 AD but the remnants of the Temple, like the Western Wall, remain a focal point for Jews. Starting in the early 300s, followers of the newly legal Christian religion established their own sites of pilgrimage here. Some of their churches, like the Holy Sepulcher,

THE GEOGRAPHY OF FAITH

still remain. In the late 600s, Muslims built the Dome of the Rock on the Temple Mount itself.

Now millions of Jewish, Christian, and Muslim pilgrims pour into Jerusalem each year to see these holy sites. On my first trip here I visited when Orthodox Easter and the Jewish holiday of Purim occurred in the same week. Happy people from all over the world jammed this city, ready to celebrate. Very much like first-century Jerusalem.

Jews then made annual journeys to the Temple Mount, especially on the feasts surrounding Passover and Pentecost. The direction of their pilgrimages, from the ends of the earth toward the Holy City, represented the direction of their faith. Their hopes were centered on Jerusalem. The Messiah would enter its very gates to rule here. He would gather Jews to the Holy City as Israel's glory was reestablished.

Then Jesus turns the geography of their faith upside-down.

"...and you will be my witnesses in Jerusalem, and in all Judea and Samaria, and to the ends of the earth." (Acts 1:8) He's telling his disciples they're *starting* here. And moving outward. Jerusalem is the launching pad. The rocket's going to Rome and beyond. They are facing the temple. He's telling them to face the other direction. To reach out, not in. He's changing them from pilgrims to missionaries.

Our natural posture is to face toward comfort and familiarity. If people are lost, they can find us! But Jesus is saying, you go find them.

THE NEW GEOGRAPHY OF FAITH
He tells them about four places to go:

Jerusalem. The center of the Jewish world.

Judea. The Roman province Jerusalem was a part of. Then it gets harder.

Samaria. The province next door, where sentiment against Jews ran high. There was bad blood, literally. In Jesus' lifetime, Samaritan terrorists broke into the Jewish Temple and desecrated it with pig blood. And then Jewish zealots attacked the Samaritan temple and spilled Samaritan blood. Hard to believe those first Jewish Christians were going to be able to spread the message there.

And as if that's not challenging enough, Jesus has a last sweeping phrase: *the ends of the earth.* From its very first days, the Jesus movement has had this daring, international, crossing-borders flavor. But pagans controlled the ends of the earth. These were frontiers filled with cultural and racial and religious barriers. How could the message go there? The Book of Acts tells the thrilling story.

And this is still the geography for spreading your faith:

My Jerusalem: Your home, the place you feel most centered and comfortable. You start by practicing the gospel here.

My Judea: The places most connected to your center. Your work, your gym, your hobbies. The people here see you a lot. So they notice how Jesus is changing your life.

My Samaria: These are the places close to home where you feel a little out of place. God wants you to reach out there too. He loves these people. And there are blessings there for you too.

The ends of the earth: These days many of us have the chance to literally go on mission trips and serve in far-flung areas. Certainly everyone can support a missionary, through prayer or encouragement or finances.

But this commission must have sounded absolutely incredible to that small band of believers. Most of them poor. Frightened. With no budget. No buildings. No proven leadership. No experienced international travelers. How in the *world* were they going to *reach* the world?

THE GEOGRAPHY OF FAITH

STARTING SMALL

And did you notice? Verse 15 says that in those days the believers numbered only about 120 men and women. That's all! That has to be one of the most encouraging verses in the Bible. *Just 120.* The total population of Judea was about four million, so this means less than one in 30,000 was a Jesus-follower.[3] Probably none of them had ever been very far from home. They were recent failures. Not well educated. Hunted by the authorities. If anything ever started small, Christianity did!

You may feel outnumbered as a believer. Maybe you're the only Christian at work, at home, or at school (My guess is that the ratio is still better than one in 30,000). But just like the first disciples, *you* are the small beginning from which God will do something amazing.

That's how God always works. All through the Bible. An infertile couple births two nations. A stuttering retiree leads slaves to freedom. A shepherd boy conquers a warrior giant. A baby born in a farm's feeding trough saves the world. And here? A clutch of anxious has-beens turns history upside down.

Maybe you're thinking, *But I don't have the ability to be some clever witness for Christ. I stumble over my words, I lack confidence...* What happens next can change the way you think about yourself — and all your obstacles — forever.

> PRAYER FOR THE JOURNEY: *Heavenly Father, help me remember that no matter how outnumbered or insignificant I may feel, you can continue transforming the world through me.*

The Temple Mount of Jerusalem, where the early believers gathered
daily according to Acts 2:46.

THE HIGHWAY SYSTEM

The most amazing accomplishment of Roman engineers was their 53,000 miles of well paved roads. These roads were incredibly sophisticated, with at least three layers of substructure and complex water runoff systems. And they were built to last. About 100 miles southwest of Rome, a 21-arch Roman-era bridge still supports the weight of modern traffic.

Much like freeway signs, mile markers (*miliaria*) detailed the distances to nearby towns and mentioned interesting sights too. They were six feet high and placed every five thousand paces all over the Empire. Romans loved them. The orator Quintilian gushed,

> It is a pleasure to measure the weary way one has come, and to know how far one has to go makes one travel more courageously...[4]

Near cities there were shaded sidewalks and even what we would call fast food service restaurants with hot stew and soup in heated pots. One ancient writer claimed the average pedestrian traveled 18 miles a day when on these comfortable roads.[5]

But not all was rosy. Like today, "Traffic accidents were the source of endless litigation."[6] While there were no speed limits, since speed was not easily measured, drivers were legally liable for pedestrian injuries, even of slaves, and required to "maintain a moderate speed."[7] One problem: there was no agreement on left or right side driving, leading to unnerving high-speed games of chicken on country roads.

Many miles of Roman road survive to this day, like this section near Corinth.

4
BABEL REVERSED

ACTS 2:1-13

This is a surprise. Jerusalem's mayor shut down the city today. No one's allowed in or out. The risks are too great. Not because of war or terrorism. But because of *snow*.

For the first time in my life, I actually did not overpack. In fact, I'm wishing I had some winter gear with me here on the edge of the Judean desert. On our second morning in Jerusalem, my wife and I wake up in our room near the Old City, stroll over to the window, and see — a blizzard. Winds blow fiercely. Snow carpets everything in sight. The city is paralyzed. There are no vehicles in sight except a handful of bulldozers clearing roads.

We go downstairs to ask the staff for tips on surviving the storm. But they tell us no one is going anywhere, because all traffic has completely stopped. Other hotel guests filter into the lobby, travelers from North America, Europe, the Middle East, Africa, Asia, milling aimlessly. Someone strolls over to the piano in the bar. An impromptu group sing-along starts. Requests pour in from the international castaways. "How Great Thou Art." "Let it Snow." "Amazing Grace." "Little Surfer Girl" (from the Californians). The frustration of cancelled tours and meetings actually dissolves into laughter.

Suddenly, international brotherhood descends on a group meeting in an upper room as a strong wind blows through Jerusalem. Where have I heard this before?

EARTH, WIND AND FIRE

In Acts 2, the Holy Spirit descends on the believers meeting in a Jerusalem room like a sudden storm, manifesting to their senses as something that sounds like a strong wind and looks like flames of fire.

What's this all about? As with much in the Book of Acts, Luke doesn't stop to explain. He just reports. He seems to be saying, don't overthink it. This all happened at such a breathless pace that the original disciples couldn't overanalyze it either. So don't discover complicated doctrine here. Just picture yourself in the moment. Don't tame it. Don't domesticate it. Let the power of it capture your imagination.

In fact, I believe God used these signs precisely because wind and fire are wild, untamable forces. Perhaps he is saying, in effect, "I am launching this, and I'm directing this. It is not a result of your strategy or strength. This is going to spread just like wildfire directed by the wind." We don't control the Holy Spirit. The wind blows where it blows. We just need to put up our sails and be ready to go with it.

And the earth is reached through the wind and the fire. The disciples start speaking in other languages from all over the globe, their speech recognized by the international crowd there for the feast of Pentecost.

This miracle foreshadows the rest of the book. The gospel will spread from here like a flame fanned by wind, to the farthest reaches of the earth.

When Luke describes the crowd, he specifically mentions people from places we would call Turkey, Rome, Egypt, Libya, Iraq, Iran, Saudi Arabia, and the Greek islands. In other words, this is a preview of all the places the disciples will reach in the years ahead. They're all here. Ideas sown in this moment will ride home with these pilgrims like seeds stuck to their clothes, landing back home and sprouting into little Christian communities ready for the later arrival of the apostles.

BABEL REVERSED

Since the very earliest days of Christianity, commentators have seen this miracle as a dramatic reversal of the curse of the tower of Babel. In Genesis 11 it says that originally all humans were able to communicate through one language and tried to build a tower to reach heaven. But God confused their language and scattered them across the world.

Thousands of years later, for a moment, in a little trailer for coming attractions, Babel is reversed.

At Babel, God made the one language into many, confusing the nations. Here he's sending one message — to reach all nations — into many languages.

Once the nations tried to build a tower to God, and here God builds a bridge to the nations.

He has made his way to all people. Even you. No matter how far away you may think you are.

MIRACLE OR MAYHEM?

As the people hear all this, some look at the disciples and think they're drunk. For whatever reason, they're not hearing the miracle. They're hearing nonsense. Others listen and realize, "They're speaking my language!"

Just like today. Some will see the enthusiasm of Spirit-filled believers and after a cursory glance assume they're out of their minds. While others listen a little longer and recognize the message is for them. If people don't always respond well to your sincere attempts to describe what Jesus means to you, remember, it's always been that way, even when the means of the message is a miracle.

Yes, some turn away. Yet thousands are baptized.

One question. Where could they have found water, here in the middle of a desert city, to baptize three thousand people at once? Ruins uncovered after the 1967 Six-Day War revealed a possible answer, as you'll see next.

> *PRAYER FOR THE JOURNEY: Help me see that your kingdom was meant to cross every boundary from the very start. I pray that this same exciting sense of forward motion would be a part of our family and our church today!*

Thirteenth-century painter Duccio di Buoninsegna was one of the first Western painters to try to capture the very moment the disciples received the Holy Spirit at Pentecost. (Photo credit: The Yorck Project, 2002)

THE ENDS OF THE EARTH

Christianity traveled far and fast from Jerusalem along Roman trade routes. Some of the distant spots touched by Christian travelers:

BRITAIN

The earliest surviving written record of Christianity here describes Christians arriving from Rome during the reign of Tiberius in the first century.

SPAIN AND FRANCE

Paul wrote about his desire to visit Spain, probably because he heard through Roman travelers of Christians already there. St. Irenaeus, a Roman transplant to Lyon, France, writing in 180 AD, described long-established groups of Christians among the Celts in France and Iberians in Spain.

AFRICA

The ancient historian Nicephorus dates Christianity in Ethiopia to the first century. It was probably started by Jewish Christians. One confirming clue: The Ethiopian Orthodox liturgy still contains many words in Aramaic, the language spoken by Jesus and the first apostles.

INDIA

The beach-fringed, lush region of India known as Kerala was part of the spice route visited by Roman merchant ships. The Christians of Kerala have historically traced their origins to Thomas, who they believe visited in 52 AD. The traditional liturgy of these churches is in Syriac, a dialect of Aramaic. Many families there have genealogies tracing all the way back to Thomas and first-century Romans.[8]

The nearly 1700-year-old Church of Our Lady Mary of Zion in Axum,
Ethiopia. The Christians here date the arrival of their faith to the
Roman era. (Public domain photo)

5
STEP INTO LIQUID

ACTS 2:14-41

I walk up the southern steps of the Temple Mount in Jerusalem. This is what many call the birthplace of the church. The launching pad of the international Jesus movement. Right here. This spot. In the time of the Book of Acts, two thousand years ago, these very steps led up to the Temple where the Jewish people worshiped God.

Hidden by centuries of haphazard development and rubble, this wide stairway was uncovered during ten years of excavation that began in 1968, about a year after the Six-Day War.

One of the lead archaeologists, Meir Ben-Dov, later brought the first man to walk on the moon, astronaut Neil Armstrong, to visit. Armstrong, a devout Christian, asked him if these were the very steps Jesus ascended on his trips to the Temple. When told they were, Armstrong said, "I am more excited stepping on these stones than I was walking on the moon!"

I'm pretty thrilled myself. Because I'm probably at the very site of the baptisms in Acts 2.

INTERNATIONAL PREVIEW

Let's do some detective work: Luke says all the followers of Christ were "together in one place." A lot of people read that quickly and assume this was the same place as in Acts 1, where they were gathered in an upper room on the Mount of Olives.

But Luke doesn't say they were in the *upper room*. He just says they were all in *one place*. Later he specifies the Christians were in the habit of meeting at "Solomon's Porch," one of the huge colonnaded

31

arcades on the Temple Mount. That's why I think, when Luke calls this place a "house," he doesn't mean a private home. He means the house of God.

Remember what happened? The crowd there for the feast heard the disciples speaking in their own languages. That's a crowd of thousands. They *couldn't* have been in one small house. If they were all there for the feast, these pilgrims would have been up on the Temple Mount.

And here's the clincher: Luke says that same day three thousand new believers are baptized. Where do you find enough water, in this desert climate, to baptize three thousand people?

Only one place.

During excavations here, archaeologists uncovered many ceremonial *mikvahs*, shallow wading pools pilgrims walked through to cleanse their feet as they approached the Temple.

Since hundreds of thousands of pilgrims visited Jerusalem on those feast days, an extensive layout of mikvahs had to be ready for them. Water from underground springs and massive reservoirs fed these pools. They would have been the obvious choice — and really, the only choice — for a massive baptism service.

And the mikvahs were right here, at the base of the steps. It's *here* that the first three thousand converts stepped into ceremonial water and emerged as disciples of Christ.

But three thousand? Why so many at once? Because of an amazing message they hear from Peter as he preaches the first sermon, after Christ, in church history.

IN A NUTSHELL

After one of the best, most attention-getting openers in public speaking history (Flames! Wind! Multiple languages!) Peter gets up and gives a short, TED-length speech to the crowd.

He lays out the basics of the Christian message. This probably gives a peek into what Jesus has been teaching the apostles during those forty days with them after the resurrection.

Peter talks about *two events* (the crucifixion and resurrection).

As attested by *two witnesses* (the prophets and apostles).

Who talked about *two promises* (forgiveness and the Spirit).

On *two conditions* (repent and believe).

I like that because it's a reminder not to amputate the message.

Don't preach the cross without the resurrection.

Don't preach the New Testament and leave out the Old.

Don't preach forgiveness for the past and not mention the Spirit's power to live now.

Don't preach belief without a call to turn from destructive behavior.[9]

And then — not only are three thousand people baptized, but they are *changed*. Into something amazing and beautiful. Luke describes that next.

> PRAYER FOR THE JOURNEY: *Lord, help me see myself as not just a saved individual, but as part of a movement that infiltrates every corner of the world with God's love and good news.*

A sudden snowstorm blanketed Jerusalem and closed all roads into the city on our first morning there.

SAILING THE BIBLICAL SEAS

As the Book of Acts was being written, Roman merchant ships were already establishing trade routes as far east as India and China. First-century Roman ships have been discovered in muddy harbors and ocean floors across the ancient world.

These vessels could reach gigantic proportions. One ancient sailor describes the maiden voyage of a ship 420 feet long and 72 feet high. "During a trial run it took aboard over 4,000 oarsmen and 400 other crewmen, and on deck 2,850 marines."[10] Most ships were smaller, but it was not uncommon for vessels to carry hundreds of passengers and crew.[11]

Ships are a key part of the Acts narrative. And they surely bore passengers with the message of the gospel to the far corners of the world, right after the first Pentecost sermon, as pilgrims to Jerusalem returned home.

Carving in the RG Museum Koeln showing the detail of the rudder of a Roman boat from the first century AD. (Public domain photo)

6
IT CAN HAPPEN AGAIN
ACTS 2:42-47

It's Sunday, a day after the sudden Jerusalem snowstorm, and roads have cleared enough for us to attend church. We ask for some suggestions and someone directs us to a congregation in a local shopping mall. To my absolute surprise, a couple greets me in the lobby with the delighted shouts of old friends. Only I've never seen them before.

They recognize me from watching videos of our church services on line. I want to be clear. We're not some famous church. We're just a local congregation in a small town, thousands of miles from Jerusalem. Yet this couple ask all about recent events in our congregation that I've mentioned in sermons. We sit together for worship. Pretty cool. Here we are, total strangers, yet we're together worshipping with the common ground of Christ and even a shared church vocabulary. There's an instant bond.

As the service starts we quickly pick up the flavor of this congregation. It's large (about two thousand people are packed in), enthusiastic, and very international. One of the pastors explains they're mostly Messianic Jews, Jewish people who follow Jesus. He identifies various groups of visitors. There are people here from the States, Europe, and Africa on that day. And such a sense of camaraderie.

The Bible describes heaven as having the same international flavor ("People from every tribe, nation, and language") and the delighted recognition of old friends we never met before. ("There's Abraham! There's Isaac!")

IT CAN HAPPEN AGAIN

And here in Acts 2 there's a preview. You've already seen how international the Jesus movement is from the very start, with pilgrims from across the world hearing the good news in their own languages. Then amazing fellowship flowers. Look at the way it's described. Doesn't this sound great? Ray Stedman summarized these verses like this:

It's a *learning* church. They devoted themselves to the apostles' teaching.

It's a *loving* church. They had fellowship every day, they shared everything, they gave to those in need.

It's a *worshipping* church. They devoted themselves to breaking bread (probably a reference to communion) and prayer and praising God.

It's a *joyful* church. It says they did all this with glad and sincere hearts, a phrase that can be translated "unaffected joy."

And it was a *growing* church. Luke says the Lord added to their number daily.

You just get this sense it was a really fun place to be. The people here were intellectually curious and humanitarian and hospitable and deeply devout and generous and welcoming, all at the same time — and people just wanted to hang out with them. More joined them every day. That's what a community of faith is meant to be. *This is our DNA. What we were meant to be.* It happened then; it can all happen again.

Here's an idea for action. Commit yourself, during the course of your study of Acts, to contribute to those five characteristics. Learn. Love. Worship. Rejoice. Grow.

Notice that here you see a thread that winds all through Acts: The generosity of early believers to the poor. Later in Acts you read about Tabitha providing for the destitute, Paul bringing aid to famine victims, the Jerusalem church helping its widows, and more. It's a Christian tradition more relevant now than ever. In the world today one billion people are hungry. Ten million Africans die each year from preventable diseases.[12] In our own communities children need food and clothes. Let's joyfully immerse ourselves in our identity as the community of Christ and reach out as Jesus enables us.

I think it's because the early Christians were immersed in this environment that they had confidence God would do absolutely amazing things. Like the amazing thing that happens next.

> PRAYER FOR THE JOURNEY: *Lord, do this again. May our church be a learning, loving, worshipping, joyful, growing church. And let all those qualities begin in me.*

Ruins of ritual *mikvahs* or ceremonial baths from the time of Acts at the ancient steps leading to the temple. Many scholars believe the baptisms in Acts 2 took place here.

WHAT EARLY CHRISTIANS WERE LIKE

A very ancient document known as the Epistle to Diognetus (c. AD 120–200) is believed to have been written by a man named Athenagoras. In one important section he describes Christians:

> The difference between Christians and the rest of mankind is not a matter of nationality, or language, or customs. Christians do not live in separate cities of their own, speak any special dialect, nor practice any eccentric way of life. …They pass their lives in whatever township—Greek or foreign… and conform to ordinary local usage in their clothing, diet, and other habits.
>
> Nevertheless, the organization of their community does exhibit some features that are remarkable, and even surprising. For instance, though they are residents at home in their own countries, their behavior there is more like transients. …[T]heir citizenship is above in the heavens. They obey the prescribed laws, but in their own private lives they transcend the laws.
>
> They show love to all men—and all men persecute them. They are misunderstood, and condemned; yet by suffering death they are quickened into life. They are poor, yet making many rich; lacking all things, yet having all things in abundance…. They repay [curses] with blessings, and abuse with courtesy. For the good they do, they suffer stripes as evildoers.[13]

Mosaic of Perpetua, a 22-year-old noblewoman who was executed for her Christian faith in 203 AD. Depictions of early Christians reveal people of every social class. (Public domain photo)

7
RISE UP

ACTS 3:1-10

The snow has melted and the city is springing back to life. As I walk into the Joppa Gate of the Old City of Jerusalem, vendors selling fresh bread and children peddling postcards shout their prices. I'm dismayed that I must look so obviously American. I like to imagine that, like a trained spy, I can blend into any culture seamlessly. Apparently not. Because I'm hearing, "One dollar, Yankee! One dollar!"

Then I hear a weaker voice. "One dollar?" I look across the sidewalk and see a woman dressed in rags holding out a cupped hand. No one stops or even looks in her direction. Not much has changed since Bible times. I think I dropped a little spare change into her open palm but what I remember most is leaving uncomfortably, wondering what more I could do.

It's a scene that's been repeated here for centuries. But on at least one occasion two followers of Jesus did what we all long to do: Make a permanent difference.

The man begging near the Beautiful Gate in Acts 3 had to be carried here every day, where every day he begs. He's probably just part of the scenery for most people, wallpaper, something they don't even notice. When Peter and John walk up, he asks for help, just like he does hundreds of times every day. But this time something surprising happens.

THEY SAW

Luke brings out a phrase he uses in the Gospel of Luke to describe a habit of Jesus Christ. It's a phrase he'll use again and again in Acts: "looked intently." It means something like a lingering stare. A deep, thoughtful look, past the eyes, right into the soul.

He says Peter and John "looked intently" at the man begging. They stopped and really saw him. Thousands of people passed him every day and glanced in his direction, but never really noticed. Peter and John are *seeing* him, really perceiving him as a human being in need of Jesus. By using a term he associated earlier with Jesus, Luke is reporting that one characteristic of Jesus and his closest followers is that they really *looked* at people, gave them their full attention.

I know someone who served for a brief time as a missionary in India and once met Mother Teresa. He told me, "The most memorable thing about her was that she really looked intently at you, as if you were the only person in the room."

I don't know about you, but I need to learn to do this. My eyes tend to dart nervously around the room when I'm talking to people, always wondering if there's something in my environment I'm missing. But the kind of intent gaze Peter and John have here shows a relaxed confidence, a steady, unhurried belief that God may have something for them to receive or give in each moment.

Do you really *look at* the people around you? How many times do you perceive people as irritants or sinners or beggars or useful resources or court jesters or stereotypes — without really *seeing* them? As Jesus' agent in the world, can you do what Peter and John did for the people around you? Really notice? The man in Acts was crippled. But some people around you are crippled by insecurity. Or fear. Or addictions. They are beaten up by life. Sick. Tired. Overwhelmed. And no one *sees*. Can you encourage them, "In the name of Jesus Christ, rise up"?

THEY SPOKE

After they look intently at him, another phrase Luke introduces will also echo through the rest of the book: Peter doesn't just say, "Stand up and walk!" He says, "In the name of Jesus Christ the Nazarene, rise up and walk!" Notice that it's the power of *Jesus'* name that counts here and everywhere they'll go. They're not about their own resources or cleverness or power. Or their own reputation or influence or brand. It's all about *Jesus.*

You and I aren't dependent on our own resources or cleverness either. And we are not here to market ourselves as the owners of great spiritual insight for the world. Aren't you glad? It's all about "the name of Jesus." That isn't some magical phrase to repeat, like "abracadabra." It means you recognize you only have any power or authority because of what Jesus did and who Jesus is.

The rest of the Book of Acts carries this theme forward. Focus on Jesus, and stuff happens. Amazing stuff. Miraculous stuff. And dangerous stuff. It's not what the first followers teach about morality or about love that gets them into trouble. It's the name of Jesus.

Specifically, it's this name that's about to get Peter and John arrested. Suddenly the whole future of this beautiful movement seems in jeopardy.

But I pray that what happened to that man will happen to you as you read this book: That you'll be swept off your feet — or rather, *onto* your feet, as in his case! Are you discouraged, wounded, paralyzed by fear? *Rise up and walk.*

> PRAYER FOR THE JOURNEY: *Lord God, help me to have this kind of impact on hurting people around me. May I see them, really look at them, and say, "In the name of Jesus, rise up!"*

The diverse group that characterized the early Christians from Acts 2 onward is captured in this fourteenth-century painting by Tomasso Masolino da Panicale in Brancacci Chapel, Florence, Italy, of Peter's speech in Acts 2. (Public domain photo)

PART TWO

NEW FRIENDS
& NEW ENEMIES

8
ESSENTIAL INGREDIENTS
ACTS 3:11-26

My adventures in Jerusalem are slowed down constantly by one Israeli temptation I cannot seem to resist. The food! I love the sesame seed sprinkled bread, the Israeli salads with cucumber and tomato, the potato latkes, and the rugelach.

Then there's the national Jewish fast food, the menu item that serves the same role in the Jerusalem food eco-system as hamburger or pizza in the States. The fabulous falafel. You can get one fast and hot on almost every street corner. It looks like a meatball sandwich served on pita bread, but it's not a meatball. It's made of chickpeas (or garbanzo beans).

But then there's my absolute favorite thing, the one item that seems to taste twice as good in Israel as anywhere else, my obsession, my love. Hummus. That amazing sauce. That wonderful dip. I could bathe in it. Swim in it. Shampoo my hair with it. I think I've made my point!

If you're not in Israel and you want to create some hummus, there are just five ingredients. Only five. Yet these very basic food items, ancient ingredients known to people in this region since prehistoric times, combine perfectly to create a bowl of food ecstasy: garbanzo beans, olive oil, tahini (ground sesame seeds), lemon, and garlic.

One observation. I enjoyed hummus from my very first day in Israel, but it was only after someone explained to me these five simple ingredients that I was able to appreciate the subtleties in each new serving I enjoyed. It was like being educated at a wine tasting (Note to self: Consider starting new hummus tasting tours of Israel). After I learned how to *make* hummus, I could really *taste* the tahini, the lemon, the garlic, in differing quantities. I began to notice the quality of the olive oil and beans.

Okay, having left my writing to enjoy some hummus, I will now continue.

Here's my point. There's a hummus factor to the speeches in the Book of Acts. Yes. If you just read them with no orientation, they're interesting. But they all contain five basic ingredients that combine very cleverly in ways that only really unfold for you if you know what to look for.

I can see the confusion on your face, so allow me to demonstrate. Look at Peter's speech here in Acts 3. It has a lot of content in a few words. But learn to appreciate and recognize the five ingredients he uses — ingredients that all the speakers in Acts combine in their own way to produce speeches cooked up for their specific audiences — and you'll enjoy it so much more.

IT'S ALL ABOUT JESUS

Peter deflects all glory, turning people's attention to Christ. When Peter's describing these events, remember, he's talking about something he witnessed. And each speaker in Acts will make his description of Jesus very personal. How *they* met him. How *they* are experiencing the risen Christ — even at that moment.

IT'S WHERE HISTORY IS POINTING

Each speaker in Acts talks about the prophecies in the Hebrew Scriptures (the Old Testament). Sometimes they even quote *pagan* writers. The point? This is not something new. It's something for which God has been prepping the world for centuries, and now it's coming true! The Scriptures are a single story pointing toward something great God is going to do one day. And that day is here. And you can be part of it.

IT'S A PERSONAL INVITATION

Peter invites his audience to "repent," meaning a change of direction, a change of thinking. Repentance is another theme in Acts. When you hear the word "repent" you might think of a half-crazy street preacher carrying a sign about the end of the world. It can sound so aggressive, so judgmental. But have you ever considered what a *gift* the invitation to repent is? "Repent" doesn't mean God hates you. "Repent" means God loves you and believes your life can be so much more than it is right now. "Repent" is a word of hope and possibility. And it's a word all through the speeches in Acts.

IT'S MEANT FOR ALL PEOPLE

Again and again this theme appears in Acts. This is not just something for the people of Israel. "In your seed *all the families of the earth will be blessed*," Peter says. (Acts 3:25)

Peter's quoting a promise made to Abraham, the very earliest of the biblical patriarchs. He's saying that the radical, barrier-busting, international flavor of the Jesus movement, which was so different from the isolationist, Jerusalem-focused culture of much of first-century Judaism, was the whole point of God's covenant—from the very beginning.

His point: The Jesus movement is simply recovering a flavor God had in the recipe the whole time. The disciples believed this from the very start, even though they had no idea how much God would blow their minds in the way he was about to accomplish this.

IT'S THE BEGINNING OF
THE GREAT RESTORATION

God will bring a time of "restoration of all things." No more tears. No more death. No more injustice. It brings so much hope when you look ahead to that day.

All the religious Jews of Peter's day believed this ultimate promise. One day the Messiah will restore the nation of Israel. There will be peace and justice.

ESSENTIAL INGREDIENTS

But don't miss verse 19. Here's the new twist the Christ-followers are bringing to the recipe. That day can be anticipated by "times of refreshing from the Lord" *right now!* When I repent and turn to Jesus, my sins are forgiven and he refreshes my soul in a way that gives me a little "taste sample" of how God will make all things new. The resurrection will not only happen one day. In a way, it has already started, beginning with Jesus. It's not just that God *will* do something fresh and new. God *is doing* something fresh and new *right now*.

All the speeches in Acts have this exciting sense of possibility! Look back over those five ingredients (not of the hummus; of the Acts speeches). This is not a list of demands. Not a negative, retreating, reactive message. It's a positive, proactive, exciting proclamation that God is at work, and inviting others to join in! Ask God to help you cast this kind of positive vision about your faith when you talk about it.

Sounds exciting to me. But not everyone loves this new recipe. Peter and John are about to stare down the biggest VIPs in their society as the pressure on them grows more intense.

> PRAYER FOR THE JOURNEY: *Lord, I marvel that today, this day, I get to be part of what you predicted in the past and what you will fulfill in the future. Help me see myself as part of your amazing movement!*

9
THE BONE BOX

ACTS 4:1-31

I'm at the Israel Museum in Jerusalem staring at an ancient terra cotta box. I may never be closer than I am this day to the physical remains of someone from Acts.

In 1990 workers in Jerusalem were digging trenches for a new park when suddenly the ground gave way. The ceiling of an ancient, forgotten burial chamber collapsed beneath them, revealing a room that had been hidden for two thousand years.

Construction skidded to a halt. The emergency office of the Israeli Antiquities Authority was called. Staff archaeologist Zvi Greenhut rushed to the scene. Lowering himself by rope through the collapsed ceiling, Zvi directed the beam of his flashlight around the chamber and quickly realized he was in an untouched tomb from the time of Jesus, filled with ossuaries (ceramic boxes containing the bones of the dead).

Light from his flashlight fell across an exceptionally well-decorated ossuary. Like the rest, this one was about 15 inches deep and 30 inches wide. But the decorations covering this box were strikingly beautiful, indicating it belonged to a very important family. Zvi realized this was the one to take back to his laboratory.

When the box was examined it was found to contain the nearly two thousand-year-old bones of two babies, two teenagers, a woman, and a man of about 60 years of age. Who were these people? Bone boxes were often shared, bearing the remains of an entire family.

But whose family was this? An inscription on the box identified the adult male as "Joseph son of Caiaphas."

That's the ossuary I'm looking at now in the Israel Museum. After many tests, Zvi Greenhut and others identified the remains of the 60-year-old man in the bone box as the same Caiaphas mentioned in the Bible, the man who presided over the trials of Jesus, Peter, and John![1] The ossuary strengthens the case for the historical reliability of the Bible by confirming the existence of one of its central characters.

I have goose bumps and I'm only facing his bone box. Peter had to face Caiaphas *alive*.

FACING CAIAPHAS

The first-century historian Josephus says this man's full name was "Joseph who was called Caiaphas of the high priesthood."[2] He describes Caiaphas, and all the high priests of his family, as "heartless when they sit in judgment," a description that fits with what we know of him from the Bible.

Josephus is an interesting first-century source because he was a Jew who was very critical of the Jewish leadership at this time. He points out that the family of Annas (which includes Caiaphas) had a stranglehold on the priesthood for decades. During that time all the high priests, who were the de facto leaders of the country, came from this one family.

That's power. Think about it. Since they controlled the Temple, they had massive economic, political, and social clout. They even had their own police force. It was more like a mafia family than a religious family.

And this is the power Peter and John come up against in today's passage. The *capo di capo*. The head man. The Chairman of the Board.

But Peter and John are not intimidated in the least.

The members of Caiaphas' family were probably accustomed to people quaking in fear when called to trial. But these two are so courageous that they're amazed. This is reflected in one of my favorite verses:

> When they saw the courage of Peter and John and realized that they were unschooled, ordinary men, they were astonished and they took note that these men had been with Jesus. (Acts 4:13)

THE JESUS EFFECT

There's something about spending time with the resurrected Jesus that changes you. It gives you confidence that can make you almost unnerving. So the temple leaders command Peter and John to stop speaking in this name of "Jesus." Even today, there are plenty of people just fine with Christians helping the poor and healing the sick. It's the *Jesus* part they wish we'd cut out.

But Peter's reply is classic. It's the foundation for the Christian relationship to government authority from here on out. He asks, "Which is right in God's eyes—to listen to you, or to God? You be the judges! As for us, we cannot help speaking about what we have seen and heard." (Acts 4:19–20)

DO YOU LISTEN TO HIM OR "THEM"?

In every culture, on every playground, in every workplace, there are the inner circle who determine what's cool and what's not cool. What to say and what not to say. What to think and what not to think. But sometimes, their word about what's acceptable and unacceptable is different than God's word.

When it comes down to it, on those issues where you have to make a choice, who do you listen to? Him? Or "them?"

A suggestion: When you feel the pressure, pray the prayer at the end of Acts 4: "Now, Lord, consider their threats and enable your servants to speak your word with great boldness. Stretch out your hand to heal and perform signs and wonders through the name of your holy servant Jesus." (Acts 4:29–30)

BACK IN THE BOX

Whatever happened to Caiaphas? He enjoyed an unusually close relationship with the Roman rulers of the region, doing all he could to quell signs of revolt. He controlled the Temple from 18 to 36 AD. Soon after Pontius Pilate was removed from office in 36 AD, the new Roman governor forced Caiaphas to resign too. But his sons continued to operate as members of the high priesthood, allowing Caiaphas to operate from the shadows, pulling all the strings for many more years.

What about all his wealth, all his power, all his influence? As I stare at his ossuary I remember a line from a John Ortberg book. Every summer when he was a child John and his family played intense rounds of Monopoly. He loved to amass money and real estate and power. But in the end, as his grandmother pointed out, "It all goes back in the box."[3]

Caiaphas was the big winner on the Jerusalem game board. But it all went back in the box. This box.

And what happened to the Jesus he so opposed? Well, *his* tomb is empty. And his disciples turned the world upside down.

When you see a person of political or social power today, be respectful. But remember: One day it all goes back in the box. Don't be intimidated. Instead, ask yourself what you are doing to store up treasure, not in some earthly box, but in heaven — where it lasts forever.

> PRAYER FOR THE JOURNEY: *Lord, give me confidence. I pray the prayer of those early Jesus-followers: Enable me, your servant, to speak with boldness. Stretch out your hand to do great things here in the name of Jesus.*

العصر الهيرودي / عصر الهيكل الثاني
ميلادية

The ossuary of Caiaphas in the Israel Museum, Jerusalem.
(Photo credit: Deror Avi, 2012)

WHAT WERE THEY SO AFRAID OF?

Why were some of the first-century Jewish leaders of Jerusalem and their Roman governors so sensitive to the apostles preaching *in Jesus' name?* Probably pride of position had a little to do with it. But from their perspective, they were also just trying to keep the peace. Messiah-fever was gripping the population. People were expecting a political revolutionary. They were trying to stop the crazies from igniting a war.

Josephus, writing after the destruction of the Temple in 70 AD, says the spark that ignited the furious anti-Gentile violence in Jerusalem which led in turn to the Roman war against the Jews was this very idea of a political Messiah.

> But what more than all else incited them to the war was an ambiguous oracle also found in their sacred writings, that at about that time one from their country would become ruler of the habitable world. This they took to mean one of their own people, and many of the wise men were misled in their interpretation.[4]

So the elite, both Jewish and Roman, were trying to smother this revolutionary fervor sweeping the country. But Luke shows in the Book of Acts how the Jesus movement was distinct from every other Messianic group at the time because it was never violent, even when faced with violence.

10
COLONY OF LOVE

ACTS 4:32-37

As I walk into the lobby of the American Colony hotel here in Jerusalem I feel like I'm entering a shrine. I'd heard of this place since I was a teen. But many of the tourists who stay here are unaware of the terrible and triumphant story that unfolded within these walls.

As I wander down the hallways I'm captivated by the large old photographs detailing the history of the small band of believers that lived here. The "American Colony" began as kind of a Christian commune in the late 1800s, started by an American named Horatio Spafford who had an incredible backstory.

In 1871, Spafford was a successful Chicago businessman, a respected leader in the abolitionist movement, and a devout Christian. Then the Great Fire broke out and destroyed all his investment properties.

Two years later the family decided to vacation with friends in Europe. At the last minute Horatio was delayed by business, so his wife Anna and their four daughters went ahead. On November 21, 1873, a British ship rammed their ocean liner and it sank. Anna was picked up unconscious on floating wreckage and taken to the coast of Wales, where she was given the news that all her girls had drowned.

After receiving Anna's grief-soaked telegram, Horatio immediately boarded a ship to join her in Great Britain. While crossing the Atlantic, the ship's captain informed him when they passed over the exact spot his daughters had perished. Horatio returned to his room, took a sheet of Chicago hotel stationery that he happened to have packed, and as he wept he scratched out the lyrics to a hymn still sung today:

When peace like a river, attendeth my way,
When sorrows like sea billows roll
Whatever my lot, thou hast taught me to say
It is well, it is well, with my soul

It is well
With my soul
It is well, it is well with my soul

Though Satan should buffet, though trials should come,
Let this blest assurance control,
That Christ has regarded my helpless estate,
And hath shed His own blood for my soul[5]

The family tragedies continued. A son, Horatio Junior, born after the tragedy, died at age four. Seeking some consolation from God after all this sorrow, the Spaffords set out for Jerusalem with friends, rented a house there, and decided that since they'd lost so much already, they might as well try to live as closely to Luke's description of the early church as they could. They held all property in common and devoted themselves to Bible study and good works.

Their philanthropy earned them a very good reputation, and a nickname, "American Colony." They housed and fed refugees from Yemen, along with many others, during their early years. They also became critical of what they called the "malfeasance" of the American consul in Jerusalem. These charges were eventually proven true, and President Theodore Roosevelt changed the U.S. representatives there based on the Colony's observations.

The little Christian community grew, and moved into a large house outside the city walls, where they became nearly self-sufficient, with their own dairy, bakery, butchery, blacksmith shop, and hostel for foreign visitors. Their photographers became world-famous for their pictures of Israel, eventually contributing to early *National Geographic* magazines. The children of the colony spoke fluent Arabic and grew up to become key members of the foreign diplomatic corps, facilitating massive relief efforts during World War I. Eventually they took charge of six Jerusalem hospitals, opened an embroidery business that employed 300 women whose husbands had perished in the war, and a soup kitchen that fed over 1,000 people a day. As the director of their food outreach said, "We make no distinction in nationality or creed, the only requirement being if they absolutely need the help. We have Syrians and Arabs... Latins and Greeks, Armenians, Russians, Jews, and Protestants."[6]

In many ways the story of the American Colony mirrors the story of the very first group of Christians here.

SNAPSHOT OF SELFLESSNESS
The description of the early Jesus movement in Acts 4:32–37 is the kind of community every one of us would love to be part of: There's no one in need, because everyone pitches in to help.

This is the aspect of the early church that usually captures our imagination. We can see it as almost unattainable today, some past Eden-like innocence at the very dawn of the church age. But in reality, this can — and does — still happen today. I think we just don't notice it. As we share our goods through church offerings and garage sales and thrift shops, needs are met all over our communities. May the Book of Acts inspire us to do even more.

IMAGINE ASTONISHMENT
Imagine the excitement of the movement at this point. Believers must have known there was something new and fresh and powerful happening here. Consider the deepening dimensions of friendship and prayer and teaching they see unfolding all around them, the sheer joy of helping the needy in their midst.

The early Jesus followers believed *the kingdom of heaven was at hand*. That's a poetic way of saying, God is going to restore earth to heavenly perfection, and he is starting right now, in small pockets, one heart at a time. *So live as though heaven is on earth.* Treat others that way; live with those values.

Don't settle for a bleak life, a bland Christianity. No, your church won't be perfect. But don't shut the door on the possibility that your church and your life can be a place where people are swept up in the excitement of the kingdom of heaven being made visible here on earth! It can be a place of love, of generosity, of knowledge, of friendship, of Spirit-directed good works. Don't let the cynical world grind all the idealism out of you.

Even when church people are revealed as corrupt hypocrites. Which happens next.

> PRAYER FOR THE JOURNEY: *Father, may the joy and generosity that characterized the early church increasingly characterize ours — starting with me.*

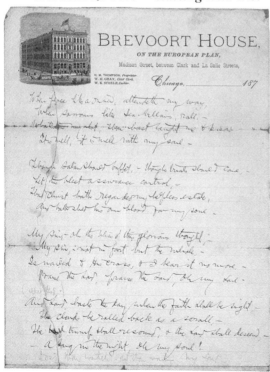

The original handwritten lyrics of "It Is Well With My Soul" by Horatio Spafford on Chicago hotel stationery, now on display in the American Colony hotel in Jerusalem.

11
POSERS

The American Colony hotel I explored still hosts visitors to Jerusalem, and the Spafford Children's Center still cares for more than 30,000 children each year. But the commune itself dissolved in the 1950s. There is no more Christian community at the American Colony. After surviving world wars and terrorist attacks and corrupt government officials, the church here was undone by internal division.[7]

And it's internal division that becomes the most serious threat to the existence of the early church.

NO RELIGIOUS POSING

In Acts 5, a couple named Ananias and Sapphira sell some property and apparently make quite a big deal of the fact that they're giving 100% of their proceeds to help the poor. Only... they're lying. They are only giving a percentage. And there would have been absolutely nothing wrong with that. Peter makes clear in verse four that they're free to do whatever they want with their possessions; the problem is not their finances. The problem is their hypocritical showboating.

God's community should have no room for this religious posing and fakery. Why? It alienates people from the life-giving gospel when they see religious hypocrites. And people can smell hypocrisy a mile away.

But there's another reason not to pretend you're more spiritual than you really are: You don't get the help you need to change.

That's why hypocrisy, religious play-acting, was the only aspect of his culture that Jesus himself consistently and severely criticized. And he aimed his criticism at the religious leaders, the Pharisees. As one scholar, Warren Wiersbe, writes, "The great sin of the Pharisees was hypocrisy based on pride. Their religion was external, not internal; it was to impress people, not to please God... They loved titles and public recognition and exalted themselves..."[8] And here, that kind of hypocrisy appears for the first time in the Jesus movement. And Peter makes clear it does not belong.

DESCRIPTIVE VS. PRESCRIPTIVE

Both Ananias and Sapphira drop dead after they are confronted. I have to be honest. I do not understand why this story ends like this. I don't like it. Why couldn't they just have been scolded?

But two points you need to notice: First, it actually does not say they were *struck* dead. It says they fell down and died. Could they have simply died of heart attacks or sheer fright? Maybe this story shows the immense pressure we put on ourselves when we wear self-righteous masks.

Second, this is clearly not a story meant to show what *always* happens when we are hypocrites. *We instantly die!* There are other hypocrites in the Book of Acts who don't die or even get sick. No, Luke is simply accurately telling what *did* happen to this *particular* couple.

And as the great scholar N.T. Wright points out, this raises a very important point about reading Acts. Many times in this book, things happen which never happen the same way again.

Here, a couple falls down dead after they're shown in public to be hypocrites. Never happens that way again.

Also in this chapter, people are healed when Peter's shadow falls on them. Never happens that way again.

Later, people are healed when they touch Paul's handkerchiefs. Never happens that way again.

Earlier, flames of fire appeared above the heads of people. Never happens that way again.

There are many more examples. That's because the Book of Acts is not *prescribing*; it's *describing*. It's not giving an exact *prescription* for how to confront hypocrisy or how to heal or how to exhibit the gifts of the Holy Spirit. It's giving a *description* of what happened in these cases.

The *prescriptive* parts of the Bible clearly teach principles that apply to every believer, like in Paul's letters where he gives detailed instruction to the churches. By contrast, the Book of Acts is *descriptive*. It *describes* what happened.[9]

And you and I need to be careful about deriving timeless principles from descriptions. Here's the rule of thumb. If you think you see a principle taught in a *descriptive* passage of the Bible, always ask, "Is this taught *prescriptively* elsewhere?" In this book I've tried to make certain the principles I see in these stories are all explicitly taught in the prescriptive parts of the Bible, and not just imagined by me.

For example, you may think Acts teaches that pastors should heal people through their handkerchiefs. But is that taught in a prescriptive passage elsewhere? In any of Paul's letters does he say, "The elders of the church should heal with hankies?" No. But does he tell us to pray for healing? Absolutely.

GOD DOES WHAT HE PLEASES

Here's why this is so important. We tend to want God to work the same way every time, to repeat himself over and over. In Western culture especially, we love systems and scalability and equations that work precisely the same way no matter what variables are involved. We like to turn even faith into a formula.

As N.T. Wright puts it,

> In our democratic age we tend to suppose that if God
> is going to do anything at all it would only be fair if he

would do it all the same for everybody, but things just don't seem to work like that... In the apostolic age they seem simply to have accepted that God can do whatever he pleases and that, when people pray and trust him, he will often do much more than we dare to imagine...[10]

So these *descriptions* in Acts are not necessarily *prescriptions* for how God *always* works. But are you *open* to God working in the same way again? If he wants to do miracles through you, are you up for it?

> PRAYER FOR THE JOURNEY: *Lord, help me stay open to however you choose to work: I don't want to demand that your Spirit works in my life precisely as you worked here in Acts; but let me not stay closed to it either. I want to be receptive to however you choose to work through me.*

12
PRESSURE BUILDS

ACTS 5:17-42

I'm back at the Southern Wall of Jerusalem, one of the last remnants of the Temple complex built by King Herod, trying to explain to a group of friends the tensions between the Jewish Temple leadership and the new Jesus movement.

Instead of painting the Temple leaders as pure villains, I want to help my little group of twenty-first-century Christians sympathize with the first-century Jewish leaders. I find myself paraphrasing N.T. Wright again, who uses a great metaphor to explain this:

Imagine you're the owner and manager of a famous concert hall like Radio City Music Hall in New York. Over the decades every famed musician in history has played at your venue. Your holiday productions always sell out. People have bought season tickets for generations.

Then a scruffy band starts playing right outside your door. At first you don't mind. But soon more and more people stop coming into your concerts and stand listening in amazement to this street band. The media reports popular opinion: This band is better than anything people have ever heard inside your doors! To top it off, the band seems to be suggesting not only that they play better tunes than your orchestra; they insist they are the new management.

That's a tiny taste of the frustration the Temple leaders must have felt with the Jesus movement. In today's passage you sense it. The people are all going after this new fad. So Peter is called to answer for his teaching. The high priest says, "We gave you strict orders not to teach in this name." And Peter responds with the classic line: "We must obey God rather than man." (Acts 5:28–29)

OBEY GOD OR HUMANS?

Dietrich Bonhoeffer was a famous pastor in Germany. As he watched the Nazis take over the Lutheran Church, he and two thousand other pastors signed and printed a pamphlet urging fellow pastors to resist Nazi influence. They called it "We Must Obey God Rather Than Man."

Although Bonhoeffer successfully persuaded many to resist the Nazis, including Martin Niemöller, who had been a pro-Nazi German U-boat captain before he became a minister, ultimately his stand cost Bonhoeffer his life. The Nazis imprisoned and executed him.

How about you? You may never face a fascist government. But you and I face social pressure to conform constantly. Your stand may cost you your social status or position. Can you say, with serene focus on Christ, "I must obey God rather than man"?

In Acts, the Christians are very good at resisting pressure from the outside authorities. But their biggest challenge, one that wrecks churches to this day, comes from a surprising source in the very next chapter.

> PRAYER FOR THE JOURNEY: *Lord God, I want to obey you rather than humans, even my own all-too-human compulsions and insecurities. Help me, in large and small ways, to consistently follow you when other culturally dominant influences say not to.*

The well-preserved remains of the first-century southern steps leading to the Temple Mount. These are the steps that Jesus and the apostles would have used to access the Temple area.

WHO WAS GAMALIEL?

Luke describes Gamaliel In Acts 5 as a teacher of the law "well respected by all" (Acts 5:34). He calmly persuades the furious religious council not to put the apostles to death.

Gamaliel is well known from Jewish sources in the first century and later. He's considered one of the greatest rabbis of all time, a man who knew the law thoroughly, taught it brilliantly, and lived it consistently.

At this stage in the development of Judaism there were two schools of interpretation of the law, named after two famous teachers who lived before the time of Jesus: Shammai and Hillel.

Shammai tended to always take the hard line, politically and theologically. He even taught that violence against those who broke the law, though regrettable, was understandable. *God's law must be enforced.*

Hillel took a different tack. He taught that God wanted Israel to follow the law with all their *heart*. Since it's a matter of the heart, we shouldn't fight to make people keep it because that wouldn't be obedience from the heart. So believers need to follow God's law with all their hearts as a good example, and let other people follow. Sort of, live and let live.

Gamaliel, as revealed in his thinking in Acts 5, is a follower of Hillel. However, one of Gamaliel's followers abandons this softer approach for Shammai's hard line as he becomes more and more frustrated with the Jesus movement. You'll meet him shortly. Saul of Tarsus.

13
FOOD FIGHT

ACTS 6:1-7

One thing I love about the Book of Acts is how *real* it is. It doesn't read like propaganda, just one improbable victory after another. In fact, Luke gives about as much time to the *struggles* of the early Jesus movement as to its *triumphs*. This is big, because we all have a tendency to whitewash our challenges. But Luke is very honest about the ways early Christians lied or disagreed or argued.

In this story an argument over food turns into accusations of racial prejudice.

The players: Hellenistic Jews (Jewish people who had adopted Greek language and culture) and Hebraic Jews (Jewish people who still spoke Hebrew and were more typically "Jewish" in culture) in the early Jesus movement (at this stage, all the first Christians identified as Jewish, not as a separate movement). There was a lot of tension between these two culturally distinct groups. In Jerusalem, the Hebrew-speaking Jews apparently held the upper hand in terms of social status. But they felt threatened by the Greek-speaking Jews because, globally, there were many more Hellenistic Jews. In fact, most of the Jews in the world at that time probably did not speak Hebrew but Greek.

The problem: The Jesus movement is mushrooming so fast friction erupts between these two groups within the Jerusalem church. The Hellenistic Jews suspect they're getting cheated of their daily allotment of food for their needy widows. Imagine what an emotional issue this was. Years of perceived prejudice boils over.

"I don't mind when they look down on me personally, but to steal food from our widows is absolutely despicable!"

The solution: It's fascinating to observe how wise the early church leaders were in dealing with this situation. This seems like a simple problem with a simple solution: better organization. But this offense is specifically along ethnic and cultural lines. So it is not simple. And it is not trivial. If Jesus intends the church to burst through cultural barriers, then even the perception of *possible* prejudice must be stopped inside the local church.

DIVERSITY IN LEADERSHIP

So the apostles urge the whole community of disciples to select seven men "known to be full of the Spirit and of wisdom" to oversee food distribution. At least one of them is a Greek convert to Judaism named Nicolas. Brilliant choice. If there is even a hint of racial divide between Greek and Hebrews in this church, then the leadership for solving the problem must reflect cultural diversity.

The result: "So the word of God spread." (Acts 6:7). Interestingly, even "a large number of the priests," the same priests who had opposed the early Christian movement, become believers. When the church overcomes prejudice, people notice.

I see a great leadership principle here. Even the apostles couldn't do everything, so they had to delegate! But more than that I see a reminder about the sensitivities inherent in cross-cultural ministry.

It was one of the first challenges the church faced, and it remains one of our biggest today. We have this international message, yet ethnic differences remain some of the most difficult barriers we face. How can you help change that? Someone suggested this simple starting point. Decide that *no one sits alone.* Determine that if you see someone alone at church, you are going to say hello and join them. Or ask them to join you. Especially if they are somehow different than you.

Let's do all we can to promote the true nature of the gospel; it was designed to be a barrier-busting movement. That includes race, language, and ethnic barriers.

> The reason there are so many exhortations in the New Testament for Christians to love other Christians is because... the church itself is not made up of natural 'friends.' What binds us together is not common education, common race, common income levels, common politics, common nationality, common accents, common jobs, or anything else of that sort. Christians come together not because they form a natural collocation, but because they have all been saved by Jesus Christ and owe him a common allegiance. In this light we are a band of natural enemies who love one another for Jesus' sake, of mutual love among social incompatibles. —D.A. Carson[11]

So the Jesus movement seems to be gaining momentum — but you might be getting a little impatient, thinking, *All the action's been in Jerusalem. No one seems to be going out anywhere, like Jesus said they would. I thought this was a travel book.* Hang on to your hats. Things are about to explode in some very strange ways.

> PRAYER FOR THE JOURNEY: *Father God, help me reach out like a family member to believers from different backgrounds. I pray that no one, from any ethnic or language or cultural group, would ever feel unwelcome in our church. And may this welcome start with me. Open my eyes to ways I can proactively heal these divides.*

THE LOST TOMB OF THE BARSABBAS FAMILY

In 1945, Israeli archaeologists made a spectacular discovery—an undisturbed first-century tomb near Jerusalem's Kidron Valley containing ossuaries etched with cross symbols and prayers to Jesus, and the names of the people buried within. Among the names: Simon Barsabbas, Judah Barsabbas, and Matthias.

In Acts 1, Luke describes how "Joseph called Barsabbas" was one of two finalists to replace Judas as the twelfth apostle, though another disciple named "Matthias" is selected instead. Then in Acts 15, someone named "Judas called Barsabbas" is chosen to accompany Paul on a journey.

Because of the Christian symbols on the ossuaries, archaeologists concluded that the people buried in that tomb were the very disciples mentioned in Acts.

What makes this find even more astounding for historians is that, based on expert dating of pottery fragments found with the ossuaries, the tomb was sealed less than a decade after the crucifixion of Christ, around 42 AD. That the cross was already a recognized symbol of Christianity is a remarkable piece of evidence that Christ's crucifixion was seen, from the very beginning, as the center of the faith. An article in the *American Journal of Archaeology* concluded, "While it once was claimed that the cross did not appear as a symbol of Christianity until the late second century AD ...the timeframe for this symbol now must be pushed back into the first century."[12]

Eliezer L. Sukenik of Hebrew University, one of the tomb's excavators and one of Israel's leading archaeologists, concluded, "All our evidence indicates that we have in this tomb the earliest extra-biblical records of Christianity in existence. It may also have a bearing on the historicity of Jesus and the crucifixion."[13]

14
ROOTS RUN DEEP

Just across the Jordan River to the east of Jerusalem is the beautiful country of Jordan, so we decide to take a few days to explore there. I'm stunned when my Jordanian guide recites his entire family tree to me. And I mean, his *entire* family tree, going back many centuries, all the way to Bible times. And he does this by heart. Sometimes I feel like I can barely remember the names of my own three children, so I'm extremely impressed.

Every time I'm in the Middle East I'm amazed at how far back corporate memory goes. In America, national identity goes back 240 years or so, to George Washington and the Revolution. Most of us don't even know the names of our great-grandparents. In the Middle East, personal and national identity still goes back thousands of years, back to Abraham and Moses.

That's important to know when you try to understand the charges against the early Christians from their fellow Jews here in Acts. They're being accused of undermining the ancient teaching of Moses, of bringing in something new, something novel, something with no historical roots.

That's why Stephen's speech in Acts 7 is centered on the pillars of Israel's national identity and memory: Abraham, Moses, and the prophets. What he tries to show is how, when properly understood, not only does the Christian message *not* contradict those stories; those ancient stories actually *set the stage* for Jesus! The ministry of Christ (and the response of the religious leaders to it) is in fact *exactly* what you'd expect if the Messiah came to Israel.

He paints five pictures from Israel's fascinating history to show a pattern emerging:

ABRAHAM: GOD'S CHOSEN PEOPLE ARE FIRST ENSLAVED

God promised Abraham that something new would arise from his descendants. A blessed nation! But first the Israelites would be despised and enslaved for 400 years. Then they would emerge from slavery to fulfill the promise!

JOSEPH: ISRAEL'S SAVIOR IS FIRST REJECTED BY HIS BROTHERS

God was with Joseph, but Joseph was despised and rejected by his own brothers. Later he became the agent of their salvation from starvation.

MOSES: ISRAEL'S LEADER IS FIRST REJECTED BY HIS PEOPLE

God made Moses a powerful leader from birth, but first he would be rejected by his own people, who said, "Who made you to be a ruler and a judge over us?" Moses disappeared into the desert, but later emerged to lead the Israelites to freedom.

MT. SINAI: GOD'S LAW IS REJECTED BY HIS PEOPLE

God spoke to Moses on Mt. Sinai, but meanwhile the people made a golden calf and worshipped that instead. The prophets saw this as a sad template for the way Israel turned away from God again and again.

SOLOMON: THE TEMPLE IS BUILT; BUT GOD LIVES IN NO HOUSE

Eventually Solomon did build a temple for God, though the Scriptures say God cannot dwell in some man-made house. Stephen seems to be making a dramatic parallel between the way the Israelites made idols, and the way they are now idolizing the Temple.

Then Stephen summarizes his uncomfortable but accurate message: This habit of rejecting God's prophets is a consistent pattern in Israel's history. So really, rejecting Jesus is exactly what any observer would expect, if Jesus really was sent from God.

He's showing the logical fallacy of his opponents' position. They are appealing to public opinion, and to their own authority, to show Jesus is not the Messiah. But Stephen's pointing out that the true Messiah might very well be rejected by the public and religious authorities, because they have gotten it wrong in Israel's history time and again. He's saying, "So you want history? You value the old ways? Well, you're sure right when you say you're keeping the old customs alive: The old custom of persecuting God's anointed, and focusing on idols!"

At this point the religious leaders have had enough. They don't even wait to ask the Romans to execute Stephen. Enraged, they drag him out of the city and stone him to death.

Watching Stephen's brutal, bloody murder, giving his hearty approval, is a man radically bent on destroying the Jesus movement. He is about to make things very dangerous for all of the Jesus followers.

> PRAYER FOR THE JOURNEY: *Lord, thank you that you keep pursuing us humans through history, though we keep rejecting you. And thank you specifically that you pursued me. Through all my failures and rejections of your ways, you kept seeking me. May I live in gratitude of your pursuing love today and model it for others.*

FROM JUDAISM TO CHRISTIANITY

It's impossible to really understand the Book of Acts, or any of the New Testament, without understanding the relationship between Jews and Christians in the first century. The main thing to get is this: No Christians at the time saw themselves as starting a new religion. They thought of themselves as Jews completing their God-given mission. That's why, repeatedly in the Book of Acts, Jesus-followers make the case that they're solidly in the Jewish tradition and are in fact fulfilling the Jewish Scriptures.

SHARED HISTORY

The shared background of Judaism and Christianity in a very small nutshell: About 1800 years before Christ, Abraham, the father of the Jews, has faith in God's promise and leaves his home for the Promised Land, the land of Israel.

His son Isaac and descendants, the Israelites, are later slaves in Egypt for 400 years. But Moses leads them out of slavery back toward the Promised Land, and God gives the Israelites the Law of Moses. The most famous section of this law is the Ten Commandments, but there are many other rules and interpretations of the rules that later became rules themselves, such as the kosher food restrictions against eating meat with dairy products. The oldest part of the Jewish law goes back even further. Male circumcision started way back in Abraham's time. This history and these laws became essential aspects of Jewish identity.

PROPHESIES OF A HERO

Fast forward through many important kings and battles to the time of the prophets, from about 800 until about 400 years before Christ. The nation of Israel is in decline, and the prophets foretell a "Son of Man," a heroic Messiah who will be sent by God to restore the fortunes of Israel and begin a "new covenant" between

God and Man. In this new covenant, God's law will not be written on stone tablets, but on the hearts of transformed people. The new covenant, it is said, will even spread to the Gentile nations of the earth, and their hearts will be turned to the one true God as well.

THE FIRST-CENTURY SITUATION

Now fast forward again to the time of the New Testament, about 2,000 years ago. Most Jews no longer live near Jerusalem, or even speak Hebrew. They are scattered throughout the Greco-Roman world and mainly speak Greek.

Many pagan Romans and Greeks who meet these Jews find their idea of one true God appealing and attend synagogue regularly. These Gentiles are known not as Jews but as "God-fearers" because to completely convert to Judaism would require adherence to all the kosher Jewish laws, which many Gentiles find burdensome. This creates a situation where many Greeks and Romans live between two worlds: They're not believers in the pagan gods anymore, but they're not fully embraced in Judaism either.

Meanwhile, the Hebrew-speaking Jews in Israel are under the control of the Roman Empire. The elite members of Jewish society there cooperate with the Romans and adopt many Roman customs, even sending their children to be educated in Rome.

But the Jewish masses hate the Romans and long for the Messiah to appear and set them free. Several revolutionaries arise during this time, but the Romans crush these uprisings violently. The wealthy Romanized Jews assist the Romans in suppressing these Messianic movements because they're afraid the Romans will completely wipe out their culture if things get out of hand politically. And they would be proven right. The Romans destroyed the Temple in 70 AD, and Jerusalem was levelled in 135 AD.

THE MESSAGE OF THE JESUS MOVEMENT

Into this framework step the early Jesus-followers, with their message that Jesus is the Messiah, yet his mission is not to overthrow Rome and reestablish Israel politically, but to reach beyond all borders with a message of grace from the one true God of the whole world. This is a new twist on the idea of the Messiah. They believe this development was foretold in the law and the prophets: This is a fulfillment of God's promise that through the Jews would emerge a light to all nations.

To the elite Jerusalem Jews this still sounds uncomfortably like political insurrection with its talk of a new "kingdom of God" — so they oppose the Jesus movement. Even the Jews who long for a Messiah don't all take to the Jesus movement. They long for a nationalistic *ingathering* of Jews back to Israel, not an evangelistic *outreach* to all nations. The emphasis on reaching the Gentiles is hugely offensive to them. And both these groups argue the Jesus-followers are teaching against the old traditions because they seem to be minimizing the importance of the religious law.

So the Jesus-followers have a case to make on several fronts. They need to show the Jews that they are not anti-Jewish, but are in fact solidly in the tradition of Jewish Scripture. They need to show the Romans they are not anti-Roman, but socially beneficial and reasonable. And they need to persuade the "God-fearers" that this is precisely the kind of monotheism they've been longing for, a faith where they are fully accepted without having to keep 600 rules first.

You see the apostles' speeches in Acts all addressing these important concerns.

ACTS ODYSSEY

PART THREE

SWORD & SORCERY

15
PAIN TO GAIN

ACTS 7:54-8:4

While in Jordan I'm invited to a church in Amman, about 60 miles from the Syrian border and 200 miles from Iraq. In Bible times, Amman was on the King's Highway, one of the two major roads leading north from Jerusalem to the rest of the world.

I'm far from the only foreigner at church today. The local Jordanians are vastly outnumbered by worshippers from across the borders, refugees from cities in Iraq and Syria where Islamic extremists are specifically targeting Christians. After church I chat over coffee with several of them who speak English perfectly. Most are professionals: doctors, lawyers, engineers, and architects. All have lost nearly everything.

Yet strangely there is an atmosphere of lightness and laughter. And love. One doctor, an Iraqi refugee, tells me of his own spiritual awakening that happened, he says, as a result of his devastating losses. His family barely escaped as extremists took over their city. They now live in a tent in a local refugee camp. But in some ways, he says, their lives have never been better. "God has taken this terrible thing and is working through it," he asserts with confidence. They've discovered a vibrant faith in Christ.

And he tells me of a revival among other Iraqis too, a revival like he has never seen in his lifetime. He describes it this way: "It's like something out of the Book of Acts."

PAIN TO GAIN

PAIN TO GAIN

Beginning in Acts chapter 8, the Jesus movement begins rapidly exploding outward. Finally, Jesus' promise that it will spread beyond all borders starts to come true. What's the catalyst?

Persecution. Clearly God isn't encouraging persecution of his own people. Yet he takes this terrible thing and makes it result in something really great. Like he always does.

You know what I think? Sometimes we get so comfortable where we're at... that we don't move where God wants us to go.

That seems to have been the case with these first followers of Jesus. Even though Christ told them they'd go to the farthest ends of the earth, there's no evidence they made it much further than the gates of Jerusalem. Maybe they needed time together to get over the shock of Christ's resurrection and the new reality they were living in. Maybe their numbers needed to grow so they would survive the coming persecution.

But now the hammer comes down. And they scatter. Prodded by pain that God turns to gain.

In the same way, God will take terrible things that happen to you, and — in his time and by his power — use those bad things to help you move forward to where he wants you to be. For the first disciples that meant a literal, geographic move. For you and me it often means a different kind of move. Moving from addiction to sobriety. Moving from careerism to treasuring family. Moving from the urgent to the important. We know we should make those moves. But for a lot of us it just doesn't happen until we're prodded by pain, until we hit bottom.

GOOD FROM BAD

And this becomes a theme of the Book of Acts. As I immerse myself in it during my journeys, it becomes increasingly odd to me that many people think of Acts as a record of unbroken successes propelled by miraculous moments.

Yes, there are miraculous deliverances in Acts. I believe God still does miracles today! But most of Acts describes one obstacle after another. It's a parade of problems. The theme of Acts is definitely not, "The good news equals good luck. If you follow Christ, good things will happen!" It's more like, "If you follow Christ, expect problems. Big problems. But ultimate victory."

Again and again in Acts you see this play out. Doing God's will is not painless. There will be trouble. There might be disaster. But don't despair. God will turn anything, even death, into ways to bring the kingdom of heaven to our world.

Going through a dark time? Be confident: *God is still working in the dark*. One way or another you will get through this. It will not usually be quick. Or easy. But God will use this. He will *always* bring good from bad.

THIS TRAIN CANNOT BE DERAILED

One thing's for sure: The persecution meant to destroy the early church instead serves to keep the gospel train rolling, in the exact direction God wants it to go.

And in many persecutions since, the same thing has happened. Because that train can't get derailed. God's purposes cannot be thwarted. He will get ministry done. He will see salvation offered. He will bring the kingdom of heaven to earth. In refugee camps. In hospital halls. In prison yards. In divorce courts. No matter the tragedy, God will use it to reach people with his love. And he will use *you*, in any circumstance, to be his witness.

Even when the circumstances are really *super* crazy. Like they're about to become for these first disciples.

> PRAYER FOR THE JOURNEY: *Heavenly Father, when things go wrong in my life, help me remember these examples from Acts, how you even used persecution to accomplish your work. Help me stay positive, flexible, and undaunted.*

HOLY SPIRIT RIPPLES

One of the many curious things about the Book of Acts is this: The Holy Spirit seems to descend on some people *after* they believe. Why does it sometimes happen this way in Acts, when Paul says in Ephesians 1 that the Holy Spirit is given to us *when* we believe?

I think God had to make something very clear: He accepts each subsequent wave of "outsiders."

It happens with the Samaritan believers in Acts 8. They were viewed by some as an ethnically inferior "mixed" race of Jews who had intermarried with Gentiles. They were also considered religious heretics. They had their own temple, their own scriptures, their own priests. In every way, they were seen as off-brand, corrupted versions of true Jews.

So after some Samaritans become Jesus-followers, Peter and John go check out this surprising situation. And God shows them, by having the Holy Spirit come upon the Samaritans in a dramatic, visible way (which resembled what Peter and John had experienced themselves in Acts 2) that he approves of this new wave of believers.

You see that pattern throughout Acts. As the gospel bursts through barriers, there is a visible initiation into the family of God through a spectacular baptism into the Spirit. Luke does not seem to be teaching this is prescriptive for every believer, but it was definitely important in the spread of Christianity. God is saying, with each new wave of the Spirit, "These are my people too." These "outsiders" are now insiders.

16
SORCERY IN SAMARIA

ACTS 8:5-25

What happens next sounds very weird. Especially to modern ears. Almost like something out of a J.K. Rowling story, a "sorcerer" named Simon becomes a believer in Jesus. And he seems sincere, following Philip and then Peter around like a curious cat.

In the first-century world, sorcery and magic were widely practiced. Josephus describes how magicians would hire themselves out to conduct healings and exorcisms, using supposedly enchanted objects like charms or bowls of "magical water" to do their tricks. They'd perform in front of large audiences, appearing to dramatically cast out spirits and sicknesses.

He describes watching one sorcerer place a subject in the middle of a series of bowls filled with water. When the magician commanded the demon possessing this person to leave, bowls stretching in one direction all tipped over in a row, apparently showing the path the invisible evil spirit was taking as it left the room. Josephus is very skeptical, but he shows how these gadgets were an inseparable part of the magician's act.

THE FOR-PROFIT PROPHET

Simon had a very nice business doing this sort of thing before his conversion. In fact, he'd been a local celebrity sorcerer known as "The Great Power of God" (Now that's a gutsy stage name!). But the Holy Spirit's empowering presence is something he's never seen before. People's lives are *really* being changed. With no stage props. You can almost hear the wheels in his brain turning: *Imagine how much respect I could command if I could give people the courage and joy they're receiving through the Spirit!* So he actually offers Peter money for the secret. And Peter severely rebukes him.

Simon still longed for "greatness" and power even after becoming a believer. And that's a temptation for people in ministry today. Pastors, authors, worship leaders, even home Bible study leaders and Sunday School teachers, can be subtly twisted by the temptations of power, by the reputation of having some almost magical connection to God. Some people just love to be looked up to as The Great Teacher of God. And this can go badly wrong, very quickly.

THE SIMON SYNDROME

Here are some warning signs of Christians leaders who have "Simon Syndrome." They use their position for personal profit or ego-driven affirmation:

- Their personal fulfillment is more important than caring for people.

- They promote themselves, creating a cult of personality.

- They're basically insecure, looking to spectacular results for validation.

- They're motivated by acclaim and power. They love titles!

- Most tellingly, they think the secret to ministry success can be bought. They value *technique* above all else. They're all about the "how" instead of the "who." In our technique-driven culture, where success in everything from sex to parenting is boiled down to marketable techniques, this is a particularly common temptation for pastors.

- Because they need results and validation, and believe ministry success depends on technique, they transfer those values to their congregations. So people in their churches are also willing to pay money to learn the latest secrets to spiritual power and success.

The Christian life becomes less about God's grace than about trading up to the best technique.

Acclaim and public reputation may, for a season, surround a church or pastor. In Acts 2, the early church had favor with the people in Jerusalem. But if you ever see a ministry leader *motivated* by acclaim and power, or who promotes the idea that God's power can be packaged in marketable techniques, back away quickly. They may have Simon Syndrome. And God does not endorse that.

Just as Jesus rebuked abusive, authoritarian religious leaders, Peter also rebukes Simon. "You have no part or share in this ministry, because your heart is not right before God!" (Acts 8:21) The good news? Unlike Ananias and Sapphira, Simon the Sorcerer seems to have been humbled by Peter's rebuke. "Pray to the Lord for me," he says.

If you're a leader, take care that you don't fall into this all-too-common trap. If someone tells you that you're becoming acclaim-driven or technique-oriented, take it at least as well as Simon took Peter's rebuke, humbling himself.

And if you've been abused by such a ministry, know that Jesus offers something entirely different — grace-rooted, freely available, humble, loving care in the family of God. Don't give up because you've had a negative experience with the showboating sorcerer types. There are still Christian leaders who value ministry focused on Jesus, and not on them.

TOTAL ABANDON AND TOTAL QUALITY

I see two dynamics in Acts that often seem mutually exclusive in churches today: *total abandonment* and *quality control*.

On the one hand there's a sense of total abandon, absolute surrender to whatever the Holy Spirit wants to do, however he wants to do it. *Anything is possible.*

Yet there is also very strict quality control, particularly of *theology* and of *leaders*. There are councils held by the leadership in Jerusalem to examine closely the theology of Peter and Paul among the Gentiles. There is a rejection of profit-oriented or hypocritical leadership, as you see here with Simon.

Both of these principles are taught throughout the Bible. But in churches today I usually see one or the other.

Either it's, "We are open to whatever God wants to do, and that means mistakes are going to be made, but, oh well!" And these churches do take amazing risks and see wonderful results. But many wind up with cult-like leaders teaching nutty, unbiblical truth.

Or it's, "We are solidly based on a foundation of Scripture and bad theology SHALL NOT PASS!" And these places are bastions of excellent doctrinal teaching. But many wind up withered, dry, and dead, straining at theological gnats but swallowing the camel of religious pride and self-righteousness.

My prayer is that as individuals and as a church we would recover this first-century mentality where we have *both*. Wild abandon. *And* excellent quality control.

> PRAYER FOR THE JOURNEY: *Lord, help me understand that spiritual power comes not from technique but from time with you, my Savior. Please help us as a church to be a place of total abandon and quality control.*

ANCIENT MAGIC KIT

Magic and sorcery were as much a part of the first-century Roman world as the established religions. So-called magicians were not seen as illusionists, but as actual sorcerers with real power.

Archaeologists have discovered a complete "magician's kit" in Pergamum, near the coast of Turkey close to Ephesus. This is not like the kit you got for Christmas when you were twelve.

It contained a bronze table and base covered with "magic" symbols, a dish also decorated with symbols, a large bronze nail with magical letters inscribed on its flat sides, two bronze rings, and three black polished stones inscribed with the names of spirits. Josephus describes how magicians would use these supposed magical tools to "cast out demons." Imagine how many desperate people sought help from charlatans alleging great spiritual power.

Replica of the "prognosticon," one of the elements of the magic kit, made by the Pergamon museum in Berlin. (Photo credit: Pergamonmuseum)

17
OUTSIDER TO INSIDER

ACTS 8:26-40

Turns out sometimes the legends are true.

I'm standing on top of a hill outside the ruined walls of a Greco-Roman city called Hierapolis. It's just a few miles down a narrow valley from the ruins of Colosse in modern Turkey. Friends and I wander through the remains of an ancient church built here to commemorate the martyrdom of Philip the Apostle, who was allegedly hung upside-down and then buried on this hill.

But you know how it is with these medieval legends about the saints. Who knows if they have any basis in fact? In the Dark Ages anything connected to a saint gained a lot of traction as a pilgrimage destination. That's probably why so many ancient churches claimed to be the final resting place of this saint's finger or that apostle's head.

A lot of modern scholars scoff at these legendary connections. But this particular legend was viewed with a little more interest because of a letter written by a man named Polycrates to Victor of Rome toward the end of the second century. He claims the graves of Philip "of the twelve apostles," and two of his virgin daughters were in Hierapolis. However, no trace of the graves had ever been found.

Then in 2011 the archaeologist Francesco D'Andria made an exciting discovery in a hillside just 40 yards outside the church ruins: a first-century tomb. After intense study his team made a stunning announcement. They had finally found the legendary grave of the martyred apostle Philip.[1]

I pause at the gravesite and think of his ministry. The Book of Acts doesn't describe Philip's martyrdom here. But there is a fascinating story about his encounter with a person forced to the fringes of faith.

THE ULTIMATE OUTSIDER

The story starts when one of God's angels (the Greek word literally means "messenger") prompts Philip to take the road that leads from Jerusalem to Gaza. It's described as a "desert road" and the phrase "go south" in verse 26 is an expression that in Greek could also mean "go at noon."[2] Not exactly an ideal time to be traveling in the parched wilderness. But then he realizes why the instructions were so specific. God has a divine appointment for him.

As he is walking along the road he encounters an African, the chief treasurer to the Ethiopian queen (Her name is sometimes mistakenly translated as "Candace," but that was actually a title, like "Caesar." She was "The Candace," a title that meant she ruled over Ethiopia, at that time a well-established state south of Egypt). This African is also a eunuch.

In ancient times males chosen to serve in royal courts would sometimes be castrated (have their testicles removed), usually before puberty. Of course this would have major hormonal effects. They would retain high, feminine voices for the rest of their lives, and they would never develop many male physical characteristics. They were valued as royal advisors and servants because they were seen as more trustworthy around women than typical testosterone-driven men.

However, not everyone liked eunuchs. They were frequently unwelcome in the homes of the very religious. Most importantly for this story, eunuchs were even forbidden to worship at the Temple. *"We don't serve your kind here,"* this eunuch must have often heard.

So this person represents the ultimate outsider. In terms of race, culture, gender, geography, and politics, if there's anyone in Acts who represents the "other," it's this eunuch.

Yet the eunuch was seeking God, just returning from Jerusalem. Worship there must have been a melancholy experience. The eunuch could stand outside the temple and worship, but could never enter the actual courts.

He still has an unfulfilled longing for God when Philip sees him in his chariot reading the Bible, specifically Isaiah 53. Apparently the chariot is moving, but slowly, the horse clip-clopping forward in the hot midday sun. The eunuch is sitting down in the back, perhaps to take advantage of the small shade afforded by the sides of the chariot, reading Isaiah out loud, legs probably dangling over the back of the cart. This is the only time a chariot is mentioned in the New Testament. It was a luxury item, like a sports car today, owned only by the very wealthy or the well connected.[3] Although he enjoyed aspects of the queen's wealth, the eunuch was still a spiritual seeker, looking at the Temple from the outside in.

DIVINE APPOINTMENTS

We'll get back to that scene in a moment. But first, an observation. The eunuch didn't have a neon sign pointing to him reading, "Great chance to share your faith!" Although an angel set him on the road, Philip still had to have his eyes and ears open to the opportunity. Same with you and me. Because moments like this are all around us.

One night while I was driving back from the Reno area radio station that employed me, my car stalled and then stopped entirely. This was just before cell phones took over the world, and the only public phone booth was a couple miles away, inside a small diner at Zephyr Cove, Nevada. Then I glanced at my watch and realized the diner would likely close in just half an hour, at 9:00 pm. So I sprinted for the restaurant, sliding through the doors just as the lone waitress turned off the neon OPEN sign.

After phoning my wife I collapsed into a booth and ordered a soda. The server looked at me sideways, and then said, "I can't believe it's you, you're the guy who did that funeral I attended last month!" She went on, "I was just thinking that I need to get right with God, and that I should give that pastor a call, and here you come, walking right into my restaurant at closing, the only time all day I could have chatted with you!"

What felt to me like bad luck looked to her like answered prayer. My guess is, we've all had those "God moments" when his timing supersedes our own and perfectly sets the stage for ministry.

And here in Acts 8 you see another example.

THE CONVERSATION

The eunuch invites Philip into the chariot, and asks a question a lot of people have about this same passage: "Who is this about?"

Luke says Philip began with that very Scripture and explained the good news of Jesus. Isaiah 53 is still an excellent bridge to explaining the mission of Christ. If you have time, check it out today. Written hundreds of years before Jesus, it explains the Messiah's mission, even forecasting details about his death and burial.

Luke doesn't specifically say, but I like to think Philip went forward just a few chapters to Isaiah 56, where it says:

> "Don't let foreigners who commit themselves to the Lord say,
>   'The Lord will never let me be part of his people.'
> And don't let the eunuchs say,
>   'I'm a dried-up tree with no children and no future.'
>
> For this is what the Lord says:
> I will bless those eunuchs
>   who keep my Sabbath days holy
> and who choose to do what pleases me
>   and commit their lives to me.
>
> I will give them — within the walls of my house —

> a memorial and a name
> far greater than sons and daughters could give.
>
> For the name I give them is an everlasting one.
> It will never disappear!
> …My Temple will be called a house of prayer for all
> nations.
>
> For the Sovereign Lord,
> who brings back the outcasts of Israel, says:
> "I will bring others, too,
> besides my people Israel." (Isaiah 56:3–5,7b–8 NLT)

I love the eunuch's response: "Here is water! What can stand in the way of me being baptized?" Great question! He's probably had barriers to God thrown in his face his whole life. But now he gets the gospel, really *gets* it. If the message of grace is true, what can stand in the way of his full acceptance into the people of God? Absolutely nothing!

BRINGING IN THE OUTCASTS

Do you ever feel left out? Know this: The gospel has come so that all people, everywhere, beyond any possible barrier, can know the love of God and the community of his people.

And the gospel keeps blazing forward, past one barrier after another.

But not everyone is amused. One very dangerous, super-religious zealot is determined to stop the spread of this subversive message before it goes too far. But he has no idea who he is up against.

> PRAYER FOR THE JOURNEY: *Lord, thank you so much that you came for the outsiders. Like me! Help me see your "divine appointments" today.*

The Tomb of Philip, discovered in Hierapolis in 2011. (Photo credit: Carl Rasmussen at www.holylandphotos.org)

18
TERRORIST TO EVANGELIST

ACTS 9:1-9

"Yeah, that's under ISIS control now."

We're peering down from the Golan Heights into Syria, currently one of the world's most dangerous hot spots. I'm visiting with Kenny Garon, an energetic Israeli grandfather and veteran of intense battles fought here during the Yom Kippur war.

Kenny has brought us to bunkers used by the Israeli army in that conflict. He points out a city just a few miles across the border. It's currently occupied by radical Islamists who are battling other rebels and the Syrian government for control of the territory. It's a dramatic, strange reminder of the tensions gripping this part of the world.

Government forces oppose various religiously motivated rebels. Each of those sects in turn seems intent on fighting the others. Foreign empires are also on the scene, navigating a contentious relationship with locals. But one thing they nearly all agree on — they must eliminate the newest group of fanatics which endangers them all.

It's all eerily like the tensions gripping this same corner of the world in the first century.

Only in those days, it was the Herodian government, divided among feuding brothers, in an uneasy truce with the Jewish Temple authorities. That group was itself fractured into different sects, the party that had the upper hand at the time being the strict, fundamentalist

95

Pharisees. Roman troops were also on the scene, a foreign empire trying to quell rebellion, intent on control, suspicious of everyone.

And as uneasy as these factions were with each other, they eventually agreed on one thing: they adamantly, even violently, opposed a new sect called The Way.

This new group claimed to follow a man resurrected from the dead, the Messiah of Israel. That was religiously unacceptable to the Jews and politically unacceptable to the Romans. The spectacularly enthusiastic followers of this new movement sounded very alarming, with their talk of a new King above all other kings, with a kingdom that crossed any carefully carved-out borders. They seemed to endanger not only the fragile political status quo, but also the ancient traditions of the Jews. These people had to be eliminated before their movement took root in Damascus.

MAN ON A MISSION

Unlike Jerusalem, which was out of the way except for religiously motivated pilgrims, Damascus was built on the crossroads of the world. The major north-south and east-west roads ran right through the city. From the perspective of the established authorities, if the Christian cancer got here, it might metastasize to the rest of the world. The situation was urgent. Followers of The Way had to be stopped. Stat.

And the Pharisee dispatched as an agent with a license to round up the opposition was a very unique man named Saul.

He was born in Tarsus. That fact alone put him among the elite. The Roman geographer Strabo described Tarsus as having "surpassed Athens, Alexandria, or any other place that can be named where there have been schools or lectures of philosophers."[4] Visited by luminaries like Julius Caesar, Mark Antony, and Cleopatra (when Cleopatra heard her lover Mark Antony was visiting Tarsus, she quickly sailed there from Egypt and travelled upriver on an elaborate barge dressed as the goddess of love, Aphrodite), Tarsus was a gem, something like Oxford today.

Tarsus was held in such high esteem that it was given a unique honor for a city so far from Rome. Everyone born there received Roman citizenship, as if they'd been born in Rome itself. That meant Saul spoke at least three languages: Greek (the language of education); Hebrew (the language of his faith, Judaism); and Latin (the language of Roman citizens). He was educated by one of the most renowned rabbis of the time, Gamaliel.

The Pharisees saw this cultured yet zealous man as the perfect foil for the mostly Galilean Christ-followers, who seemed undereducated, rural rubes by comparison.

Standing now near the ancient road from Jerusalem to Damascus, I imagine the scene of arguably the most far-reaching conversion in history. The story's told three times in the Book of Acts, in chapters 9, 22, and 26. Everything the Apostle Paul says and does for the rest of his life flows from one sudden and shocking moment on the road I'm on right now.

Since the road to Damascus goes over mountains that rise suddenly from the desert, late afternoon thunderstorms tend to accumulate, with spectacular lightning strikes. I imagine a storm brewing and distant bolts of electricity flashing as Saul begins striding purposefully with his entourage toward Damascus (I wonder if that explains why, in his descriptions of this life-changing event, Saul says his companions saw the bright light but did not hear the voice. Could they have perceived it as a lightning strike? Just a thought).

Saul describes his motivations at the time like this: "On the authority of the chief priests I put many of the Lord's people in prison, and when they were put to death, I cast my vote against them... I was so obsessed with persecuting them that I even hunted them down in foreign cities." (Acts 26:10–11b)

THE SURPRISING GOD

Saul is a man on a mission. Then, somewhere on this road, he suddenly sees a blinding light, brighter than the noonday sun. And he hears a voice: "Saul, Saul, why do you persecute me?" (Acts 9:4b)

Don't miss what happens next. He asks, "Who are you, Lord?" (Acts 9:5)

This detail is fascinating to me. Saul was at the top of his class. Religious expert. Fanatic fundamentalist. But when God appears *Saul doesn't even recognize Him.* All his life he confidently believed he had a clear picture of who God was, and what God wanted. But when God shows up, all Saul can squeak out is, "Who are *you*?"

So much damage is done by cocky religionists who think they have God all figured out. They reduce God to a list of rules and requirements. But if God showed up, they probably wouldn't recognize him. Eventually they will all discover you just can't put God in a box.

The answer comes back: "I am Jesus, whom you are persecuting... Now get up and go into the city, and you will be told what you must do." (Acts 9:5b,6)

LEAN FORWARD
I want you to note how much time Jesus spends reviewing all Saul's sins. How long does he read him the riot act? How much time does he rake him over the coals? Look again.

Other than to confirm that, when Saul was persecuting the church, he was persecuting Jesus, the Lord doesn't say anything at all about Saul's past. Instead he immediately launches into what Saul's life is going to look like moving forward. *No need to rehash your old mistakes. Here's your new life mission.*

Don't you love that? It reminds me of Jesus' post-resurrection appearance to Peter. No need to dwell on the mistakes, Peter. Let's lean forward.

And he does the same for you and me. We're the ones who get obsessed with our past, not God. God says, move forward. He doesn't center on your sins or wallow in your wasted opportunities. So why should you? Look ahead to what he has in store for you — today!

TERRORIST TO EVANGELIST

STILL CHANGING TERRORISTS

In my travels I met a Palestinian man who told me he was once determined to kill Jews. He threw rocks at Israeli soldiers as a teen. He dreamed of joining the intifada. Then in a dream he saw Jesus calling him to follow. Intrigued, he found a Bible and then a church where he began learning more about Christ, eventually learning to love the Jewish people.

As we talked, he took out his phone and showed me pictures of him on a stage washing the feet of two men. I looked at him puzzled and he explained that at a church service in Jerusalem he told his conversion story and at the end of his talk, he asked a Christian pastor and a Jewish rabbi to the stage so that he could wash their feet. Now he travels into war-torn Iraq at great risk to his own life in order to share the gospel with beleaguered villagers there. To this day, he still texts me pictures from his travels as he preaches in bombed-out churches.

How can someone change so radically? Only one way. They meet the living God, the risen Savior, the empowering Spirit.

This moment changes not only Saul's plan for his trip to Damascus; it changes his entire life — and the world. And this stunning turn of events develops in a rather humorous way next.

> PRAYER FOR THE JOURNEY: *Lord, help me not to rehash my past, but to lean forward into the mission you have in store for me now. Thank you for your grace.*

To go from Judea to Damascus, Paul would have had to travel over mountainous and rugged terrain, like these hills near the modern border of Israel and Syria.

WHAT DID PAUL LOOK LIKE?

Although Luke describes Paul's personality well, he leaves out a physical description. The earliest written source for that comes from around 200 AD, in the *Acts of Paul and Thecla*. In that account, a man named Onesiphorus is standing on the road to Lystra, looking for Paul based on a description Titus provided: "And he saw Paul coming, a man small in size, bald-headed, bandy-legged, of noble mien, with eyebrows meeting, rather hook-nosed, full of grace. Sometimes he seemed like a man, and sometimes he had the face of an angel."[5]

Does this description contain any trace of Paul's actual appearance? Bible scholar Mark Wilson observes: "[While] the description of Paul is a conventional one, found as a standard feature in second-century biographies… the bald head is the sole feature out of character for such descriptions and thus perhaps is a genuine recollection of Paul's appearance."[6]

Ancient fresco of Paul and Thecla, probably the earliest depiction known of Paul, discovered in a cave on Mount Bülbüldagh in Turkey. (Public domain photo)

19
GOD SURPRISES

ACTS 9:10-31

I'm at dinner in Jerusalem and bump into a man on the way to my table. We make some small talk and when he discovers I'm a pastor, he comes alive and starts telling his story. I invite him and his wife to join our family and I'm riveted for the next two hours as he shares.

He was raised with a strong Jewish faith, but moved into atheism and materialism as a young man. He says he tried desperately to fill an aching hole inside his soul, first by reaching the height of his profession as a diamond merchant. When that didn't provide satisfaction he tried travel, moving to exotic places all over the earth. Next he plunged into Eastern mysticism, and then rose to the highest levels of a martial art order.

Finally, in desperation, he turned to the person he'd opposed and mocked his whole life. He turned to Christ. And he tells me through tears that his life has never been the same. His wife is with him, and she nods vigorously. "He is a completely new man," she tells me, "like he's had a personality transplant."

I ask him what his friends here in Jerusalem think. He replies, "At first they don't believe me; they think I am joking when I say I follow Yeshua (the Hebrew word for Jesus). They are still sort of suspicious of me. Really, they don't know what to think. But my parents are glad that at least I am happy!"

I always love hearing stories of how people come to faith in Christ.

But it's intriguing to me when their own friends and even other Christians don't know what to make of their conversions.

One of my friends is a scientist, a marine biologist who was a lifelong atheist before he became a believer. He tells me that his scientist colleagues were surprised but accepting of his new faith; it was other, non-scientist Christians who were so shocked that they almost couldn't believe it. They wanted to debate him about all his scientific views before they felt he could be safely accepted into the fold. They didn't believe he was a "true Christian."

That's what happens to Saul. It's actually pretty funny. When this vicious persecutor of the faith shows up in Damascus, no one believes he's changed his tune, least of all the Christians. God has to appear in a vision to a disciple named Ananias to announce Saul's conversion. He tells Ananias that he is to heal Saul of his blindness. And Ananias basically says, "Lord, are you kidding me?"

NOT THIS GUY!

He says, "Lord, I have heard many reports about this man and all the harm he has done to your saints... and he has come here with authority from the chief priests to arrest all who call on your name!" (Acts 9:13–14).

It's funny how we think we need to give God news updates. "Lord, in case you haven't been checking lately, here's why I can't do what you're asking of me..."

Of course God knows more than you and I know. He's the divine chess master, planning all the moves. And he has lots of other pieces on the board besides you and me. Before you do your part, God is already moving other pieces into play. So just do what he asks of you. And watch the big picture start to take shape.

THE SURPRISING PEOPLE GOD USES

Then God tells Ananias something truly amazing: "This man is my chosen instrument to carry my name before the Gentiles and their kings..." (Acts 9:15).

This man? Your chosen instrument? This man zealously focused on arresting and even killing believers? Couldn't you use any of the other apostles? Two other times in this chapter (verses 21 and 26), people simply cannot believe this fierce opponent of Christianity is now a friend.

Saul is blazing a trail for many other famous opponents of Christianity who became articulate spokespeople for the faith, including Peter Hitchens, brother of outspoken atheist Christopher Hitchens; Oxford professor C.S. Lewis, who went from atheist to evangelist; and the lyricist of *Amazing Grace*, John Newton, a radically converted former slave ship captain and atheist who described himself as a man "appointed to preach the faith he had long sought to destroy." But God used them in part because of their antagonistic past, not in spite of it.

THE SURPRISING WAY GOD WORKS

I've seen it again and again at the church I pastor. What people see as footnotes or even embarrassments in their past are the very things God uses to give them amazingly productive ministry.

God used Saul's unusual combination of strict training in Judaism, plus first-hand knowledge of pagan culture in his hometown of Tarsus, to bring the message of Jesus to both Jews and pagans across the Empire.

And God knows how he can use parts of your own background that you may see as irrelevant or even incompatible with your faith.

Here's the takeaway. Just release yourself to God. Do what he directs. Then watch him move you, using and redeeming elements of your past, in ways that surprise even you.

> PRAYER FOR THE JOURNEY: *Lord, I entrust you with every element in my past, all the accomplishments as well as all the hurts and mistakes. Please use it all for good. I know you will, because you are the Redeemer!*

20
RADICAL PICNIC

We've driven from the high country of Jerusalem to the tiny port of Joppa (or Jaffa, as it's known today). It seems almost abandoned tonight. I wander through its ancient stone alleys as amber light from second-story windows gives the wet cobbles a warm glow. Fishing boats bob in the harbor while their nets dry on the rocks. I can hear a baby cry. Someone's playing music. The smell of sautéed onions and garlic drifts through the breeze. Tonight it's easy to imagine this place back in Bible times.

Joppa may be the very oldest port city in the world; many of the other ports from Bible times are long-abandoned or silted up. Not Joppa. It's always been Israel's portal to the rest of the world.

The cedar logs Solomon used to build the temple were floated down the coast to Joppa.

The prophet Jonah hopped on a ship here to try to escape God's call.

And in Acts 10, Joppa becomes the portal through which the message of Jesus goes international, in ways the disciples never expected.

CLEAN AT ALL COSTS

Remember, at this point all the disciples are Jewish, 100%. Even the Gentiles in the church (like the Ethiopian eunuch) enter the faith as converted Jews. They all try their best to keep the kosher laws, and they all still think of the Messiah primarily as Israel's king who will restore the country to glory. Sure, the other nations will be blessed through the Jewish Messiah. But they all still need to get to the Messiah through the portal of conversion to Judaism.

Then everything changes.

Peter's here because the Joppa Jesus-followers summoned him. Their beloved Tabitha, a woman well known for her goodness and generosity, has died. I suspect they simply wanted Peter there to pray and mourn with them. But instead he prays and raises her up.

Peter ends up staying in Joppa for several days at the house of a Jewish believer in Jesus named Simon who was a tanner by trade. This is an interesting detail in light of what follows, because tanners were considered unclean by strict Jews due to their constant contact with the hide of dead animals.

Here's the situation: Like today, in Peter's time religiously observant Jews did not eat non-kosher food, like shellfish or pork or fish without scales (such as eels). And there were many, many more dietary regulations. Even plates or bowls used to serve non-kosher food were considered unclean.

And this was not just a matter of personal holiness. The influential Pharisees taught that the Messiah would come to Israel only when the entire nation was holy. That meant *everyone* needed to rigorously keep the food laws (and all the rest of the religious law too). The Messiah was watching, scanning the land to see if the Jewish nation was holy. In their definition that meant religiously observant.

To put it bluntly, the belief was something like this. "You better watch out; you better not cry. You better not pout, I'm telling you why: Messiah King is coming to town. He knows if you've been kosher. He sees what's on your plate. He knows if you've been bad or good, so be good for all our sakes!"

If you weren't keeping kosher, you were preventing the coming of the Messiah for the entire country. Like Linus' belief that one molecule of insincerity in a single person will keep the Great

Pumpkin away, everyone needed to be on exactly the same perfect page. That's pressure!

All this meant it was virtually unthinkable for a Jewish person to eat at the home of a Gentile. Even if the food they served was kosher, who knew what was in the kitchen, or what had touched those dishes?

Now you'll understand why Peter's vision so disturbed him.

THE NON-KOSHER PICNIC

Luke says Peter was hungry. Then he has a vision where he sees something like a picnic blanket let down from heaven with all kinds of food in it. That might not seem like a surprising dream for a hungry man. But this picnic has both kosher and non-kosher food in it, all jumbled together. Then he hears a voice telling him to get up and eat whatever he wants.

He seems to be thinking this is a test. "Of course not, Lord!" he objects.

Then he hears these momentous words: *"What God has made clean, you must not call unclean."*

Peter is puzzled. And as we will see, these are not words just about food. They're also about people.

THE ITALIAN JOB

Meanwhile, a few miles north, a Gentile has a vision. And not just any Gentile. This is a Roman. And not just any Roman; this is a Roman soldier. And not just any soldier; this is a centurion, a commander of a regiment. And not just any regiment. This is "The Italian Regiment." So this man, Cornelius, is a Gentile of Gentiles. About as far from a Messiah-preaching, kosher-keeping Jew as you could imagine.

Yet he's also a God-fearer, the term we've already seen used to refer to Gentiles who were not Jewish, but still believed in only one true God. They did not bow to the vast pantheon of Roman deities. Cornelius has been sincerely seeking this God, praying and showing compassion for the poor. Then in this vision, he's told to send servants to Joppa to find a man named Peter.

MEETING FRIENDS

Peter's about to discover something about going into all the world as a missionary. When you do that, you're not just bringing a new idea to total pagans. You're actually discovering sympathetic souls, people raised in completely different cultures who actually already believe something of your message, before you even meet them. Sometimes they've even come to their conclusions through visions, like Cornelius. I've heard missionaries describe this phenomenon again and again.

This is not meant to imply that people don't need to hear the complete message of the gospel. The point is that God is preparing people you meet, long before you meet them. When you share your faith with friends and neighbors, don't expect to encounter only atheists and doubters. You'll also meet people who resonate with some things you're describing, and have been asking the very questions you're answering!

People like Cornelius.

Peter takes a deep breath. He walks into this Gentile house and starts explaining about Jesus. But first he says something that becomes the barrier-busting template for the rest of Acts:

> "I now realize how true it is that God does not show favoritism but accepts from every nation the one who fears him and does what is right." (Acts 10:34–35)

This is a huge statement, a massive development in the Jesus movement. Peter is realizing that God wants to make one kingdom out of all the diverse nations on the planet. The point we often miss is the revolutionary idea that *they do not have to become Jews first*.

This was a major turning point. Apparently up until this moment the disciples believed that, yes, they were to go into all the world with the gospel. But they were to tell people of the Jewish Messiah and convert them to become Jews in order to follow Jesus. Now Peter sees that God took a divine shortcut straight across ethnic lines and reached these Italians before they ever converted to Judaism.

This is going to absolutely blow the minds of the first Christians. As you'll see, it takes the apostles years to figure out exactly what to do with these Gentile Jesus-followers. Their constant question becomes, *How Jewish do Christians have to be?*

Peter then summarizes Jesus' ministry and ends with this invitation: "...everyone who believes in him receives forgiveness of sins through his name." (Acts 10:43)

And even Peter is astonished at what happens next. Before Cornelius and his family can even verbalize the "yes" that's in their hearts, the Holy Spirit is poured upon them, *the same way Peter and the Jewish disciples experienced their conversion in Acts 2.* This is God showing Peter that he approves of the believers behind this new broken barrier. And everything changes.

AND THAT INCLUDES YOU

Do not miss it. I will say it again. This is a lightbulb moment for Peter. A world-altering concept is thought by a human brain for the very first time: The idea that Gentiles can be Jesus-followers *without first converting to Judaism.* That is about to bring lots of energy and lots of controversy to the early Jesus movement.

And never forget: This message of radical inclusion extends to *you.*

Maybe you've felt excluded by a lot of people in your life. Excluded from family. From teams. From work. Did you know that you are chosen? Invited to belong? That God's perfect plan for his people includes you? No matter who may have excluded you, God wants to *include* you in his new, international, barrier-busting family.

Of course this doesn't mean God validates all our opinions or behaviors. As N.T. Wright puts it:

It means there are no ethnic or geographical or cultural or moral barriers any longer in the way of anyone and everyone being offered forgiveness and new life. That is a message far more powerful than the easygoing laissez-faire tolerance which Western society so easily embraces. Cornelius didn't want God to *tolerate* him. He wanted to be welcomed, forgiven, healed, transformed. And he was.[7]

Fair warning: Not everyone thinks this kind of radical inclusion is such a wonderful idea. As Peter is about to discover.

PRAYER FOR THE JOURNEY: *Heavenly Father, thank you that I am chosen by you. And I marvel that you are already working in the hearts of people with whom I will have conversations about the faith.*

SEASIDE CAESAREA

Caesarea Maritime is a major city in the Book of Acts, the most "Roman" outpost in Judea. Herod the Great built this city as the largest man-made seaport in the world at the time. It had stunning new marble buildings, running water, a sewage system, a massive theater, not one but two arenas for chariot races, beautiful temples, one of Herod's elaborate palaces built right on an ocean cliff with a swimming pool in the backyard. It was all cutting edge. The breakwaters here were built with what was then the brand new technology of hydraulic cement.

The beautiful ruins of Caesarea Maritime along the coast of modern Israel.

This was the headquarters of the Roman Army and government, not Jerusalem. That means it was home base for Pontius Pilate. A famous inscription with his name was found right here at the theater. Until it was unearthed, some scholars surmised Pilate was a fictional character imagined by the gospel writers. But now we know he really existed.

Caesarea appears many times in the Book of Acts. In Acts 21, Philip preached and lived here with his four prophetess daughters. In Acts 10, Peter has his revolutionary encounter with the Italian centurion. In Acts 12, Herod Agrippa dies here after accepting the idolization of the crowd. Paul visited the city voluntarily three times, in Acts 9:30, Acts 18:22, and in Acts 21:8–16. Then at the end of Acts Paul is hauled back to Caesarea from Jerusalem after his enemies incite a riot. He spends two years in prison here before being sent on to Rome.

The Pilate inscription found at Caesarea, the first evidence outside the Bible for his existence.

21
PRIDE AND PREJUDICE

ACTS 11:1-18

A few days after our visit to the beautiful and relaxed seaside ports of Joppa and Caesarea, I'm back in Jerusalem for my third visit, walking up a new wooden stairway to the Dome of the Rock in Jerusalem. As security guards pat down nervous visitors it's easy to sense a lot of tension.

The ancient platform rising above the Old City of Jerusalem was originally built more than 2,000 years ago by Herod the Great as a rectangular plaza that would incorporate his Temple complex. Though the Temple itself was destroyed by Romans in 70 AD, some of his retaining walls, staircases, and other structures remain to this day.

The custodianship of this area, significant to Jews, Christians, and Muslims, has caused riots in our time just as it did in the days of Acts. A council of Muslim leaders called the *Waqf* currently has custody of the area, and while non-Muslims are usually allowed on the Temple Mount during certain hours, they can no longer enter the beautiful Dome of the Rock building. Now only Muslims may enter. The rest of us must be content with enjoying its beauty from the outside.

As we slowly walk around the building, a scuffle erupts in the plaza. Young orthodox Jewish boys have entered wearing religious medallions and praying loudly in Hebrew. Any religious display from non-Muslims is forbidden because of the tension here, and sure enough, some older men yell at the boys in Arabic and a chase begins. It stops when police grab the boys and take them out. I read later that three minors were arrested for disturbing the peace. It's all so similar to the tensions surrounding this very same piece of real estate in the first century.

In those days only Jews were allowed into the area nearest the Temple. Archaeologists have found an engraved stone from the first century that proclaims in Greek:

> NO FOREIGNER IS TO GO BEYOND THE BALUSTRADE AND THE
> PLAZA OF THE TEMPLE ZONE. WHOEVER IS CAUGHT DOING
> SO WILL HAVE HIMSELF TO BLAME FOR HIS DEATH WHICH WILL
> FOLLOW.

The exclusion of Gentiles from the Temple is one of the criticisms leveled by Jesus against the religious leaders:

> "It is written, 'My house shall be a house of prayer for
> all nations. But you have turned it into a den of thieves.'"
> (Mark 11:17)

And now the early church is falling into the very same trap.

INTERNAL BARRIERS

It's here that we meet, for the first time, a group that becomes a major plot point in Acts: Christ-followers from the Jewish community in Jerusalem. They're sincere believers in Jesus, but they cannot understand how non-Jews can possibly become part of their movement without first converting to Judaism, including the symbolic rite of circumcision for males. There is both pride and prejudice at work here. Pride in their own purity. And prejudice against Gentiles.

Before you judge them too harshly, here's where they're coming from. Way back in Genesis, God gave the circumcision ritual to Abraham as a very personal, intimate sign of dedication to the one true God. By the time of Acts, circumcision had been part of the Jewish tradition for nearly two thousand years. So how can Peter now suddenly declare that someone could be fully part of God's people without undergoing this Jewish ritual?

PRIDE AND PREJUDICE

At least, that is their surface concern. But underneath that supposedly religious point of view, there is something else. Note their first question: *How could you even visit and eat with them?* Visiting the homes of Gentiles was never prohibited by the Bible, but the strict religious teachers had drawn such thick boundary lines between Jew and Gentile that even dining with a non-Jew became taboo. Their religious rules, as often happens, turned into personal prejudice.

Max Lucado has written some great words on this:

> People are prone to pecking orders. The affluent over the destitute. The educated over the dropout. The old-timer over the newcomer. The Jew over the Gentile. An impassable gulf yawned between Jew and Gentile in the days of the early church. A Jew could not drink milk drawn by Gentiles or eat their food. Jews could not aid a Gentile mother when she gave birth. Jewish physicians could not attend to non-Jewish patients.[8]

Unless that Jew was Jesus. He kicked off his ministry in his hometown synagogue with a sermon about how the Jewish prophet Elijah helped a Gentile widow and healed a Gentile warrior. And the people were so furious with Jesus they wanted to throw him off a cliff.

So Peter has two voices in his head: The Jesus he knew said to build bridges. The culture he knew said to build walls.

He listens to Jesus.

Peter tells these religious inquisitors that, after the Holy Spirit baptized Cornelius and his family in a repeat of Pentecost, *he remembered the words of Jesus* telling them how the disciples would soon be baptized in the Spirit. He realizes God is showing, through the very same sign, that these Gentiles are also accepted as Christ-followers.

When they hear Peter explain it this way, the believers in Jerusalem

"...had no further objection. They praised God, saying, 'So then, even to the Gentiles God has granted repentance that leads to life!'" (Acts 11:18)

But this unity does not last. By Acts 15:5 this opinion seems to be reversed. Then, later in that chapter, the leadership decides (again!) that Gentiles *are* welcome. But then, when Paul returns to Jerusalem in Acts 21, the prejudice *against* Gentiles is even stronger!

RELAPSE HAPPENS

This back-and-forth opinion about Gentiles continues. It's a reminder that relapse is natural. And I'm not just talking about relapse into sin. I mean relapse into a works-oriented view of our relationship with God and a pecking-order view of the world. You can get excited about the fact that God accepts us by grace alone, and not works. But slowly, insidiously, you and I will always slip back into a works emphasis and a stratified view of the world. You'll begin to feel your acceptance with God is based on something other than grace: good deeds, church attendance, moral perfection. And you can start judging others the same way. What's the solution? As Tim Keller says, you need to keep preaching the gospel — *to yourself!*

GRACE IS MESSY

Maybe that Jew-Gentile divide is not what's troubling you. But there's probably some other divide, if you're honest. You wear flip-flops and shorts and judge those uptight people in suits and ties. You drive a Prius and eat vegan and are sure you must be better than the SUV-driving BBQers you notice just over your fence. You're a progressive tree-hugger who can hardly imagine being friends with the redneck conservatives you see when you venture to their part of the county. Or reverse any of those sentences.

And it gets more complicated. What about those women from the drug treatment center who have to attend church each week. Can't someone tell them to dress a little more... appropriately? What about those teenagers over there smoking? I wouldn't want my kids in youth group with the likes of them.

You know what? Grace is messy. That comes through loud and clear in Acts as these early Christians try to figure out the implications of the gospel.

New believers don't always conform to our perfect idea of what a mature Christian should be like. That same exact tension has been occurring in the Jesus movement from day one.

Be welcoming. Give others time to grow. And orient them toward the grace of God that will change them from the inside out.

> PRAYER FOR THE JOURNEY: *Father, may I welcome new believers with real joy and not skepticism. And thank you for rescuing me.*

MEANWHILE IN JERUSALEM

As Acts unfolds, the international Jesus movement gradually becomes friendlier to Gentiles. Meanwhile back in Jerusalem, the opposite is happening to Temple Judaism.

First-century Jewish writer Josephus recounts how intense the anti-Gentile emotion was getting:

> At the same time Eleazar, the son of Ananias the high priest, a very bold youth, who was at that time governor of the Temple, persuaded those that officiated in the Divine service to receive no gift or sacrifice for any foreigner. And this was the true beginning of our war with the Romans, for the priests rejected even the sacrifice of Caesar on this account...[9]

The Jesus-followers were letting the lowest ranking Gentile into the family. At the same time the Jerusalem Temple would no longer allow even the highest Gentile's sacrifice. Imagine the tension for Jerusalem-based Jewish followers of Jesus as they heard of Gentiles flooding into their movement.

PART FOUR

GOING GLOBAL

22
LITTLE CHRISTS

ACTS 11:19-30

Antioch. This is where the Jesus movement really starts to explode. In the first century it was a bridge city between East and West, between the Roman world and the world of the Jews and Egyptians. One scholar estimates that about half of all international travelers in the first century eventually came through Antioch![1]

It's a slightly confusing name because there were several cities named Antioch in those days. But this one, also known as "Syrian Antioch," was the biggest. It was about 15 miles inland from the sea on the river Orontes. Because ships could navigate from the ocean upriver to the city, and the major north-south and east-west Roman highways ran right through the town, this was a very strategic spot.

And it's here that followers of Jesus were first called "Christians." The nickname stuck. "Christian" was probably a pejorative that believers eventually enjoyed and adopted, like when American revolutionaries gleefully accepted the British insult "Yankee."

"Christ" was the Greek word for "Messiah," which means the anointed one, the one chosen by God. The followers of Jesus talked about the Messiah so much that people labelled them "Messiahists," or Christians. You could also interpret the word as "little Christs," again, because they incessantly spoke about and acted like Jesus Christ.

It's worth asking whether people today would label us the same way. Is it Jesus Christ they hear us emphasizing? Or would our conversations have us labeled Good-deed-ians or Positive-thinking-ists or Moralists? Or Fear-ists and Withdrawal-from-the-world-ists?

I want to live worthy of the nickname *Christian*. I want to stay on message. I hope to make Jesus so much the center of my speaking and living that it's clear I am one of those Jesus people.

This is so helpful when people obsess on things about the Bible or Christianity that seem hard to understand. Ultimately I am not even a Bible-ian or a Moses-ian or a Religion-ian. I am a *Christ*ian. I have chosen my path because I love and trust Christ, not because I know every answer to every Bible problem or because I feel I have to defend the church against every charge.

GLOBAL POSITIONING

Antioch is where the "Messiah-ist" message starts going viral. As merchants and travelers come through town, many hear and believe this message about the Messiah for all people, and take it along the trade routes to the rest of the known world. This may be the reason why, as we'll see later, there's apparently an established Christian community in Rome long before any of the apostles visit.

The Jerusalem church hears about these exploding numbers of Jesus-followers in Antioch, a group they have had little to do with. Luke says the Antioch community is started by Greek-speaking Jews from Cyprus and Cyrene, not from Jerusalem. So the Jerusalem Christians send Barnabas to check it out. And he looks around. And sees a motley crew of various nationalities and social classes.

These Antioch Christians were probably rough-and-tumble sailors and wealthy merchants and lowly slaves, just the mix you'd expect to see in a busy port town. Barnabas could have wrung his hands at what was surely a less polished, less knowledgeable, less... *Jewish*... form of the Jesus movement than he knew in Jerusalem. Yet the text says he "saw what the grace of God had done" and was glad.

ENCOURAGE NEWBIES TO MAJOR ON THE MAJORS

When God is doing something in the lives of "outsiders" who may not know the right terminology or the traditional way to express their faith, can you and I, like Barnabas, see the grace of God and not just chaotic, awkward people?

Like I said, grace is messy. I've seen ex-cons, drug addicts, alcoholics, atheist scientists, competitive business leaders, and homeless people find Christ at the church I pastor. And at first many are very raw. Like, *extremely* raw. More than once I've heard a brand new believer express delight in their freshly discovered faith through language that would be R-rated if it was in a movie. They're just using the most emphatic adjectives they know.

I find I often need to resist the temptation to immediately swoop in and correct all the little ways I might think they need to be brought into line with Christian culture. I need to see their awkwardness through a different lens. They're babies, taking their first wobbly steps. And so I need to be encouraging. Like a dad. Like Barnabas. If kids only hear constant correction from authority figures, pretty soon they'll become discouraged.

Instead of nitpicking, I need to give new believers the big picture, a great north star to navigate by, so any smaller corrections can happen naturally. That's what Barnabas does here. He urges them to stay faithful and fully committed to God. Because that's where all life change starts. Major on the majors, not the minors. Believe in the power of the Holy Spirit. Relax. Be patient.

DEVELOP NEW DRAFT PICKS

And look: there's Paul, still called Saul here. Barnabas, who sees potential in this former hater, taps him on the shoulder. Maybe it's because Saul speaks Greek fluently and was raised as a Roman in addition to his first-rate Jewish education. Whatever his reasons, Barnabas sees an ideal teacher for this very international crowd in Antioch.

LITTLE CHRISTS

Like Barnabas, can you look for new emerging "stars" to help
disciple others? This is often the hardest thing for me. But it really
is a pattern in Acts, isn't it? God doesn't have these disciples func-
tioning as gurus everyone else must visit as they alone dispense
wisdom. The apostles are more like coaches constantly looking for
the next draft pick to train and guide.

GOD WORKING EVEN THROUGH BAD THINGS

And remember what started this international spread of the Jesus
message? Luke mentions it back in Acts 8:1 and repeats it here.
That repetition means it's important: "Now those who had been
scattered *by the persecution that broke out when Stephen was killed*
traveled as far as Phoenicia, Cyprus, and Antioch…" (Acts 11:19).
The gospel advanced because of tragedy. That doesn't mean God
wanted Stephen killed. It means God works through bad things.

In our time we also see God working through the tragedies of
religious persecution and war and refugee crises and other calamities
to reach many people who may never have heard the gospel before.
Friends who minister to refugees in Greece tell me they have never
seen such an openness to the gospel. And I've seen God working
through cancer patients to bring the gospel to doctors and through
prisoners to bring the gospel to guards. This doesn't mean the war
or cancer or crime were the will of God. It means God is able to
work *through* all things, even the worst things imaginable.

I have a suggestion. No matter what you're going through right
now, think of it as a chapter in the Book of Acts. How would Luke
have written about your troubles? He certainly wouldn't downplay
the degree of difficulty. In fact, he would show you painted into a
corner! But then he would show the Holy Spirit working *through*
the catastrophe or the delay or the injustice.

Here's the thing. The story of your life is still being written. Don't
stop in the middle of the book. Keep reading. Watch for what God
does next.

HELPING THE POOR

In this passage you also see how collecting offerings for the needy has been part of the Jesus movement's DNA from the very start.

In my modern journeys through the geography of Acts, I've met Christians in Athens who feed Syrian refugees every single night. I've visited a church in Amman, Jordan that opened a medical clinic for people fleeing Iraq. I've worshipped at a church in Jerusalem that regularly assists the Palestinian poor.

When you feel that longing to help the hungry, the poor, the oppressed, that's because it's as much a part of your identity as your own name. If you're a follower of Jesus, a *Christian*, his Spirit is changing you into someone who resembles Christ more and more. His heart goes out to the poor and oppressed. That's why yours does too. Go with that.

So now the movement really starts to pick up steam. Despite the persecution, it's making great gains. And Herod decides he is just the person to stop it. By killing its leaders.

> PRAYER FOR THE JOURNEY: *Lord, may I live in such a way that if a nickname was chosen for me, it would be "Christian." Help me major on the majors, and not the minors. Help me stay on message.*

WHICH HEROD?

There are actually six different Herods in the New Testament, all related to each other, so this can cause a lot of confusion. Herod started out as a personal name, and then the first King Herod decided to name all his kids Herod too, like George Foreman naming all his boys George (One of Herod's daughters is even named Herodias!). Then it becomes a title, like Caesar. Here's a quick scorecard to help clear things up:

1. HEROD THE GREAT (RULED 37-4 BC)

The first Herod, the guy in the Christmas story. He begins construction on the massive Temple expansion in Jerusalem and builds many other spectacular monuments to himself.

2. HEROD ARCHELAUS (RULED 4 BC-6 AD)

One of the three sons of Herod the Great mentioned in the Bible. After Herod the Great's death, three of his sons divided his empire. This one got the part around Jerusalem. The most unstable and violent of the bunch (and that's saying something). He was so crazy the Romans replaced him with a Roman procurator, or governor, after a few years.

3. HEROD ANTIPAS (RULED 4 BC-39 AD)

Second son of Herod the Great mentioned in the Bible, he ruled Galilee (the northwestern part of modern Israel, from the middle of the Sea of Galilee west into the hills). This is the guy Jesus compared to a "fox," the one who killed John the Baptist. While visiting Jerusalem one fateful Passover, he's asked by the Roman procurator Pilate to weigh in on Jesus' trial.

4. HEROD PHILIP THE TETRARCH (RULED 4 BC-34 AD)

Third son of Herod the Great mentioned in Scripture, this one ruled over the land east of Galilee full of Greeks and Syrians. He was much less Jewish in character than the rest of Judea (That's why Jesus was constantly crossing the Sea of Galilee to get to "the other side," as the gospel writers put it. He's running for the border, heading into another territory until things cool down).

5. HEROD AGRIPPA THE 1ST (RULED CA. 37 AD-44 AD)
Grandson of Herod the Great. This Herod killed James the brother of John and put Peter in prison in Acts 12. He thought he was awesome (kind of a fatal family flaw). One day while basking in the worship of all his fans he has some sort of stroke, is incapacitated, and finally "eaten by worms." I know! Gross! But I think Luke includes this to show it's not just good guys who suffer. Once in a while bad guys do get their comeuppance.

6. HEROD AGRIPPA THE 2ND (RULED CIRCA 50 AD UNTIL DEATH AROUND 93 AD)
The last Herod mentioned in the Bible, the great-grandson of Herod the Great. He's the one who presided over the trial of Paul in Acts 25–26.

Sixteenth-century woodcut depicting Herod Agrippa II. (Public domain photo)

23
SEE WHAT YOU GET

ACTS 12:1-25

Our little band of travelers is back in Jerusalem, excited to visit the Church of the Holy Sepulcher today. It's the ancient church built over the spot that early Christians believed was the empty tomb of Jesus.

There's a thick human traffic jam inside the church today. It's so crowded people can barely move. A shoving match starts between two different Christian denominations, jostling the mob (I can almost hear the Lord saying, "So, you want a journey through the Book of Acts, René? Okay, here's some mob anger. It's exactly like Acts!").

Then we hear breaking glass and somebody screams and a fight breaks out. People begin to push in panic. Our Jerusalem guide Kenny says, "Time to leave. Right away." So we get out.

If you've read my book *Jesus Journey* you know what happens next. After a quick count in the alleyway outside the church we realize a member of our tour group, Marlene, is missing. We send a couple scouts back into the chapel, but crowds make any search impossible. Kenny says we have no other choice but to move on, that either Marlene will find us or he'll go back and find her later in the day, so we go to the next spot on our itinerary minus a member.

We plod along for an hour. But we're distracted and worried. So I tell Kenny I'd like to stop and pray for Marlene to be found. We circle up, hold hands. Marlene is such a gentle, soft-spoken senior citizen I simply can't imagine her all by herself in the rather rough-and-tumble crowds choking the old city that hot afternoon.

"Lord," I pray, "you said you came to seek and save the lost, so please find our little lost lamb Marlene today."

Something tells me to be specific. I feel kind of silly saying this out loud, but I pray: "God, specifically, please remind Marlene that our guide Kenny's mobile phone number is on the back of the name tag she is wearing around her neck, and help her to figure out how to place a call to him. Right now. In Jesus' name, amen."

Seconds after the "amen," before anyone has a chance to say another word, Kenny's phone beeps. He answers it. We watch as his face goes pale. He blinks twice. And after a brief conversation, he hangs up and says, "Uh… that was Marlene. She said she suddenly remembered she had my number on her name tag. Then she realized she could ask a priest to use his phone."

A rousing cheer goes up from our group. Right before this, everyone had been so dejected. Now there's euphoria! But I can tell Kenny's a little shaken by the immediacy of the result. Later I ask him if he sees that as an answer to prayer. Feeling more collected now he says, "Well, sure, you could choose to see it that way. And maybe Marlene just remembered what I told her about that name tag!"

HOW DO YOU SEE IT?

That's how it usually is with miracles, isn't it? When strange things happen, we tend to explain them through our pre-existing world view. You see it right here in Acts.

Peter's imprisoned by Herod. An angel wakes him up and leads him right out in the middle of the night. And, at least at first, absolutely no one believes it's happening. Not the other Christians. Not Herod. Not even Peter.

Luke says Peter believed he was only seeing a vision of an angel leading him out of prison. It was the middle of the night, so he probably thought he was dreaming. Then as he suddenly wakes up in the dark street, he realizes he's truly outside the prison bars. Best sleep walking outcome ever! Peter finds a friend's house and knocks on the door.

And in the funniest scene of comic relief in Acts, the servant girl Rhoda (her name is a nickname for "rosebush," so the English equivalent would be "Rosie") answers the door, hears Peter's voice, and leaves the door locked in her excitement as she runs to tell her family. I imagine Peter outside in the dark street nervously glancing around as Rhoda tells the prayer group that Peter's at the door. And she is told, basically, "That's impossible! Now pipe down with your crazy talk about Peter being released. We are trying to pray for Peter to be released."

Then when she keeps insisting it's really Peter, these giants of the faith conclude, "It must be his angel (meaning his ghost)." In other words, they decide he's dead.

I find this super comforting, don't you? This story has such a ring of truth to it. You pray for a friend to be healed of cancer. Then when the tests come back clear, you say, "What a surprise!" You ask for God to open doors. He does. And you hesitate. "Is this really God directing?" You pray for a family member to have a safe trip. Then the phone rings, it's their number, and you think, "There's been an accident."

It really is possible to be a faithful believer in Jesus, sincerely asking God for help. And then, when it happens, to be revealed as someone who didn't think God would answer after all. That's called being human. Jesus said miracles would be done with just a mustard seed of faith. So he understands when there are other seeds mixed in. As a father requesting a miracle once said to Jesus, "I believe. Help my unbelief." (Mark 9:24) I love that prayer. And love that Jesus works with it.

But you need to be honest with yourself: You see your *needs*. You probably pray about them often. But do you see God's *answers*? You and I are surrounded by answered prayers every day. Prayers you've prayed about your church, your family, your worries. Ask God to help you see what you receive from him. Live with eyes wide open to the miracles.

One of the most cryptic parts of Acts follows the funniest. Peter can see he's a liability to the Jerusalem church, attracting the unwanted attention of the authorities. He quiets down everyone in the house, instructs them to tell James (a different James than the one Herod killed, of course. This is probably James the brother of Jesus), and then he leaves town for parts unknown. Luke mysteriously says Peter went "somewhere else." Some believe this is the first time he went to Rome, although that's just a guess.

The next morning Herod, looking forward to another beheading, discovers Peter is missing. He questions the guards, and does not come to the conclusion this was a miracle. That doesn't fit his reality. He figures the guards must have let Peter go. In his world view that's the only explanation, because believing Peter was set free by God would mean he, Herod, is wrong. That is unacceptable. So, having promised a beheading, he kills all the guards instead.

It's a brutal move. And Luke reports that Herod gets his just desserts. This does not always occur, not in the Bible, or in the world today. But you can tell that Luke feels a measure of relief as he's able to report that it happens once in a while. Herod dies soon afterward. While accepting the fawning worship of an audience in Caesarea he is "struck down," incapacitated, and as mentioned before, soon eaten by worms, a grisly end to a violent man.

WHERE ALL ROADS LEAD

It's a fitting finish to the first half of Acts: The king of Judea tries to silence the message of the King of Kings. He fails, and the new kingdom begins to radiate outward to the whole world. End, part one. So far Acts has focused on Peter and his companions, mostly in Jerusalem.

Now the baton is passed, and part two is about to start, featuring Paul and his friends headed toward Rome. Just like the plot of

SEE WHAT YOU GET

Star Wars leads to the Death Star and *The Wizard of Oz* to the Emerald City, Rome looms in Acts as the place the Jesus message is ultimately headed, if it's going to go in spectacular fashion to the ends of the earth.

STAY OPEN AND AWARE

All the characters in this story are touched by a miracle. Yet none of them see it that way at first. Some never do.

How about you? Are your eyes open and is your heart open to see the ways God is at work all around you? Don't sleepwalk through the miracles.

A tip that works for me: Look for opportunities to thank God throughout your day. You'll catch him in action a lot more often that way.

> PRAYER FOR THE JOURNEY: *Lord, help me see what I receive from you. I want to live with eyes open to answered prayer all around me.*

THE COLORS OF CHRISTIANS

The five teachers mentioned as leaders in Acts 13 couldn't be more diverse:

SIMEON CALLED NIGER

Simeon is a Jewish name. The nickname *Niger* means "black," probably referring to a dark complexion and/or African descent.

LUCIUS OF CYRENE

This was part of Africa that includes modern Libya. Lucius is a Latin name.

MANAEN

That's a Greek version of the Hebrew name *Menachem*. He is called a *syntrophos* of Herod. That means he was something like his foster brother, and was raised with him in Rome.

BARNABAS

A Jewish man we met earlier. Acts 4 says he's from Cyprus, the large island Paul's about to visit next.

SAUL FROM TARSUS

His hometown is an influential university city near the coast. In 66 BC, after being conquered by Pompeii (yes, the same famous general the volcano-doomed city was named after) Tarsus was made an official outpost of Rome. That meant all its inhabitants were automatically Roman citizens, just as if they'd been born in Rome. Several Caesars were even buried here. Latin was the official language.

So what do we have here? Two Africans, one Cypriot, one Roman, another guy raised in Rome. They're still all Jewish. No Gentile has yet attained leadership in the Jesus movement — but these men are much more internationally experienced than the original disciples. They're all familiar with navigating multi-cultural situations. Which is precisely what the movement is about to need.

PAUL'S NAME CHANGE

One interesting side note (and personal source of amusement). Did you notice Saul is called by the Roman name *Paul* for the first time in Acts 13? Ever wonder why? Many writers have pointed out that his original Hebrew name, Saul, when translated into Latin, sounds very much like a rude first-century word for an effeminate man. So perhaps simply to avoid the distraction, Saul reasoned, "Uh, know what? Call me Paul." And let me just say, as someone named "René" who grew up in America and heard many would-be junior high comedians making mirth, I think Paul made a very wise choice here.

24
TO THE BIRTHPLACE OF APHRODITE

As I fly over the Mediterranean after my stay in Israel I look out the airplane window and see the beautiful island of Cyprus, where Paul and Barnabas sail next. It's where Paul's traveling companion Barnabas was from, so maybe that's why they go here first.

They journey right to the island's capital city, Paphos. The mythical birthplace of the Greek goddess of love Aphrodite, the city of Paphos was the most non-Jewish, pagan city Christian missionaries had visited to this point in Acts. Paphos has a connection to the musical *My Fair Lady*, which is based on the George Bernard Shaw play *Pygmalion*, which in turn is based on the Greek myth of Pygmalion, the man who fell in love with a statue of Aphrodite he made. And that story was set right here in Paphos!

Paul and Barnabas set up a meeting with the Roman governor (also known as the "proconsul"), Sergius Paulus. He was a very influential person, known from other first-century sources to have been a trusted senior member of the staff of the emperor Claudius. A boundary stone with his name on it was found by archaeologists in Rome, indicating that, after his time here, he became one of the curators of the Tiber River that ran through Rome.

That was a rare honor. So he's a pretty big deal. To win his favor would be a huge coup for the Christians. But there's a magician in town and he doesn't want to lose his influence over this important Roman ruler.

TO THE BIRTHPLACE OF APHRODITE

MORE ROMAN MAGIC

The magician's name is Bar-Jesus, but Luke tells us he's known as *Elymas* (which means "Wise One" in Arabic. It must have been his exotic-sounding stage name).

As we saw earlier, in the first-century Roman world, a belief in magic was widespread, though not universal. Josephus says he mocked his fellow Jews who feared magic:

> I ridiculed the nonsense of any arguments about charms, noting that the Romans would not be maintaining so many tens of thousands of soldiers if it were possible to defeat one's enemies by means of sorcerers![2]

Nevertheless, many believed. There were two kinds of "magicians" in the first century, and you see both in Acts. One sort were the *oracles*, who were fortune-tellers claiming to commune with guiding spirits. The others were *magoi*, sorcerers who claimed to be able to cook up curses to create a desired effect. Many of their books of spells and potions survive today, and they read like something out of a fantasy book: "Take the eyes of a bat..." The idea seems to be that if you concoct the right potion, and say magic words over it in just the right way, you get the result you're hoping for.

The really expanding market for magicians in the first century was making personal "curse tablets," little pieces of jewelry you wore around your neck that contained secret spells written on tiny pieces of parchment. Many thousands of curse tablets have survived, containing phrases like, "May Trophimus go blind!" or "May Claudius be impotent!" Curses for blindness were particularly popular.

Of course this meant everyone also wanted protection *against* curse tablets. In fact, you could go to the same local sorcerer who sold curse tablets to your enemies and purchase amulets guaranteed to ward off those very curses. Nice little business model! It was like a software company selling apps for hacking and protection against hackers at the same time.

STRUCK BLIND

So this local sorcerer sees his patron start to show interest in Paul's message. If Sergius Paulus converts, then Elymas loses his celebrity endorsement. His clients may all follow! You can tell he's practically feeling the money slip through his fingers. So he whispers in Sergius Paulus' ear like Wormtongue manipulating King Theoden: "Paul is a no-good troublemaker."

Most of the time in Acts when Paul finds opposition, he counters it through submission to local authorities and logical argument. Or he just slips away. But once or twice, he is forceful and pro-active. Like here. He pronounces a kind of curse on Elymas: *You will go blind for a time!*

Now why does he do that? I think for two reasons. First, he's speaking a language the locals understand. They believed in the power of curses, and now Paul is showing what the real power of God can do. And there's an element of justice here too. It's like he's saying, "So for all these years you thought it was profitable and amusing to curse people with blindness? How's it feel to be on the receiving end of that?"

But most important, I think Paul is hoping for Elymas' repentance. Luke mentions an interesting detail. Elymas the sorcerer is Jewish!

Okay. Everyone who remembers another Jewish guy in the Book of Acts who was harming Christians and had to be struck blind before he repented, raise your hands.

You got it. Surely Paul's remembering how his own conversion took place when he was stopped in his destructive tracks by sudden blindness. I believe he's longing for a similar positive U-turn from this sorcerer. Perhaps he sees something of himself in Elymas. We never learn what became of this sorcerer, because Luke moves on with Paul back to the mainland. But I like to think he changed.

TO THE BIRTHPLACE OF APHRODITE

RELATIONSHIP OR MAGIC RITUAL?

Magic in the first century was really just a folk expression of what pagan religion had become: Rituals designed to obtain the favor or guidance of the gods. Do this ritual, you get that result.

It all sounds so exotic and strange, but has our world changed so much? Books guaranteeing supernatural prosperity formulas abound on Amazon, and even in many churches. It's "Christianity as magic." Learn to say the right prayers in the right way, do the right things (like go to church or refrain from certain sins), then you get what you pray for. If things go wrong, you must be doing something wrong.

But God wants a real relationship with us, not a series of tricks and trades. This story's a reminder to ask myself, "Is my faith a relationship with God, based on his unconditional love for me, or is it based on some sort of magical thinking?" That's a harder question to answer than you might think.

Things seem to end well here on Paphos. But soon Paul will encounter a less exotic but more effective enemy tactic that will dog his steps for the rest of his life.

> PRAYER FOR THE JOURNEY: *Lord, may my faith be grounded in a relationship with you, a confident belief that I am your beloved, and not in any magical or superstitious thinking. Let me spot little superstitions and legalisms that can creep into my life and poison a faith based on grace alone.*

THANK GOD FOR TOURISTS

In about 5 BC in the heart of Rome, the emperor Augustus unveiled a massive public map of the Roman Empire. And unintentionally invented an industry.

Author Tony Perrottet describes the map as etched in stone and as large as a drive-in movie screen. Meticulously designed by the war hero Marcus Agrippa, it was the most complete map of the ancient world. To gather data, Agrippa dispatched an elite corps of land surveyors to the farthest corners of the Empire. They charted every river, mountain range, harbor, and town. The map showed all the Roman highways and shipping routes, recording accurate distances between cities.[3]

Descriptions of the map began circulating widely. Members of the public could calculate distance and travel time to any spot in the known world. Within a generation, relatively safe, rapid journeys to any destination became common. The Roman writer Aelius Aristedes proclaimed, "Cannot every man now go wherever he wishes, without fear? Aren't all our harbors busy? Aren't the mountains just as safe as the cities?"[4]

It was the beginning of the golden age of travel for the common man. For the first time in history, large numbers of people traveled just for the fun of seeing new sights. And it arrived at the perfect time for the spread of the gospel.

> "...we travel through every nation... happily reliving ancient times, gazing at stones which moved great artists to song and string." —Anonymous Roman poem extolling the virtues of tourism, first century AD.[5]

The rapid development of the cottage industry for these first tourists meant better infrastructure for the travel-loving early disciples. Thank God for tourists!

Roman mile markers like this one marked the distance to the nearest towns and often also listed inns and attractions along the way. (Photo credit: Júlio Reis, 2004)

25
THE SCANDALOUS MESSAGE
ACTS 13:13-52

It's just us and the archaeologists.

This is the kind of scene I'd imagined when dreaming up this trip. Under moody, cinematically cloudy skies, our small group has complete freedom to explore the ruins of a once-great city.

We enter through the spectacular remains of the massive main city gate. The only other souls here are the archaeologists and their students working excitedly in one small area. They're clearly on to something major judging by their vigorous digging and excited conversation. The college interns have friendly smiles for us as they walk wheelbarrows of sifted dirt away from the site. But as we approach the archaeologists themselves (did they always wear those Indiana Jones hats, or is that a thing now because of the movies?) they wave us away: "Go! Come no closer! No picture! Everyone walking away now! Thank you! Bye-bye!"

We never do find out what they're discovering, but there's a lot already unearthed here in the ruins of Pisidian Antioch.

BUILDING A NEW ROME
This was a very unusual, extremely beautiful city in Paul's day. The Roman Empire built essentially a newer, better copy of Rome right here in Asia Minor. Just before the New Testament era thousands of Imperial Army veterans were moved here as Roman colonists, and to make them feel perfectly at home, the official language was not the Greek of the surrounding countryside, but their native Latin. A massive, still-impressive temple to Caesar was constructed on the

highest part of the city. Pisidian Antioch was even built on seven hills, just like Rome. In many ways Paul could not have had a better dry run for the other Romanized cities he would later encounter, or, eventually, for Rome itself.

This was a gorgeous city in its day. As I walk along I observe remains of a shallow, stepped waterfall that ran along one side of the entire main boulevard. Thirsty travelers and their horses must have loved that sight! Also lining the beautiful colonnaded streets are ruins of shops and temples dating back to New Testament times. Well-worn grooves in the pavement still seem to whisper the sounds of the chariots and wagons that traveled here.

And then I notice something else scratched into the first-century streets: Christian graffiti.

It looks like a pie cut into eight sections. Some scholars believe this was the first symbol of the faith. It's a combination of the first Greek letters of the phrase, "Jesus Christ, God's Son, Savior." Long before Jesus-followers had church buildings of their own, they met in homes. This little symbol may have been one way travelers could identify where local Christians were meeting.

The "wagon wheel" graffiti found throughout the ancient Roman world. Many scholars believe it to be among the earliest Christian symbols, combining the cross with the first letters of the Greek phrase, "Jesus Christ, God's Son, Savior" (*"Iesous Christos, Theou Yios, Soter"*), ΙΧΘΥΣ, pronounced "ichthus."

And amid these sprawling ruins, beneath the crumbling remains of a Byzantine-era church, is the outline of a first-century building scholars believe may have been the very synagogue where Paul preached.

I stand here with my son David. Neither of us say a word for a long, long time. There is something about this place, on this day, with towering clouds promising a stunning sunset, that makes us feel linked to the profound historical moment that took place right here.

PAUL'S REVOLUTIONARY MESSAGE

For the very first time in the Book of Acts, Paul preaches a sermon. Luke's summary gives us a peek into the messages he spoke in Jewish synagogues for the rest of his life.

He really has just one point. The prophecies about the Messiah have come true! He recounts Jewish history, describing how God patiently led his people to the places he wanted them to go. They didn't always obey, but he led them the whole way anyway. God raised up good leaders, including David, all the way to John the Baptist. But the prophecies always seemed to point to another leader, one who "would not see corruption." Even John the Baptist said he was pointing to another greater person.

Now, Paul says, all those prophecies are fulfilled in Jesus, who was raised from the dead as proof he is the Messiah. He will be the Savior of many. But beware, Paul warns: Those same prophecies also foretell that some of his own people will reject him. *Which will you be?*

ROMAN VETERANS PACK THE SYNAGOGUE

You can tell from Paul's speech that there are many unconverted Gentiles in his first audience, because he keeps referring to them as "God-fearers." And the second week there are even more. Luke says "almost the whole city" shows up to hear Paul. Wait. *This* whole city? That means most people in the crowd were Roman army veterans! Imagine the tension between them and the Jews as they sat elbow to elbow in the crowded synagogue.

And in this second speech Paul says the Messianic promise was not for the nation of Israel alone, but for the whole world.

> "For this is what the Lord has commanded us:
> 'I have made you a light for the Gentiles,
>   that you may bring salvation to the ends of the earth.'"
> Acts 13:47

This is an amazing verse, one of the key sentences in the entire Book of Acts.

Want to know the internal gyroscope of the first Jesus-followers? This is it. Contained in these lines are both the promise that keeps motivating them and the scandal that keeps endangering them: The inclusive, international, Gentile-friendly invitation that was part of the Jesus-movement DNA from the very start. And Paul's opponents are outraged.

THE SCANDAL OF THE GOSPEL

To sympathize a little with Paul's enemies, remember the political situation of the Jewish people. Oppressed by Rome, they hoped for a Messiah not as Savior of the world, but as Savior of Israel. He would be the one who would judge the Roman oppressors and teach everyone a lesson about exactly who God's chosen people were.

To them God's Messiah promise was a precious, holy, sacred teaching reserved for those who were purified. To all the rest? "Go! Come no closer! Everyone walking away now! Thank you! Bye-bye!"

But Paul is saying, yes, we Jews *are* God's chosen people. We *still* are! We are the people he prepared to bring the amazing good news to the whole world. And now his blessing flows through us to the whole planet! God is not inviting people to meet with him behind closed doors. He is leaping through those doors and into their lives, hoping they will turn to him.

But that's not acceptable to many people here. They stir up trouble against Paul and Barnabas, who have to leave.

EXPECT OPPOSITION

It's a frequent occurrence in Acts, and it bears repeating. When you share the message of Jesus, even if you share it in the most positive, culturally sensitive, endearing, personal way, some people will still not receive it. Even to the point of making things really ugly for you.

Maybe you've already experienced this. Your beliefs have been caricatured. Made fun of. You've been ostracized from the inner circle at work. Frozen out by friends. Made to feel unwelcome even at home.

It helps to know that the brilliant Paul experienced the same. Over and over. So you and I can expect we will too.

This is exactly what is happening in modern Turkey, the Asia Minor of Paul's time. Turkish Jesus-followers number less than 153,000 in a country of 76 million. Persecution is ratcheting up. A nun I met at a church there told me of the increasing pressure and anti-Christian graffiti. She fears it will get much worse before it gets better. We need to pray for our brothers and sisters there.

NOTICE BLESSINGS

As the chapter ends things keep getting worse. Scandalous rumors spread. Threats are made. Paul and Barnabas are expelled. And how do the disciples react? This next verse, coming as it does at the end of one trial after another, makes me smile:

"And the disciples were filled with joy and with the Holy Spirit." (Acts 13:52)

Amazing attitude! They focused on the positive that was happening, even in the midst of the negative: Many, many Gentiles were coming to faith.

Don't let criticism and persecution blind you to the positive outcomes all around you. Ask God to help your eyes stay open to the blessings he is effecting in and through you, by his grace.

CONTROL WHAT YOU CAN

Famed management researcher Jim Collins studied leadership in crisis moments. He and his team looked at over twenty thousand companies to discover what kind of leaders survive and thrive through tough times. He concluded, "They are not more creative. They're not more visionary. They're not more charismatic. They're not more ambitious. They're not more blessed by luck. They're not more risk-seeking. They're not more heroic. And they're not more prone to making big, bold moves... They all led their teams with a surprising method of self-control in an out-of-control world."[6]

In other words, you can't control most of what comes your way. But you can control your response. That's what you see in Paul and Barnabas. They focused their thoughts. They disciplined their reactions. In an out-of-control world, control yourself.

Paul and Barnabas could never imagine what's about to happen next. They're driven out from sophisticated Pisidian Antioch to the very pagan, rural countryside. Where they will be mistaken for gods.

> PRAYER FOR THE JOURNEY: *Gracious God, please strengthen me so that criticism does not blind me to the positive outcomes all around me! Help my eyes stay open to the blessings you are creating in and around me by your grace.*

Ruins of Pisidian Antioch, the Roman colony where Paul preached his first sermon in Acts.

WHY THE ROMANS LOVED JESUS

Luke says the Gentiles at Antioch loved this message almost instantly. To understand why, you need to know a little more about the state of their religions at this time.

Thomas Cahill writes, "At the center of Greek religion is the belief that, though we can at times successfully invoke the mercy of the gods… we must pay for our sins… and if the sins are big, we must pay big time."[7]

In other words, there was *no grace*. Ultimately you *always* paid for every tiny offense to the gods, even if you were unaware you'd done anything wrong! And the gods themselves were motivated primarily by jealousy and anger, so you needed to *constantly* appease the endless list of potentially offended deities. It was like having a bunch of super high-maintenance relatives. Who were also rich and powerful. And never talked to you. But could ruin your life.

Cahill goes on: "Roman religion was basically a businessman's religion of contractual obligations. Though scrupulous attention was paid to the rituals… it was all pretty much in the spirit of, 'you scratch my back, I'll scratch yours.'" For Greeks and Romans, worship was "a public exercise… and tended toward the bland predictability of a stadium of Americans reciting the Pledge of Allegiance."[8]

No grace. No personal relationship. No assurance. Can you imagine how awesome the gospel sounded? "What are you saying, Paul? There's only one God, so I don't have to scurry around trying to win the favor of every obscure deity? And this God is motivated not by anger but by love? And I don't need to do zillions of little sacrificial rituals because the only sacrifice God wants has already been paid for me through Christ?"

The time was right. Greco-Roman religion was beginning a long decline in popularity. Some intellectuals were openly teaching that the "gods" were just manifestations of philosophical principles. But no new religion was really catching the fancy of the people. Until this.

One more aspect of Christianity that would have been novel to the Greeks and Romans. They saw their future in terms of *fate*. You were basically doomed. But Christians saw it in terms of *hope*.

As Daniel Berrigan puts it in his "Advent Credo":

> *It is not true that creation and the human family are doomed to destruction and loss* — This is true: "For God so loved the world that He gave his only begotten Son, that whoever believes in Him shall not perish but have everlasting life."

> *It is not true that we are simply victims of the powers of evil who seek to rule the world* — This is true: "To me is given authority in heaven and on earth, and lo I am with you, even until the end of the world."[9]

26
MISTAKEN FOR GODS

ACTS 14:1-28

It's a drizzly day as we drive through the eye-popping beauty of one of the amazing national parks of Turkey, traveling through a valley that stretches from the coast to the interior, just as Paul and his companions did. Our faces are glued to the bus windows. Our son David says what we're all thinking: "I knew there'd be cool ancient ruins in Turkey but I had no clue it would be so beautiful!"

The landscape surprises nearly every foreign visitor. Luke hardly mentions it. He is very accurate. Detailed. Plot-driven. But he's no nature-enamored poet.

IT'S NOT A DESERT PLANET

Then into this vacuum of imagery enters... Hollywood. Bible movies. *Ben-Hur, The Ten Commandments, Jesus of Nazareth, The Passion of the Christ.* So we imagine the landscape of the Bible as those films present it: brown, dry, scorched. That's because every one of those movies was filmed in places like Morocco and Tunisia (where the *Star Wars* movies filmed their desert planets). Not because these are accurate reflections of Bible geography. But because they're cheap.

However, in Asia Minor and Greece, Paul and Barnabas were not walking through landscapes that looked like Tatooine or visiting crummy outposts like Mos Eisley. They were walking through Ansel Adams scenery and into cities as sophisticated as San Francisco.

To imagine the actual geography, picture the journey from San Diego to Northern California. Jerusalem and Judea are a lot like

Southern California. Asia Minor's more Northern California, with an interior as sculpted and bountiful as the beautiful valleys and peaks of the Sierra Nevada, coastlines as twisty and stunning as Big Sur, cities with structures as elaborate and elegant as the Legion of Honor in San Francisco. It's a nice place.

The natural beauty of Turkey (biblical Asia Minor) surprises many visitors. (Photo credit: Daniel Kunzler, 2006)

MISTAKEN FOR GODS

After enjoying the beauty, we pull onto a side road, and stop at a rounded hill. Only it isn't a hill. It's a tell. That's the archaeological term for a man-made mound that looks natural but is actually the dirt-covered remains of an ancient settlement. We're here because archaeologists believe this particular tell hides the remains of an important site in the Book of Acts: the Roman colony of Lystra.

As we wander over the site, spotting bits of shattered marble and pottery peeking through the wildflowers and weeds, I recall the fascinating adventure that occurred right here. It's important because it's the first place Paul preaches to pagans without first approaching them through the foundation of Judaism. And they only listen because he is mistaken for a god.

Here's what happens.

THE GODS ARE AMONG US?

As Paul enters this village, he heals a disabled man. And the crowd concludes, "The gods have come down to us in human form!"

Why in the world did they jump to that conclusion? There are ancient texts describing the gods Zeus and Hermes descending to earth to see whether they'd be treated hospitably by ordinary mortals. There's even evidence that these stories originated in the very part of Turkey Paul and Barnabas are visiting here.[10] So these villagers were always on the lookout in case it happened again.

Luke wryly includes a detail about the townspeople proclaiming Barnabas as Zeus and Paul as Hermes. In Greek mythology Zeus is the bearded, beautiful, stately father of the gods, and Hermes is his little, fast-talking, fast-walking messenger. Luke seems amused by the conclusion: *That tall beautiful bronzed athletic one? Like a statue of Zeus come to life. And the short motor-mouth? Must be Hermes.*

Luke specifically states the villagers shouted in the Lycaonian language, which explains why Paul and Barnabas didn't stop them sooner. They didn't understand what was going on. I picture them watching dumbfounded as the priest of Zeus leads a happy procession from the temple. Leaping dancers throw flower petals, joyous acolytes put garlands on the confused visitors, the elders trundle out the village's prize ox for sacrificing. It's the best day of these villagers' lives. The gods are here!

Slowly realization dawns on Paul and Barnabas that they're being worshipped, and just as the sacrifice is about to occur, they wave their hands and yell, "Stop!"

Kind of a funny story. But the reason it's instructive is what Paul says next as he tries to keep the villagers from worshipping him. He knows (very well by this point) that these people are pagans. So *he adjusts his presentation.* Unlike his teaching to Jews, he does not start with the Hebrew Scriptures. He starts from *nature.* He is not a visiting god. But he tells them about the God who did visit.

His argument:

- God is One
There's not a god of the sea and another of the sky and more still for each planet. One God made it all. Idols are worthless to represent him because he's beyond our imagination.

- God is Good
This creator is good. He gives rain and crops and food and every moment of genuine gladness. As I said, this is a gorgeous, fertile area, so I think Paul is likely trying to tap into their appreciation of nature's bounty.

- God is Calling
The creator has been patient with everyone but is now calling us all home, home to a living relationship with Him.

Paul's speech is fascinating because it shows how the Jesus-followers were already teaching that God had not only prepared the *Jews* for the Messiah. He has been actively at work in *all* people, even the pagans, preparing them for Jesus too, through the ways he blesses them in nature. Later in Athens, Paul even quotes Greek poets to show that there are threads of truth in their philosophies too, threads that can connect to the whole truth of Christ Jesus. It's not that all paths lead to God, but that God has left clues everywhere that point to him.

It's like the seashell paths laid by Dory's parents in the Pixar film *Finding Dory*. Their daughter is lost. So they leave signs that point back home. "He has not left himself without testimony," Paul says.

THE JOY OF ONE GOD

The main thrust of Paul's argument here is that there is one true, reliable God. Even for modern pagans this teaching can bring such freedom.

A woman told me after one of our church services that she found it such a relief to make Jesus her only Lord and Savior. She'd spent years deeply immersed in a movement where there was always some new technique or new regimen to try: Chakra tuning, aura adjusting, colon cleansing, diet altering. She worried she was missing some small but necessary component of spiritual health. But when she began to believe there was one God who loved her sacrificially, she felt a new peace. "It's like one-stop spiritual shopping," she told me. "I have everything I need, every blessing I can imagine, freely given to me through Jesus."

IT GETS WORSE. AGAIN.

Most inconveniently for Paul, at this very moment some of his opponents arrive and recognize him from Antioch and Iconium. And they rile the crowd even more. They see their chance to manipulate these pagans into murderous rage.

Egged on by Paul's enemies, the villagers get furious with the very people they almost worshipped. Somebody probably shouts, "How *dare* they impersonate Zeus and Hermes!"

"Yeah!" someone else agrees. And now they don't want to slay an ox for Paul and Barnabas. They want to slay Paul and Barnabas.

They pick up stones and throw them at Paul, who is apparently struck unconscious and left for dead outside the city. But a small group of believers helps him back to someone's house and the next day he slips away.

HARDSHIPS HAPPEN

So far in Acts 14, Paul and Barnabas are driven out of Iconium because of lies told by a coalition of Jews and Gentiles. Then pagan villagers try to kill them in Lystra. *Yet watch what takes place next.* Even after they're forced to flee for their lives, in verse 21 we find out they circle around and visit these very spots again. Their message to the new believers there?

"We must go through many hardships to enter the kingdom of God." (Acts 14:22)

They're not saying we earn a ticket to heaven through hardships. They're just saying the road from here to there is full of tough times. No avoiding them.

Don't imagine that if you go through trials (even to the point of people plotting against you, lying about you, and trying to kill you, like Paul), you're doing something wrong, or God is mad at you, or you don't have enough faith. Paul and Barnabas were doing God's will in amazing ways, yet they have one difficulty after another.

Bad things happen, and it's not because you're a bad person. It's because that's life. Regardless of your circumstances, and even regardless of how you got there, the important thing is how you're responding now.

If you want to respond like Paul, say, "I don't like it. I don't get it. But I trust you, God. I believe I still have a purpose. This is not a cave. It's a tunnel. There's a way through this."

Next Paul and Barnabas return to Jerusalem to report on all these adventures. And that visit turns into an event that will rock the world, and change the course of religious history, even down to the present day.

MISTAKEN FOR GODS

Prayer for the Journey: Help me hear the message of Paul to these new believers: I must go through many hardships. Not because I'm bad. But because that's life. Strengthen me for those times. And help me live with the same unbeatable spirit I see in Paul and Barnabas, no matter what comes my way.

MOTEL 6 AD

The first-century Roman world was the first golden age of hotels. Travelers had four classes of hotel to choose from, ranging from the *hospitium* at the top end of the luxury scale down to the *stabula*, which was the horse equivalent of a motel.

I visited a well-preserved first-century *hospitium* in the ruins of Pompeii for a glimpse into the niceties available then to travelers with means. It had rooms for at least 50 guests, a large garden, and a spacious restaurant with several indoor bathrooms. After the collapse of the Empire this level of luxury wouldn't reappear until Boston's Tremont Hotel installed indoor restrooms in 1829.[11]

27
STAYING ON MESSAGE

ACTS 15:1-11

I'm back in Jerusalem. It's been a few years since my last visit. The tension between Israelis and Palestinians is apparent. But what surprises me is the increasingly contentious relationship between groups of fellow Jews. It's even on the front page of the *Jerusalem Post* newspaper tonight.

Photos show the entrance to an ultra-orthodox Jewish neighborhood. Signs are posted everywhere, warning non-orthodox not to enter during the Sabbath, and spelling out in detail exactly how women should dress when visiting at any time. The placards ominously state that if the reader disregards these warnings, the neighborhood cannot be held responsible for ensuing violence. The article reports that some secular Jewish college students were beaten up that very week for not dressing modestly enough.

I feel the tension myself on a ramble through the Old City later that day. I observe people dressed in modern European garb. And ultra-orthodox wearing their Russian-style fur hats and long black clothes. One thing becomes very clear. Things are not warm between these groups. No one even makes eye contact. People are keeping their heads down these days.

BOUNDARY MARKERS

Sociologists would say I'm seeing evidence of the phenomenon of "boundary markers." All subcultures have them.

When I visit Orange County, California, I'm always amused at how many people there dress in identical workout clothes, drive identical SUVs, and even dye their hair with the identical bot-tle-blond color. In my hometown of Santa Cruz, even the surfer subculture has boundary markers. They dress a certain way, buy certain clothing brands, wear certain haircuts. They even use their own slang. I often see a van parked near the beach when I go for runs. It's covered with stickers that read, "Animals are friends not food." "Animal Liberation Front." "I think, therefore I'm vegan." The windows have silhouettes of gorillas aiming machine guns at hunters. Pretty clear boundary markers! It's all a way to identify who's in your group. And who is not.

But boundary markers take on an added dimension when they involve religion.

As John Ortberg points out, "A boundary-oriented approach to spirituality focuses on people's position: Are you inside or outside the group? A great deal of energy is spent clarifying what counts as a boundary marker. But Jesus consistently focused on people's center: Are they oriented and moving toward the center of spiritual life (love of God and people), or are they moving away from it?"[12]

In Acts 15 the disciples face a major problem about what it means to be a follower of Jesus, since so many Gentiles are becoming believers. *What's our boundary marker?* What follows may be the single most important meeting in the entire history of the church.

HOW DO YOU BECOME A CHRISTIAN?

The question: Do Gentiles first need to convert to Judaism and keep its laws in an orthodox way in order to be considered Christians? The phrase "the law of Moses" means the Ten Commandments plus all the hundreds of other laws in the first five books of the Hebrew Scriptures and all the extra rules that religious traditional-ists added. That included circumcision, kosher food rules, pilgrim-ages to Jerusalem, and much more.

To most of the Jerusalem-based Christians at the time, the answer was obvious. Yes! Jesus was Jewish, so his followers should be too. *Strictly* Jewish.

STAYING ON MESSAGE

Not so fast, says Peter. He reminds them they discussed this already (back in Acts 11) when he led Cornelius' Italian family to Christ. God affirmed those Romans were accepted as believers by pouring the Holy Spirit on them instantly, before they could commit to any sort of kosher system. And the Jerusalem leaders concluded back then that Gentiles did *not* have to keep kosher rules to be followers of Jesus. He says backtracking on that decision would be rebellion against God. "Now then, why do you try to test God by putting on the necks of Gentiles a yoke that neither we nor our ancestors have been able to bear? No! We believe it is through the grace of our Lord Jesus that we are saved, just as they are." (Acts 15:10–11)

Did you see the word? Grace.

This brouhaha about Gentiles won't be the last controversy to rock the church. But that's the word Christians eventually come back to again and again, one controversy after another, century after century, as they try to return to the core message. What a beautiful word.

Grace.

"We believe it is through the grace of our Lord Jesus that we are saved..."

Grace means it's a gift. From God. You don't earn a gift. You earn a salary. By definition, a gift is simply *given*. That means our salvation is all God. Imagined by God. Initiated by God. Paid for by God. Given by God. Finished by God. The more you see that, the more you'll love him and others. *Because you've been graced.*

That's the center of our message.

No other belief system, no other philosophy, emphasizes grace so radically. For the rest of Acts and the entire New Testament, the main battle is to stay on message, not to get distracted by the boundary markers, the controversies, and legalisms that constantly swoop in like buzzing bugs on a summer day to divert our attention from the gospel.

WE ALL NEED AMAZING GRACE

Peter's argument is this: Even we Jews, if we stop to think about it for a second, know we're not saved by keeping the law of Moses, because no one keeps it perfectly. It's only by God's grace that anyone is ever saved. So... why put the burden of the law of Moses on the Gentiles? It is completely unnecessary. He's not saying the law of Moses is bad. He's saying they're forgetting its purpose. It's there to lead us to grace.

After Peter takes his stand, Paul and Barnabas describe what they've seen among the Gentiles.

Finally James gets up to speak. Imagine the moment. Most scholars believe he was the half-brother of Jesus. Perhaps some even saw a resemblance to Christ in his voice or his mannerisms. Clearly James is the leader of the Jerusalem believers. And the Jerusalem fellowship is still the leading group in the growing Jesus movement. So whatever he says next will forever flavor the message.

Everyone holds their breath. He clears his throat.

And he starts, not with his own experience or opinion. He goes to the Bible. Always a good move whenever there's a church controversy. He points out how the Scriptures foretell that after the Messiah comes, "...the rest of mankind may seek the Lord, even all the Gentiles who bear my name..." (Acts 15:17)

So, he says, if Jesus is really the Messiah, we should *expect* to see Gentiles pouring into the Jesus movement. The Gentile presence is not an abomination; it's an affirmation!

And then here's the history-making verdict:

> "It is my judgment, therefore, that we should not make
> it difficult for the Gentiles who are turning to God."
> (Acts 15:19)

And the gates are flung open to the rest of the world. The sign on our neighborhood says, "Welcome."

STAYING ON MESSAGE

RE-EXAMINING ASSUMPTIONS

The tension created as the gospel rolls into new territory is always good. It forces Christians to define the essentials of the gospel more clearly, to ask: Are my expectations of what a Christian looks like shaped by my culture, or are they shaped by God's word and real *Christian* thinking?

This chapter is not about innovation vs. tradition. It's about how easily cultural preferences and assumptions can creep in and begin to squeeze out the gospel message. You might remember when a good Christian never played cards (UNO cards were okay), or never went to movies (Disney movies were okay) and never smoked (pipes were okay if you taught at Oxford and wrote Christian fantasy).

Obviously there will always be behavior that is inconsistent with healthy Christian living. The Jerusalem council writes a letter to the Antioch Christians instructing them to stay away from sexual immorality; from a certain kind of non-kosher food (they specify "strangled meat and blood"); and from meat sacrificed to idols.

But the stand is made here for salvation by grace.

You and I replay the scene of the Jerusalem council in our heads throughout our lives. We hear the accusing voices demanding that we do more to secure our standing before God. But can you hear the voice of Peter?

"It is through the grace of our Lord Jesus that we are saved."

> PRAYER FOR THE JOURNEY: *Lord, help me always stand for grace against legalism in my life and in the lives of others.*

WHY THESE RULES?

It's been a topic of debate for 2,000 years. Why did the Jerusalem council in Acts 15 specifically prohibit "food polluted by idols, sexual immorality, the meat of strangled animals, and from blood"? Obviously these are not the only rules that apply to Jesus followers. The other moral laws of the Hebrew Scripture also apply: Do not lie, steal, murder, etc. The council in Acts 15 certainly was not suggesting that anything they *didn't* mention in their letter was okay. They didn't mention murder, but we can't go around killing people.

So what was this all about? Why do they only mention these four rules?

One common interpretation is that they are referring to the "Noahic Covenant," the covenant between God and all humanity addressed to Noah in Genesis 9. Centuries after Christ, Jewish rabbis coined the term "Noahic Covenant" and discerned seven distinct commandments in Genesis 9 that predate the Jewish law and apply to all people. However, the events in Acts 15 occur long before the idea of a Noahic Covenant appears in rabbinic literature. So maybe the Acts 15 rules are about something else.

Bible scholar Ben Witherington III points out:

> There are a variety of hints in the text of Acts 15 that what is being prohibited is the attending of pagan temple feasts and all that they entail. Each of the four prohibitions in their letter referred to four activities known to transpire in pagan temples.[13]

James introduces these four prohibitions by saying what should be avoided is "the pollution of idols" (Acts 15:20). That's actually a single word in Greek which means "the pollution resulting from contact with idol worship."[14] Then he defines this pollution four ways:

Meat of strangled animals: Pagan priests believed that strangling animals in temples caused the animals' life force to transfer to the god. For example, these instructions to followers of the god Eros:

> Take also on the first day seven living creatures and strangle them... do not make a burnt offering of these; instead, taking them in your hand strangle them while holding them up to your Eros, until each of the creatures is suffocated and their breath enters him.[15]

Blood: Ancient literature describes pagan priests tasting the blood of their sacrifices.[16]

Food sacrificed to idols: The earliest known Christian commentator on the Book of Acts, John Chrysostom, points out that this instruction in Acts 15 could not refer to any meat purchased in a marketplace that had once been sacrificed to idols, or the words of Jesus about no food being unclean would be contradicted (he cites Jesus' words in Matthew 15:11 and the vision of Peter). He says the issue here must be eating meat while worshipping at the temples.[17]

Sexual immorality: The Greek word used here is *porneia*, which in its most basic meaning referred to prostitution, including temple prostitution, common in some first-century pagan cults. Any sexual immorality is off-limits for Christians, but in this specific instance, combined with the other prohibitions, this seems to be referring to prostitution as an element of pagan worship.

In other words, the Jerusalem council is saying the Gentile believers need to make a choice. They cannot be both Jesus-followers and idol worshippers. Jesus is not a god to be added to their pantheon. He is the one Lord of all. It's worth considering how this applies to Christians today. Are we merely adding Jesus to our lives, or are we changing our lives to follow him?

28
DISCERNING DIVINE DIRECTION
ACTS 15:12-16:10

I'm enjoying my first visit to Greece, strolling through the scenic ruins at Delphi, the beautiful spot high in the foothills where the ancient Greeks made pilgrimages to see the Oracle. The Oracle at Delphi was a woman who functioned something like a fortune-telling prophet. People asked her questions like, "Should I plant wheat or corn? Should I leave or stay in my city? Who should I marry? Where can I get some hummus?" And this priestess would go into a trance and give direction in rhymes and riddles.

Why bring up the Oracle of Delphi when Acts 15 and 16 are set in Jerusalem? Because in these chapters you find huge help with a question every believer has: "How can I know the will of God?"

I think a lot of Christians wish they had a place like Delphi, an oracle to consult and get direction on every little thing. But in the Book of Acts you don't see Jesus-followers relying on prophets or oracles before they make decisions. Of course there are times in Acts that God leads through visions or prophecies. But even in Acts, those moments are rare.

So how do you make wise choices if God's not giving you a sign at every fork in the road?

The council in Jerusalem is debating, "What is a Christian?" That's a pretty major deal, way more important than deciding where to move or what car to buy. So how will they determine God's will on this huge question? Here are some very important principles for discerning God's guidance.

DISCERNING DIVINE DIRECTION

1. NOTICE HOW GOD IS MOVING

Don't just ask God to bless your decisions; look to see what kinds of decisions God is already blessing. Luke says "everyone listened quietly" as people talked about God moving among the Gentiles. Then James, the leader of the meeting, summarizes. He says God has already answered the question for them by converting Gentiles without asking anyone's permission.

2. LOOK TO SCRIPTURE

James says he can accept the Gentile conversions as genuine because they're backed by God's Word. He quotes Amos the prophet, who said this would happen. Don't just decide based on experience. Ask if experience matches Scripture.

3. SEEK GODLY COUNSEL

After James puts together the actions of God and the word of God, the Jerusalem council comes to the unanimous conclusion that it's God's will for Gentiles to be Christians.

This is what you do between times of extraordinary direction from God. See what God's already blessing, search the Scripture, and seek godly counsel. Don't make major decisions in a vacuum.

4. THEN TAKE GODLY INITIATIVE

Later Paul says to Barnabas, "Let's go back to all the cities where we preached and see how all the new believers are doing." (Acts 15:36) There's no vision, no angelic call, no bright light, no special word. No oracle. There's just the logical, responsible concern of Paul for the people he's led to Christ.

God doesn't want to give you orders about every step you take. He's not interested in robots. He doesn't want cult followers who have to wait for some special feeling before they act. You're free to take initiative. You can do what's on your heart, as long as it's godly and sensible. Don't wait for supernatural direction. If you see an opportunity to act in a Christian way, do it.

In the next paragraph there's kind of a side note. Barnabas and

Paul disagree so sharply about who to take along that they part ways. *Even when two godly people try to do God's will, there are times when there are differences of opinion.* That's just going to happen. It will happen in churches, in ministries, in families, on mission trips, and when it does, act in a way that doesn't permanently break the relationship.

5. ASK WHAT'S BEST FOR THE GOSPEL

In chapter 16, Paul goes back to Lystra (where they once mistook him for a god) and meets Timothy, whose mother was Jewish and a believer, but whose father was a Greek. According to Jewish law, this makes Timothy a Jew.

Fascinating detail here: Paul asks Timothy to go through the circumcision ritual. Now why did he do that, if he had just preached that circumcision does not make you a Christian? In fact, later in the Bible, in the book of Galatians, you learn that Paul took Titus, who was a Greek Gentile, with him to Jerusalem. The Jewish Christians there pressure Titus to be circumcised, but Paul absolutely refuses. So why does he resist in Titus' case, and not in Timothy's? Because allowing circumcision for Titus would have been a concession to the idea that you had to become a kosher-keeping, religious-law-abiding Jew in order to become a Christian.

But the case of Timothy is different. Timothy's already considered a Jew, and in order not to offend the Jews, in order to keep the door of Timothy's ministry open to them, Paul okays his circumcision. His governing principle is, "I became all things to all men, in order that I might win some…" (1 Corinthians 9:22).

This is always the will of God. Whenever there's controversy, or you wonder what course you should take, always do what's best for the advancement of the gospel.

6. TRUST GOD TO DIRECT SPECIFICALLY WHEN HE CHOOSES

This is huge. In Acts 16:6–8 you see how Paul doesn't wait for directions from God about where to go; he just tries to go to the next logical place. But the Holy Spirit doesn't want him to go there, and shuts the door. Doesn't say how. Maybe roads were closed. Maybe Paul just couldn't find transportation. However it happened, the door was shut.

So Paul and his companions try to go to the next spot. That doesn't work out either. Now they don't know what to do. And in the city of Troas, near ancient Troy, Paul has a vision of a man of Macedonia (a Roman province in today's northern Greece) begging him, "Come over to Macedonia and help us."

MOVE THE CAR

Here's the point. It's easier to steer a moving car than a parked car. God is sovereign, and he can choose the way he wants to direct. Just start moving in what seems to you to be a God-honoring direction. Trust God to redirect you — or stop you — if he has other plans.

Paul *expects* God to lead him. He doesn't doubt it. But he doesn't *wait* for a vision or some inner prompting. He simply acts and expects God to correct him if he's wrong. And even when he gets what seems to be direction from God, he checks it out with godly companions. They all agree, and off they go.

Then — talk about breaking down barriers! These mostly Jewish missionaries go where they have never been before — to Europe.

LUKE JOINS THE PARTY

One more detail. This is where Luke joins the party. Did you catch it? In verse 8, Luke says, "...*they* went on through Mysia to the seaport of Troas." But in verse 10, he says, "...*we* decided to go to Macedonia..."

We don't know where he came from, or how he got there, or how he knew Paul. But now he's there. Perfect timing, now that they're going to Europe, since Luke is a Gentile. And he stays with Paul until the very end, as you see in Paul's final letter, Second Timothy, written from a Roman prison.

So how will God guide you? Where will God guide you? The important thing is that, wherever you go or whatever you do, you stay confident of Jesus' power in you, and you trust in him completely to direct and empower you.

And remember, God's guidance does not mean everything will go smoothly, as Paul is about to experience in an adventure that involves fortune tellers, riots, and earthquakes.

> PRAYER FOR THE JOURNEY: *God, help me move forward confidently, knowing you will direct me as needed. May my decisions be wise ones based on biblical principles, godly advice, and observations of how you are blessing today. Thank you for your guidance. Amen.*

PART·FIVE

RIOTS & REVELATIONS

29
FIRST DAY IN EUROPE

ACTS 16:11-15

We pull into the ruins of Philippi as dusk falls on a beautiful night in October, lending an almost magical look to the surroundings. Our first night in the Greek countryside reminds me of soft golden summer evenings in the rolling hills of California wine country back home. A small river meanders through hills dotted with oaks; instead of wineries I see ancient ruins. We stroll to the riverbank and read Acts 16.

It's such an unspoiled, rural setting that it's easy to squint my eyes and imagine all the history in this spot. Two world-changing events took place here.

First: About 35 years before Jesus was born, right in this valley, the future Caesar Augustus and Mark Antony defeated the armies of Brutus and Cassius. That brought an end to the Roman Republic and started the Empire.

Second: Around 49 or 50 AD, the apostle Paul visits this city and in many ways changes the whole course of European history. I'm sure that if emperor Claudius, who was Caesar at the time, had been asked to name the most significant events at Philippi, he would never have dreamed of suggesting Paul's visit (As Ray Stedman points out, that's how little we understand the history we're living through in our own lifetimes).

But this is a very significant moment. Paul has crossed another barrier — geography. He's bringing the message to a new continent.

FIRST DAY IN EUROPE

And the Jesus movement here takes root in a completely different way than we have seen before.

SHE SELLS SEASHELLS

Paul walks into the city and, as usual, looks around for a synagogue. But it's a different world over here in Europe. There *is* no synagogue. That means there are probably not even ten Jewish men in the city. (The law was very specific. You had to have ten adult male Jews in order to have a synagogue.)

The city of Philippi probably had so few Jewish people because it was a Roman colony. Retired Roman soldiers, mostly from Italy, could purchase property here at low prices in order to colonize the place. Even more than other cities Paul has visited so far, the people here are culturally Roman. They wear Roman clothes, speak the Roman language, and follow strictly Roman laws. This is a place of Roman pride.

Some of us might have been discouraged right away. "So God said to come to Europe, and there isn't even a synagogue where I can start teaching? What am I supposed to do now?" Well, it gets more complicated.

Paul, Silas, Timothy, and Luke walk along the river outside the city walls to see if they can find an outdoor prayer meeting, which was the custom of Jewish people in the Roman world if there was no local synagogue. They find a group of women and have a conversation. One of them becomes the first convert in Europe: Lydia.

That's a Gentile name. Lydia is wealthy, a successful dealer in purple, which was a luxury commodity. The term used to describe her profession, *pupularius*, specifically refers to a dealer in purple dye extracted from certain shellfish in the Aegean Sea. She's on a business trip from Thyatira, which is back across the Aegean in modern-day Turkey.

Lydia's described as a "worshipper of God." Remember, that's the term used for Gentiles who find Jewish monotheism appealing, but stop short of converting, usually because of the daunting kosher requirements. For Lydia, conversion to Judaism would have been a real problem. Her constant contact with the product of dead shellfish would have made her ritually unclean.

Can you see why she would have responded so enthusiastically to Paul's message? The gospel means she can be saved by God's grace through Christ, and not by keeping kosher laws! She's so enthusiastic that she's immediately baptized, and insists that Paul and his group stay at her house (indicating her home is large enough for this whole group, another sign of her wealth).

WOMEN IN THE EARLY CHURCH
This is the beginning of another pattern in the early church. The Christian message is very appealing to Gentile women and particularly to women of means. Sociologist Rodney Stark writes a lot about this in his book *The Rise of Christianity*.[1] He points out that Christianity offered an equality to women that was found nowhere else in the ancient religions. So another barrier in the very male-dominated world of the first century is crossed — the gender barrier.

STAYING FLEXIBLE
Paul was looking for a synagogue. He found an outdoor prayer meeting. He was looking for Jewish men. He found Gentile women. But he stayed flexible and open.

Often we make plans to serve God in one way, and God puts a completely different opportunity in our path. Can you keep your eyes open for the unexpected divine appointments?

Paul's first European convert is a woman; but it's Paul's care for another oppressed woman in Philippi that's about to get him into deep trouble.

> PRAYER FOR THE JOURNEY: *Lord, help me to live flexibly, knowing that even delays and disappointments can lead to exciting opportunities to serve you.*

THE ROLE OF WOMEN
IN THE EARLY CHURCH

One of the least known facts about Christianity is the huge role that women played in the early church.

In the letters Paul writes to the early churches, he mentions women again and again as key leaders. At the end of Romans alone, he refers to Phoebe, calling her a deacon; Priscilla, who had a teaching ministry with her husband; Mary, Tryphena, Tryphosa, Narcissus; Persis, who he calls "a dear friend"; Julia, Rufus' mother, Nereus' sister; and Junia, who he even alludes to as an apostle.

In Second Timothy, Paul refers to Lois, Eunice, and Claudia, the wife of Pudens, a Roman senator.

And there's a little nugget in the letter he writes to the Corinthian church. He's writing in response to a concerned letter from a woman named Chloe, so she must have been an influential woman in the church there.

People who try to paint Paul as anti-woman usually quote one or two verses with a cultural context so obscure that their meaning is difficult to discern. But when you look at the many easy-to-understand verses about how Paul actually lived, you see someone who highly valued the contributions of women.

And this continued for some time. Many early Christian women were ardent students of the Bible and of Hebrew and Greek. The circle of Roman women who studied with Jerome in the late 300s became famous. Augustine declared that "any old Christian woman" was better educated in spiritual matters than male philosophers.[2]

In the second century, Bishop Cyprian of Carthage said, "Christian maidens were very numerous," and there were so many female Christians that it was difficult for them to find Christian husbands. It all paints a picture of a church disproportionately populated by women.

For the rest of Acts, you'll see Luke making careful note of all the Roman and Greek women who begin streaming into the early Jesus movement. And that all starts with the conversion of the wealthy woman named Lydia in Philippi.

30
PRAISES AT MIDNIGHT

ACTS 16:16-40

The preaching of the gospel always seems to attract colorful characters, as Paul and Silas soon discover. A female slave follows them around Philippi, shouting to all passers-by, "These men are servants of the Most High God!" After several days of this, Paul is increasingly annoyed and, Luke says, casts out the spirit that is vexing her.

Problem is, she's been making money for her owners by predicting the future for paying customers. This "future-predicting" probably happened in the same way ancient writers report other Greek oracles prophesying. The oracles, always women, entered a trance and uttered cryptic phrases that were considered prophetic puzzles to be solved by advice-seekers.

Now that she's sane, this woman no longer experiences the delirium that apparently sent her into these prophetic states, and her owners realize their hope of making money off her misery is gone.

Infuriated, they drag Paul and Silas to the marketplace, where the town authorities have their offices. The site of these very town offices on the Philippian marketplace has been uncovered by archaeologists. "These men are throwing our town into an uproar by advocating practices illegal for Romans to follow!" the men accuse. Paul and Silas are flogged and thrown into jail.

That night an earthquake hits. Philippi is on a fault line, and suffered from many damaging quakes in its history. But in this quake the prisoners are set free! The jailer's about to kill himself, because the

Roman punishment for failing as a prison guard is death, when Paul says, "Stop! We're not escaping. We are still here." (Which is amazing. I would have been so out of there! But Paul is more concerned with this man's soul than his own freedom). The jailer accepts Christ and he and his whole family are baptized.

PRAISING AT MIDNIGHT

It's a riveting story. The most impressive aspect of this adventure to me, though, is not the strange fortune-telling woman, or the earthquake, or the fact that the chains came off their wrists. It's Paul and Silas singing in jail.

Imagine it. Your plans are derailed. You're thrown in prison. You're beaten. Your back is raw and bloody. You've suffered an injustice.

And Luke says it was "at midnight." Everything, all the pain and the heartache and disappointment, is always worse in the middle of the night, isn't it? But they're not wallowing in self-pity. They're reveling in praise.

I see three very important applications here:

GIVE THANKS EVEN IN THE HARD TIMES

Keep giving gratitude, stay focused on God, even when all the wheels seem to be coming off. Paul tells these same Philippians, "Rejoice in the Lord always," in his letter to them. And he practices what he preaches.

GOD HAS A PLAN HE IS ALREADY WORKING

God directed Paul to Europe because he had plans in the works. He already had a woman named Lydia right there, prepped for the gospel. And he has plans already in the works for you to be a part of.

THE STORY IS STILL BEING WRITTEN

Things could not have gone worse for Paul and his group—from a human perspective.

Yet the story of the Christianity at Philippi did not end with this seeming defeat. It was still being written. This church at Philippi grows and grows and when you read Paul's letter to the Christians here, you can tell they're full of joy. It was a strong church that started in the fire of a severe trial.

That means you can take heart. The worst of times can produce the best, most long-lasting results.

The next morning the magistrates free Paul and Silas, who promptly go to the next city, probably hoping for a little less trouble. But even more violence and intrigue await them there, and they will make some even more persistent enemies.

> PRAYER FOR THE JOURNEY: *Father, help me sing praises even at midnight, knowing you are working your plan.*

THE ROAD TO THESSALONICA

Thessalonica is almost 100 miles from Philippi, so the trip here for Paul would have taken several days. But it was travel in relative comfort. When they walked from Philippi to Thessalonica, Paul and Silas were on the famous Roman highway called the Egnatian Way which connected the Adriatic Sea with the Black Sea.

The cities mentioned in Acts 17 are all on that road. It was almost 700 miles long, about 20 feet wide, and paved the entire way. Horse stables were located about every ten miles, and there were inns for travelers at least every 20 miles. It was safe, patrolled by two kinds of Roman troops: Special imperial soldiers called *stationarii*, who kept an eye out from elevated watchtowers along the way, and *beneficiarii*, who patrolled the roads helping travelers.

A surviving portion of the ancient Egnatian Way. (Photo credit: Marion Golsteijn, 2013)

31
MOB MENTALITY

ACTS 17:1-15

First night of our stay in Turkey, our son David comes running into our hotel room. "Mom, Dad, look out the window right now. There's a mob rioting outside!"

We pull back the curtains. Sure enough, there's an angry, chanting crowd filling the sidewalks and the entire street right below our window. They smash the glass walls of the bus station right across from our hotel and soon pull the structure down. We look at each other nervously. Are we safe in the hotel? Well, we aren't going down there, that's for sure. Someone turns on the TV. There's our street, helicopter view.

The rioters make it just a block further and then a line of police in riot gear approaches from the other direction. We watch tensely as water cannons and small tank-like vehicles stop the mob's progress.

The next morning all is quiet. The front page of the paper has a damage assessment: A lot of property destruction. No lives lost this time, thank God.

Great history lesson for David about the power of the riot. The ancient Romans in this same area experienced mob action frequently enough to have a word for it: *ochlocratia*, which means "mob rule." They saw it happen many times. In an instant, an inflamed crowd can cause vast damage and threaten lives, as Paul discovers repeatedly in Acts.

BUSTLING CITY

Weeks after the Istanbul riot, toward the end of our long trip through Turkey and Greece, we pull into Thessalonica. And it occurs to me that a greater contrast to the quiet countryside surrounding Philippi could not be found. Thessaloniki, as it's now known, is a bustling, modern port city with crowded sidewalk cafes, busy shopping malls, and huge public parks.

It was big and busy in Paul's day too, renowned even then for its traffic jams. The famous Roman orator Cicero was exiled here, and in one of his letters he complains about the road congestion. He reports that he has to time his travel in order to miss the daily vehicle backups (sounds familiar!).

We imagine Athens as the crown jewel of Greece, but actually in the New Testament era that honor went to Thessalonica. Many celebrities of antiquity lived here, including Cleopatra, Pompey, and many more, attracted by the wealthy, popular seaside city. But with the right spark, the large crowds of Thessalonica could quickly be ignited into rage. Under a later Emperor a murderous riot here led to violent Roman reprisals and a massacre of thousands. Thessalonica was like a box of matches waiting for a spark. Just call Paul "Sparky".

MORE WOMEN RALLY TO THE CAUSE

In Acts we've already seen the Jew-Gentile barrier being broken, and once the gospel gets to Europe, the barriers start to fall left and right. Not only Jews and Gentile converts but outright pagans flock to the new movement. And economic and social barriers fall too. Not only tradespeople but city leaders are turning to Christ. And did you notice that among those leaders, Luke is careful to point out, are "quite a few of the prominent women of the city" (Acts 17:4)?

These were educated women who found Greek myths full of degrading ideas about women. The gospel came with the good news that, in Jesus Christ, there is neither male nor female, slave nor free,

Jew nor Gentile, or any other distinction (As Paul says in Galatians 3:28), and these women found this liberating and fulfilling.

But. Whenever long-standing barriers are crossed, people get upset. And often when people can't defeat opponents by logic and reason, they resort to slander and violence. And that's just what happens here.

BARRIER-BREAKING LEADS TO TROUBLE

Some of Paul's opponents form a mob and start a riot. I can imagine them marauding down streets like the crowd we saw from our hotel window. The rest of the city might not agree with them, but no one is stopping them. Windows are shut and doors are barred as the mob marches past. When they can't find Paul and Silas, they burst into a home known to be Christian and drag out a man named Jason who's been housing Paul there. They take him and his friends to the city authorities and say, "These men have caused trouble all over the world, and now they're here too!" (Acts 17:6)

They continue with the most politically charged accusation they can think up: "They're all defying Caesar's decrees, saying that there is another king named Jesus!" They knew they had to paint Paul and Silas as political insurrectionists to get interest from the civil authorities.

The Christians here don't even wait for Paul to be put on trial. They know the unreasoning power of a mob. That very night they smuggle Paul and his companions out of the city.

And they bring them to Berea, which today, just as it was in Paul's time, is a very nice, picturesque town in the foothills of the Olympic Mountains. A more peaceful contrast to Thessalonica cannot be imagined. An ancient synagogue has been excavated in Berea that some scholars believe is the actual one in which Paul preached.

It's fascinating to me that, just as Paul found a warmer reception in Berea than in Thessalonica, we experienced something similar ourselves.

Modern Thessaloniki is exciting, but a little scary. Our guide quietly warned us of a band of pickpockets shadowing us as we walked around the old town. But in modern Berea, walking along the winding village streets, we found the townspeople to be very friendly, stopping to chat, asking where our group is from, and even inviting us to church.

MOB ACTION VS. PERSONAL REFLECTION

Luke also notes a sharp contrast between the rabble in Thessalonica, with their prejudiced minds and their impulsive mob action, and these Jewish people in Berea, who were "more noble," as the King James version expresses it. And Luke doesn't say, "They were noble, because they accepted what we said without question!" Because they didn't. Luke says they were noble because they diligently checked everything out with the Scripture.

That's a great role model for believers. When anyone brings you a spiritual teaching, don't just gulp it down like an open-mouthed baby bird. And don't be unthinkingly critical either. God's not looking for cult-like obedience or knee-jerk cynicism. He gave you a brain, so he wants you to use it. Give every teaching your intelligent, personal reflection. A fair hearing. Reasoned debate and discussion.

Three things I see here as takeaways:

1. GOD'S WILL ISN'T ALWAYS SMOOTH

In Acts, as in life, sometimes things go smoothly. And sometimes they don't. But that doesn't mean you're no longer in the will of God. Paul doesn't question God's leading to Macedonia, even though his visits ended with riots in the first two cities he preached in. You can be in the center of God's will, spreading the gospel, and encounter one obstacle and heartbreak after another.

2. THERE WILL ALWAYS BE OPPORTUNITIES. FIND THEM!

Paul doesn't find a synagogue back in Philippi (in Acts 16) so he goes out by the river. There's a riot in Thessalonica so he moves on to Berea. When things go wrong, look for ways to be a light in that darkness and for other opportunities.

3. JUDGE WHATEVER IS TAUGHT BY THE WORD OF GOD

The Bereans were praised for this. When you hear new teaching, don't immediately accept it. Judge it by the rest of the Bible. Ponder it. Put it through a grid of Scripture. And when you're the teacher, don't judge someone's response to the gospel just by their enthusiasm. Judge it by their thoughtfulness and willingness to listen, and then by their changed lives.

And we're about to roll into one of my favorite parts of the Acts Odyssey, in one of the most interesting cities in the world.

> PRAYER FOR THE JOURNEY: Lord, I see that even when I am doing your will, the way will not always be smooth. Help me not get discouraged. Help me see that there will always be opportunities — and empower me to find them.

EXPLORING FURTHER
THE SECRET PYRAMID

The Acropolis is a flat-topped steep hill in the center of Athens that bristles with elaborate temples to the Greek gods, the Parthenon being the most impressive by far. In Paul's time this edifice was already an ancient marvel, built nearly five centuries before Paul arrives on the scene.

The Parthenon was so well built that it was still completely intact in 1687 AD when Athens became the scene of a battle between the Venetian and Ottoman armies. The Ottoman Turks had taken over the Acropolis and were storing their munitions inside. The Venetians lobbed up a cannonball, which went through the roof and ignited the gunpowder. This beautiful ancient building exploded, leaving a gaping hole in three sides of the building. But centuries later that led to an amazing discovery that may have stayed hidden forever if the Parthenon had stayed intact.

As restorers in the twentieth century tried to reconstruct the monument from the fragments left like jigsaw puzzle pieces all over the mountain, they rediscovered a secret of the ancient architects. The columns and blocks are not interchangeable, though they appear identical. Each column, each brick, is precisely shaped to provide the illusion of uniformity, while actually leaning slightly inward from a variety of angles. The columns, if continued upward as lines, would all meet at a point almost exactly one mile above the structure. The apparently rectangular Parthenon is actually more like the base of a steep pyramid.[3]

The ancient Greeks understood a principle which was only redis-covered centuries later. In order to appear straight, lines of a massive building have to be tapered inward slightly. Parallel lines in a structure of this size will otherwise appear to bow outward, a dis-concerting effect you may have experienced if you've ever looked up at a skyscraper and had the feeling it was about to tip over. How did they figure this out and make the precise calculations needed for each piece of the Parthenon to fit this design all those years ago? No one knows for sure.

The Parthenon was already centuries old by the time the Apostle Paul saw it around 52 AD.

32
BUILDING BRIDGES NOT WALLS
ACTS 17:16-26

I hike from our Athens hotel to the Acropolis, the steep, ruin-crowned hill that juts from the sprawling metropolis of the modern city. Approaching the main entrance, I see a long line. So I take a detour and make my way up an almost deserted walkway that winds along the slopes of the hill.

BRISTLING WITH RELIGION

I'm nearly alone on this path despite the crowds elsewhere, so it's easy to imagine I'm back in Paul's time. The massive, partially restored buildings on the hilltop include altars to Zeus, Athena Nike, Poseidon, and Artemis. They're all roped off. Visitors can look in but not enter. However, surprisingly little excavation has been done on the sides of the hill, so the remnants of much smaller temples remain largely unguarded and unvisited here.

I clamber through shallow caves that once held shrines to Apollo, Pan, and the Nymphs. By the light of my iPhone I notice cracks at the back of these chambers. Some believe these were once secret passageways into the temples on the hilltop, used by virgin priestesses during annual rituals. I retrace my steps and blink as I emerge into daylight, spotting even more niches that once held idols of gods whose names we no longer know.

And all these little altars, as well as the massive shrines above, were visible to Paul from the Areopagus, a rocky outcropping directly across from the Acropolis. He would have seen a hill swathed in the constant smoke of sacrifices. One ancient writer says there were 30,000 gods and goddesses worshipped in Athens at the time.

That's probably an exaggeration, but his point is, this was a very religious place.

THE RELIGION POLICE

And not only were there a lot of religions in Athens; there were always more popping up. From time to time, new teachers would try to start movements. And these upstart religions had to be screened.

That was one of the responsibilities of a city council named after the Areopagus. The name means "Mars Hill," that rocky knoll next to the Parthenon where the council originally met, although by Paul's time they probably convened in a building below the hill, near the town square. Most of them were either Epicurean or Stoic philosophers (for a brief intro to their beliefs, see page 196).

Some members of the committee hear Paul preaching and insult him. They use a word translated "babbler" in many English Bibles, but literally in Greek it's "seed-pecker." It has the connotation, "What's this hick trying to say?" Others thought he was advocating "foreign gods."

By the way, don't miss the intriguing detail. They think Paul is preaching about *gods*. Plural. Some scholars believe that when they heard Paul preach on "Jesus and the resurrection," the Areopagus members thought he was talking about two deities, Jesus and Anastasia, a female name that sounds like the Greek word for resurrection, *anastasis*. They ask him to their council meeting to explain himself.

This was really a big deal. It was the most important meeting of pagan culture-makers Paul had yet addressed. And in his response to them, Paul is a role model for you and me.

BLAST OR BLESS?

Paul chooses to begin his address to the Athenian philosophers with the surprising words: "Men of Athens, I notice that you are very religious in every way, for as I was walking along I saw your many shrines…" (Acts 17:22–23a ESV)

That's almost a joke. It would have been impossible *not* to notice the shrines. Paul's senses would have been assaulted as he saw the massive marble temples, smelled the roasted meat of the sacrifices, heard the flutes and the songs and the cymbals. And unlike the pristine white friezes and columns we associate with Greece today, the temples Paul saw were gaudily painted with bright colors. Even the idols were technicolor, with painted fingernails and fake eyes that were eerily lifelike. All the color has been washed away by centuries of storms and the ivory eyeballs plundered by thieves, but then the whole scene surely stunned Paul as garish and offensive.

Yet I see him doing some things here I often forget to do when talking with people who don't believe what I believe. Be gracious. Observe. Learn. Compliment. Paul does not start by telling his audience they're all wrong. He actually compliments the Athenians for their spirituality, though Luke says their idols really disturbed him. *And you and I can do the same.* Bless instead of blast.

NOT A CULTURE WAR

I'll reveal a pet peeve: I find the expression "culture war" troubling. Some people use it to describe the battle of Christians against a secular society. *But if you see yourself at war with your culture, then it's easy to see the people in your culture as enemies* rather than people God loves.

I know. I've been there. When I was younger I saw myself and my friends as "the good guys." I became self-righteous and judgmental. I looked for things to *oppose* in the culture. But Paul looked for things in Athenian culture he could *engage* with. Of course he also saw where Greek culture opposed his faith; he didn't compromise the integrity of his core beliefs. But he worked as an agent of God's love, building bridges of understanding.

Can you build bridges like Paul did? You don't even need to use obviously "spiritual" points of connection. You can build bridges with music, movies, sports, nature – almost any interest anyone has. Affirm what's good about it, then find a way to use it as a conversation starter about faith. And you don't need to plan out all your conversational moves like some chess master. Just start the dialogue. Believe in the power of the Holy Spirit to influence further conversation.

The point? You can accept and befriend people who don't agree with all your beliefs. You can have strong convictions and still gracefully disagree. God loves them, and so should you.

Say you have a friend who's into Eastern meditation. That's something certainly open to critique from a Christian point of view, because it usually emphasizes emptying the mind of content. In contrast, biblical meditation focuses on saturating the mind with inspiring content.

But judging from how he addressed the Athenians, I think Paul would listen carefully, learn respectfully, and compliment sincerely. He might comment approvingly on your friend's interest in transcendent matters instead of just binge-watching TV or playing video games all day.[4] Then he'd explain his own encounter with the living Lord they long for.

BUILDING BRIDGES INSTEAD OF WALLS

That's exactly what he does in this speech. He starts with an intriguing hook:

> "As I walked around and looked carefully at your objects of worship, I even found an altar with this inscription: TO AN UNKNOWN GOD. What you worship as unknown, I now declare to you." (Acts 17:23)

In his ancient travel guide, *Descriptions of Greece,* Pausanias mentions several altars he saw in Athens dedicated "to gods unknown" and Diogenes Laertius wrote about Athenian altars dedicated to "the god to whom it may concern."[5] None have yet been unearthed in Athens, but an altar to an unknown god has been found in Pergamum. These were pagan idols, but again, Paul does not take this moment to be critical; he uses the Athenian's existing interest in spiritual things to build a bridge. He's not saying their worship of the idol is good; he's saying their *need* to worship points to something real.

DEFINE GOD

But as he builds this bridge, Paul astutely avoids a common trap: *Assuming people who use the same words mean the same thing.* The pagan Greeks used the identical word for god, *theos*, as Paul and other Christians. But their definition of that word differed radically.

Bible scholar N.T. Wright taught at Oxford University for many years. Students often told him, "I don't believe in God." He had a stock response: "That is interesting. Tell me about the god you don't believe in."

They would stammer out a few phrases about a being who lived up in the sky, looking down disapprovingly on the world, occasionally intervening to do miracles, sending bad people to hell while allowing good people to share his heaven. Again, he had a stock response: "I don't believe in that god either."[6]

That surprised the students. Then he explained, "I believe in the God I see revealed in Jesus of Nazareth." And the conversation could then be more productive.

When many people in our culture use "god language," they don't necessarily mean what the Bible means. Even people in religious groups may talk about "Christ-consciousness," "receiving Christ," "having faith," "the gospel," "Jesus" ...and not mean at all what the Bible actually teaches. So like Paul in Athens, listen carefully to what *they* mean, and then be able to explain clearly what *you* mean.

So since Paul's starting point is an explanation of the "unknown god" how does Paul define God for them?

BUILDING BRIDGES NOT WALLS

GOD IS CREATOR
He says God is the creator of everything and does not live in temples (Acts 17:24). Epicureans and Stoics would have agreed that temples are irrelevant.

GOD IS A GIVER
Paul goes on to say that God doesn't need us to give him anything, because he is the one who gives us everything, including our very lives (Acts 17:25–26). This is a huge point. In the relationship between God and humans, God is the giver and we are the receiver.

GOD IS NEAR
Paul shows remarkable familiarity with pagan religious literature, quoting from memory the Cretan philosopher Epimenides who said of God, "In him we live and move and have our being" and the Stoic philosopher Aratus who said, "We are his offspring" (Acts 17:28). Note: Paul is not saying *God is everything*. That's pantheism. He is saying *God is everywhere*.

Stop for a minute and think about what is happening here: Paul, a Jewish man trained as a Pharisee, learned about other religions well enough to quote their own writers by heart. He's not approving everything those religions teach. He's training himself to be culturally relevant and sensitive, showing that there's a thread of teaching even in these Gentile cultures that connects with the truth found ultimately in Jesus. Seashells leading home.

And he's setting a great example for you and me. Do you know the surrounding culture well enough to engage like this, even quoting its own celebrities and saints? You're not looking for things to approve; you're looking for things with which to connect the message of Christ. But that means you have to approach the culture as a discerning *learner*, not just a kneejerk *critic* or mindless *consumer*.

WE ARE ALL EQUAL BEFORE GOD
Then, after beginning with concepts he knows these philosophers would see as true, he brings in a concept they would have seen

as radical: *Everyone is equal before God.* God created everyone, everywhere, equally, in all nations (Acts 17:26).

See the theme of the international gospel again? This would have been a huge challenge to the Athenians, who thought they were specially crafted from the soil of Athens, and had status as "most favored nation" among all races. They even called non-Athenians "barbarians." It was essential for Paul to knock down this lie.

It's intriguing to me that Paul saw, two thousand years ago, how racism subverts the gospel. For the gospel to be uncompromised, we must all be equal: equally sinful, equally deserving judgment, and equally able to receive salvation by God's grace. No one is worse, and no one is even one step closer to salvation. It is *all* God's work.

So if we are all equal, then how does anyone find God? That's his next point.

> PRAYER FOR THE JOURNEY: *Heavenly Father, help me see my relationship with my culture not as war, but as diplomacy. I am a herald of your kingdom. Let me see how I can build bridges to the gospel without compromising the truth.*

The famous Acropolis of Athens, seen here from the Areopagus or Mars Hill, was bristling with temples in the time of Paul.

I'M IN AN ATHENS STATE OF MIND

Today Athens is a sprawling megacity, but in Paul's day it was a smallish place of about 25,000. However, its influence was felt all over the world... and still is! In many ways, our modern world is "in an Athens state of mind."

There were three major schools of thought in Athens when Paul visited.

PLATONISM: IT'S BETTER TO BE SPIRITUAL.

Plato established the Academy in Athens in 385 BC, and for nearly a thousand years it was a prestigious school of philosophy. To summarize broadly, Plato taught the physical world we live in is essentially evil. Only spiritual things are perfectly good (That's why today we called non-sexual friendships "platonic"; they focus on the spiritual and not the physical). So: Matter = bad; spirit = good. Therefore, the goal of a good person is to escape the physical and focus purely on the spiritual. This contrasts with Judaism and Christianity, which teach that God gives us physical things as good gifts (to be enjoyed within God's parameters). Platonism infected Christianity from early days, and still influences it today. When people imagine heaven as a bunch of disembodied spirits floating on clouds, those images owe much more to Plato than the Bible.

EPICUREANISM: YOU ONLY LIVE ONCE, SO MAKE IT FUN.

Named for the philosopher Epicurus who taught in Athens around 300 BC, Epicureans taught the highest goal in life is pleasure, defined as "absence of pain in the body and trouble in the soul."[7]

Does that mean to do whatever feels good? Not necessarily. Epicurus himself taught that immediate sensation should be resisted for more long-term pleasures later. Moderation is the key to true pleasure, he said, because overindulgence eventually brings not pleasure but pain. However, by Paul's day a lot of this nuance had been lost, and many so-called Epicureans taught: "Eat, drink, and be merry, for tomorrow we die." The first YOLO generation!

Epicureans were functional atheists; they didn't deny the *existence* of the gods, they simply denied the *relevance* of the gods. The gods live someplace far away, totally irrelevant to our lives today. Meditating on them might have some value, but people should have no fear of their judgment, because there is no afterlife. You find the philosophical descendants of Epicureans in college dorms everywhere.

STOICISM: LIFE IS HARD, THEN YOU DIE. SO ELIMINATE DESIRE AND IMPROVE YOURSELF.

By Paul's day the Stoics were far more influential than the Epicureans. Paul's contemporary, the Stoic philosopher Epictetus, said the greatest goal in life is personal character improvement. Here's his reasoning: The only things you can truly control are your own moral choices. Absolutely everything else is outside your power. So to desire things like wealth or reputation or someone's love or a more beautiful appearance is irrational and the cause of misery because you're longing for something outside your complete control. Happiness can only be found in letting go of all these desires.

Unlike Epicureans, Stoics believed God is not far away, but in and around everything. God is the "Divine Reason" (they used the Greek word *Logos*) in all creation. They believed humans have the divine spark within them, and at death, this spark returns to the Logos. They also believed every single thing that happens is somehow part of the Divine Reason. Are you starting to recognize Stoicism? You've seen a version of it in *Star Wars* movies as the philosophy of the Jedi. Minus the light sabers.

Once you know the basics of these Greek philosophies, you can see how Paul is using some of their ideas as a bridge to the gospel in his Acts 17 speech. Like the Epicureans, he says the physical world is a good thing. In fact, life is a gift from God. Like the Stoics, he teaches God is all around us, and cannot be limited to temples made by humans. But he offers something appealing that's not in either of these schools of thought, a relevant, personal God who wants a relationship with us. And unlike Plato, he affirms a physical resurrection, because God loves the physical world as much as the spiritual.

Paul himself seems harshly critical of something that sounds like Epicureanism in Philippians 3:19 ("Their god is their appetite... they think only about this life here on earth" NLT) and Stoicism in Colossians 2:23 ("These have indeed an appearance of wisdom in promoting ... asceticism and severity to the body, but they are of no value in stopping the indulgence of the flesh." ESV) but here in Acts 17 he keeps his criticisms to himself. If he had started critically, he never would have had an audience with the council. He doesn't say out loud every single thought he had about these people. He looks for bridges. You can do the same.

33
YOU CAN'T CONTROL RESULTS

ACTS 17:27-34

On the sun-drenched Greek island of Rhodes I hire an excellent cab driver named Nicholas to show me around. He careens around town in a muscular Mercedes, showing off temples to Apollo and Caesar and Artemis, and Greek Orthodox churches too. I ask him what he thinks of the thickly religious history of the area. He pauses thoughtfully, then says, "First I show you something." Pedal to the metal. We rocket past a strand of beaches with hotels catering to Russian tourists. Huge vinyl posters of their president hang from some of the walls. Nicholas gestures toward them and describes visiting the Soviet Union years ago where he saw massive statues of Lenin and Stalin.

I'm wondering where he's going with all this when he fixes me with a stare (for an unnervingly long time, considering that he is still driving at maximum velocity) and says, "One thing all this tells me. The need to worship is in our DNA. *Whether* we worship is not our choice. The only thing we choose is *what* to worship."

Wise cabbie. That's exactly Paul's point in his speech to the Areopagus. The Athenians were reaching out to God, desperately seeking something to venerate. The existence of one altar after another proved the unsatisfactory nature of their search. To paraphrase Bono, they still hadn't found what they were looking for. And still today, the essential message of Jesus for people bouncing from one god to the next — career, reputation, pleasure, money, acclaim — is the same. *I've got what you're already seeking.* He's the one true God in a sea of false idols.

Paul explains this to the Athenian council. And makes two other points that would have appealed to these inquisitive scholars:

GOD REWARDS SEEKERS

Paul says the Lord has, at some level, engaged with all the nations. "God did this so that we would seek him and perhaps reach out for him and find him." (Acts 17:27).

The philosophers Paul faced loved to think of themselves as truth-seekers. But Paul subtly changes the emphasis from knowing *about* God to *knowing God*. God wants us to seek *him* and reach out for *him* and find *him*. God doesn't want us just to look for *knowledge*; he wants us to be in *relationship*!

Jesus promised that whoever seeks, finds. Perhaps you may not yet believe in Jesus. Here's what I sincerely want to express. I'm not asking you to jump blindly into some system. I'm encouraging you to become an open-minded seeker of a person. Because I have total confidence, based on the promise of Christ, that everyone who sincerely seeks God will find him.

And then Paul says something else that would have intrigued these philosophers:

GOD NEEDS NOTHING, AND IS IMPOSSIBLE TO CONTAIN

"We should not think that the divine being is like gold or silver or stone — an image made by human design or skill." (Acts 17:29) The philosophers would have loved this. This was a position they held but rarely stated so boldly because they were afraid of offending the masses. They didn't think the idols really represented the Divine either. They would have respected Paul for this stand.

Then Paul moves to an idea that would be more controversial:

GOD IS THE ULTIMATE JUDGE

God has a plan for history, and that includes judgment (Acts 17:30–31). We are all accountable for our choices. Stoics and

Epicureans specifically taught there was no afterlife judgment. But Paul says, no, if God is personal, then that means we are accountable ultimately to this God.

You can sense the audience getting restless now. Paul seems to be laying the groundwork for his case that the perfect judge is the all-powerful and merciful Jesus. But he is stopped in his tracks, interrupted by shouts from the gallery.

And here is one of those intriguing mysteries in Acts: *What would have been Paul's next point?* In his own epistles, Paul always moved from the idea of God's judgment to the idea of God's grace.

But just as Paul transitions into a specifically Christian point, that Jesus' authority to judge is proven by his resurrection from the dead, the Greeks interrupt. The word "resurrection" seems to be the deal-killer.

Why? Here's my theory. I think the council members who had believed Paul was preaching about Jesus *and* a goddess named *Anastasia* suddenly realize he is preaching instead about *anastasis*— a reversal of death, a literal resurrection. This idea had no parallel in Greek philosophy and was specifically rejected by the Areopagus. In Athenian legend, when the Areopagus was founded, the god Apollo declared, "Once a man dies and the earth drinks up his blood, there is no resurrection."[8]

Some openly mock Paul for preaching the resurrection, but others are curious and later become believers. In fact, Dionysius, one of the members of the council, would become the first pastor of the Christian church in Athens. That's according to a man named after him, Dionysius of Corinth, writing in 171 AD. Luke also identifies a convert named Damaris, a woman who became a beloved figure in the Athens church.

YOU CANNOT CONTROL THE RESPONSE
Here's another point to learn from Paul's speech: When you share your faith, some people will stop listening if you say something they

find ridiculous or offensive, just like the people at the Areopagus stopped listening to Paul. You can only control your content; you can't control the response. As we've already seen, even a brilliantly thought-out message like Paul's wasn't universally accepted.

Not everyone will hear the "good news" part of the gospel. Just as in Athens, the two sticking points today are often the same: God's judgment. Christ's resurrection.

No matter the response, stay true to the message. That doesn't mean being insensitive or unnecessarily offensive. It doesn't excuse laziness or boorishness. Paul was never any of those things. He studied the beliefs of the Athenians and sensitively used some of their interests as launching points for the good news.

But no one gets a 100% approval rating, not even Paul. Not even Jesus. *So don't try to achieve a level of approval the Lord Himself never achieved.* Be sensitive and faithful to the gospel. Then let go of the results. Don't despair. As in Athens, some will hear and believe and even become leaders.

The need to worship? It's in our DNA for sure. So be certain you're focused on Jesus and not any false gods. Not even the false god of ministry success or evangelistic results.

Relax. Believe in the power of the Holy Spirit. And be a thoughtful witness.

> PRAYER FOR THE JOURNEY: *Heavenly Father, help me remember that I cannot control anyone's response. Let me see that I am free from trying to achieve something even Jesus never achieved: 100% approval! Let me be winsomely confident in my witness.*

A BONANZA FOR TENTMAKERS

Every two years the city of Corinth hosted thousands of visitors at the Isthmian Games. Second only in popularity to the Olympics, these athletic contests were held at the nearby "sports city" of Isthmia, built exclusively to host the games.

Archaeologists have been digging at Isthmia for about a century, and while they have found temples and stadiums, not one single house has yet been found. So where did those tens of thousands of athletes, coaches, and spectators stay every other year when the games were held? Here's the scholarly opinion: In elaborate tent cities. Tents were like the Airstream trailers of the era, where the visiting celebs stayed when on location.

And that means Corinth was the perfect place for a tentmaker like Paul. He was clearly a very entrepreneurial guy, and he, and his fellow tentmakers Priscilla and Aquila, must have seen a huge market for their skills.

The beautiful ruins of Corinth, where Paul lived for about 18 months.

34
WHAT GOD SAYS ABOUT YOUR FEAR
ACTS 18:1-23

Let's finally get back to that Athens police station where I was detained after my passport and money were stolen on the Areopagus. After hours and hours of answering the same questions from various detectives I'm finally released. But I can't leave the country. I have no passport.

My plan for this book was to retrace the geography of Acts, but now that's in jeopardy. I can still go down to see the ruins in Corinth, about an hour south of Athens, because we're still in Greece. And that's exactly the direction Paul took when he left Athens, so that's cool. But the next stop is supposed to be Ephesus, back in Turkey. And I can't get there without a passport. I'm stuck.

Questions run through my mind all night: Have I come all this way only to be blocked from completing the project? Will I be forced to return to the States? How is God going to work in this?

IN THE (LITERAL) FOOTSTEPS
The next day I walk down the main street of ancient Corinth and decide to forget my troubles and focus on the present for at least a couple hours. Relax, I tell myself. Calm down. Settle into the moment. I become transfixed by the thought that I am quite literally in the footsteps of Paul here.

I glide up and down the ancient avenue, squinting so I can better picture the ancient city in its ancient glory, which may have been a mistake, because I violently stub my toe on an ancient slab of ancient marble. As I hop around in pain, it occurs to me: Hey! I bet

Paul did this once or twice. Maybe on this same street. Consider new book title: *Acts Ordeal: Tripping in the Path of Paul.*

PERILOUS PATH

The 50-mile road from Athens to Corinth was filled with danger for unwary travelers in Paul's day. At about the halfway point were "The Sceironian Rocks," where the broad highway narrowed to a razor-thin footpath carved into a cliff. One stumble would send a person plummeting to sharp rocks far below. Making matters worse, the path was thought haunted by the ghost of the robber Sceiron. His phantom, it was said, would block the path, commanding travelers to bend down and wash his feet. When they did, he would kick them over the precipice.[9] After that came hills patrolled by the bandit Sinis, who robbed and then dismembered his victims with ropes and pulleys connected to pine trees. When Paul told the Corinthians he had "faced dangers from robbers" (2 Cor. 11:26), maybe his trip to visit them was on his mind.

But once Paul got here, what a city! Ten times the size of Athens, Corinth was a center of political and economic power. The capital of the whole province of Achaia, Corinth made money from ports on two different seas. In a quirk of geography, it sat on a narrow neck of land just over three miles wide between the Aegean and Adriatic Seas. To cut hundreds of perilous miles off their trip, sailors would disembark on one side of the isthmus and simply stroll over to different ships on the other side, passing through the impressive city of Corinth along the way.

Meanwhile, hired workers transferred cargo from one port to the other. A paved road between the two sides of the isthmus was grooved with channels for wagon wheels, much like a train track. Massive carriages shuttling freight between the twin ports traveled back and forth constantly.

As they waited for their goods to be loaded onto new vessels, the sailors and passengers threw their money at the notorious pleasures available in the gleaming city. The Greek geographer Strabo claimed the temple of Aphrodite, prominently advertised by its position on a hill 1800 feet above the city, employed over a thousand prostitutes. Plato used the term "Corinthian girl" as a euphemism for streetwalker. A typical comic relief character in Greek plays of the time was the tipsy Corinthian, showing the city's wide reputation for drunkenness.[10] No wonder immorality, drinking, and materialism were issues Paul dealt with in his letters to the Christians here.

These days Corinth is a stunning archaeological site for Christians. The city's place of judgment, or bema seat, has been discovered. It's the very spot Paul stood as he faced the Roman governor. Maybe with his toe still smarting from some stumble.

Here's what happened. Paul leaves Athens and moves to Corinth for an extended stay of about a year and a half. For much of that time he goes back to his job of tent making, sharing space with Priscilla and Aquila.

And every week on the Sabbath, Paul attends synagogue and "tries to convince Jews and Greeks alike" that Jesus is the Messiah (Acts 18:4). Gentiles, he is teaching, can become Messiah-followers without first keeping Jewish kosher laws.

THE TENSION BUILDS

Apparently in Corinth, as elsewhere, this message does not go over too well with the majority of observant Jewish people. The tension in the synagogue builds until Paul leaves in a huff and moves his teaching next door to the house of Titius Justus, a Gentile. In a funny plot twist, once Paul moves, the leader of the synagogue, a man named Crispus, becomes a believer in Jesus.

But the rest of the synagogue leadership still sees Paul as the dangerous leader of a new sect. They drag him into court, right at the very bema seat discovered here in the ruins at Corinth.

As he stands before the Roman governor Gallio, Paul surely remembers a dream he had earlier in his stay. God spoke to him, saying, "Do not be afraid; keep on speaking, do not be silent. For I am with you, and no one is going to attack and harm you, because I have many people in this city." (Acts 18:9–10)

I love the fact that God had to tell even Paul not to be afraid! It shows he was just as human as you and me. Something else I love about that vision: God is telling Paul that he's not alone, that many others "belong to God" in the city.

You and I need to hear that too. In your school, your work, your city, don't be afraid to be a witness; *you are not alone.* There are other people who belong to God there too. Even if they don't know it yet.

The Corinthian bema seat, or place of judgment, where Paul stood before Gallio. (Photo credit: Ryan, 2007)

Back at the bema seat, in a surprise move, Gallio instantly dismisses the charges, even before Paul says a word in his own defense. Gallio judges this a purely religious dispute having nothing to do with his civic responsibilities. And his decision is another clue to the purpose of the Book of Acts. Keep it in mind as you collect that evidence.

As their case is dismissed, the crowd that brought the charges against Paul is so upset that they turn on their new synagogue leader, a man named Sosthenes, and beat him up. But here's something fascinating about Sosthenes. In his first letter to the Corinthian Christians, in the very first verse, Paul writes: "Paul, called by the will of God to be an apostle of Christ Jesus, *and our brother Sosthenes...*" (1 Corinthians 1:1 RSV) So Sosthenes, the one who led the opposition against Paul, becomes a Christian, even travelling with Paul on a mission trip!

All of this is a beautiful picture of how, behind the scenes, God is always working. He used Gallio, who wasn't even a believer, to help spread the gospel. He works through the most surprising people for his strategic purposes.

He'll do it for you too. Like he did for me.

GOD KNOWS A GUY

Later that day in Corinth, my wife Laurie asks our tour guide, Dino, "I know exactly one person who lives in Greece, a man named Jonathan Macris. Do you happen to know him?"

And Dino says, "Know him? He's my best friend!"

We laugh because we think he's kidding, and he says, "No, seriously, I was just at his birthday party last night!" Incredible. In a country of fourteen million we meet the best friend of the one person my wife knows here. Turns out they're both pastors. So I ask if I can join them at church the next Sunday.

My wife, son, and church tour group must all stay with the original itinerary and catch their planned flight to Turkey that night. But I'm not alone after all.

WHAT GOD SAYS ABOUT YOUR FEAR

"Do not fear... I have many people in this city." God always does. Wherever you go.

Dino and his family pick me up for the church service the next Sunday. So many refugees and immigrants are pouring into Athens on their way to Europe that I meet people there from Afghanistan, Sudan, Lebanon, Iraq, Iran, Syria, Dubai, Somalia, the Ukraine, and of course the U.S., Greece, and Turkey. Most people are wearing headsets because the church provides simultaneous translation into all kinds of languages.

Toward the end of the service, Pastor Dino announces, without warning me beforehand, "We have with us a dear friend from California. Will you share a few words?"

I get up, put on the translation headset microphone, and simply open my Bible to the last place I'd been reading, the place where Paul visits Corinth: Acts 18. My eyes fall on verses 9 and 10. I read the words of Paul's vision:

> *This is the word of the Lord:*
> *Do not be afraid!*
> *Speak out!*
> *Don't be silent!*
> *For I am with you,*
> *and no one will attack and harm you,*
> *for many people in this city belong to me.*

A strange silence falls over the church. I look up. And see tears. These brothers and sisters of mine from Somalia and Syria and Iraq and Afghanistan are just drinking those words in. Afterward one tells me, "You have no idea how I needed to hear exactly that."

I'm humbled that my minor inconvenience has allowed me to minister to these refugees who truly do not know what their future holds.

HE CAN WORK THROUGH IT

Are you afraid like Paul was?

God's words to Paul are his words to you too: Don't be afraid. Keep on speaking for me. I am with you. You'll be okay. I have people there in your situation that you don't even know about yet.

Keep your eyes open and your heart ready!

> PRAYER FOR THE JOURNEY: *Lord, help me not to be afraid. Help me remember you are with me. And that you are already working in the lives of people I will meet at just the right time. May my eyes be open to those people in those moments.*

WHO WAS GALLIO?

Part of a rich and powerful family with many friends in high places, Gallio was the older brother of the famous writer Seneca, personal tutor of Nero, who was soon to become emperor. He was also close friends with the Roman emperor Claudius.

In the early twentieth century archaeologists found fragments of an inscription written by Claudius in 52 AD which refers to Gallio as proconsul. Why is that so important? It helps us date the rest of the Book of Acts with precision.

The famed Gallio inscription, which dates his time in Corinth to 52 AD
(Photo credit: Delphi Archaeological Museum)

35
CLEANING THE PICTURE

ACTS 18:24-19:22

The next week I'm back in Turkey, having endured the best of American, Greek, and Turkish bureaucracy at their respective embassies. The good news is I have a temporary passport and visa, so I'm once again free to travel internationally. The bad news is, my new emergency passport looks very temporary. I am stopped at every checkpoint by officials convinced it's a forgery. Hey! More opportunities to relate to the encounters with bureaucrats in Acts!

But eventually I return to the ancient ruins of Ephesus, one of the most beautiful archaeological sites in the world.

The city sparkles even after centuries under debris which a team of archaeologists is slowly scraping away. As I watch, two diggers sifting through mud suddenly smile and hold up a coin. They rinse it off and read the inscription: It's from the first century.

Beautiful hillside mansions are also emerging from the dirt here, revealing amazing paintings, huge lobbies, tiled courtyards with lovely fountains, and indoor bathrooms with sophisticated plumbing. Even the very theater mentioned in Acts where city silversmiths stage a riot against Paul is once again seating thousands and is even available for rent to large groups.

And our Turkish guide Tulu Gökkadar tells me she has a surprise: She may be able to show us part of the Ephesus site which remains closed to the public. But she knows a guy. The head guy.

We walk to a nondescript farmhouse just outside the city. Goats and a small dog romp in the yard with two children. An aging man limps toward us with a cane but his step quickens when he sees Tulu, apparently an old friend. They embrace warmly. And then she introduces him to me. He is the lead archaeologist of this secret site.

After a consultation with Tulu, he agrees to her suggestion, and asks one of his assistants to take us on a steep and narrow dirt path, through thorn bushes and an olive orchard, to an overlook on the side of the hill where the ruins of Ephesus spread out below us.

We're on Mount Bülbüldagh (That's a super fun word to pronounce. Try it. Seriously. Try it now. *Bülbüldagh.* Looks like the name of an IKEA sofa. Sounds like "Bull-bulldog." It means "Nightingale Mountain" in Turkish. But that's way less fun to say).

Soon we are *inside* Mount Bülbüldagh. The man brings us to a cave secured tightly against intruders with an iron gate. He unlatches a massive padlock. The metal door creaks as he forces it open and leads us into the darkness.

THE ANCIENT CAVE
Discovered by two priests in 1892 while they were searching for the tomb of Mary the mother of Jesus, this cave was later excavated by the Austrian Archaeological Institute.

Their research shows this has been a Christian sacred site since the first or second century. Its walls were decorated with paintings over many years, whitewashed several times, then repainted with new images. Archaeologists carefully removed centuries of dirt and pigment to discover the very earliest art underneath it all. To protect these delicate and ancient frescoes, the cave is not open to the public. But Gökkadar got us into Bülbüldagh (okay, once again, that is just a fun thing to say).

As I walk in with my wife and son, our flashlights reveal why this cave is so treasured. We see very early paintings of the Apostle Paul and Thecla, a female disciple. This is the only known depiction of

Paul at Ephesus and possibly the very earliest portrayal of him yet found. Why was this cave associated with Paul? Did he live here? No one knows for sure. What's certain is that Christians prayed and apparently hid here during times of persecution.

CLEANING THE PICTURE OF JESUS

Before we leave, my wife points to something on the very back wall, in the furthest, darkest reaches of the cavern. We go back to take a closer look. It's another ancient painting. This one hasn't survived the centuries nearly as well as the painting of Paul. It's chipped and faded, yet still recognizable. Barely.

It's an ancient painting of Jesus, one of the oldest known. It's amazing to be here next to it, not in a guarded museum, but in a cave lit only by our flashlights. So this is what early Christians pictured when they thought of him. We feel a mysterious sense of connection to the unknown artist, my brother or my sister in the faith, all those centuries ago. My wife reaches out her hand to clear away cobwebs, and the entire image crumbles off the wall and slides to the cavern floor.

Just kidding about that last part.

But we did see that picture of Jesus in the back of the cave. Laurie did not touch it. Here's my point. Like that fading fresco, the picture of Christ in your heart can begin to grow dim. It gets obscured by layers that tend to accumulate over the years: guilt, distraction, busyness, and unbiblical doctrine.

That's why, in nearly every sermon in Acts, one of the followers of Jesus performs what you could call an art restoration.

It's essential. Clear up the picture of Jesus.

FUZZY IMAGE

In today's passage, several people have a fuzzy picture of Christ.

First you meet a Jewish man named Apollos, from Alexandria, Egypt. Although Apollos taught accurately about Jesus, Luke says he "knows only the baptism of John." (Acts 18:25) Then the same thing is said of another group Paul meets in the next chapter (Acts 19:3).

How can believers in Jesus "know only the baptism of John"? You might not realize it, but you meet them all the time. Even today. In fact, maybe that describes you.

"The baptism of John" refers to John the Baptist, a hugely popular teacher (and Jesus' cousin) before Christ's ministry began. As Paul tells the people in Ephesus, "John's baptism called for repentance from sin." (Acts 19:4)

Repentance. That means, turn around. Rethink your life. Be sorry for your wrongdoing and recommit your life to God in light of his coming judgment.

That was okay as far as it went. The apostles' sermons in Acts speak of repentance too. But the message of repentance in the teaching of John was incomplete. It pointed to the Messiah. But now the Messiah had come, with something powerful to add to John's call for repentance: *The power of the Holy Spirit to change you once you realize you're powerless to save yourself.*

That's why the baptism of Jesus is likened in the New Testament to a death and resurrection, which was never said of John's baptism. We die to our old self-centered lives, and are raised with Christ into a new life that was simply not possible before.

The baptism of John was a baptism *only* of repentance. The baptism of Jesus is a baptism of *resurrection* that follows repentance.

THE "TRY HARDER" NON-GOSPEL

True confession: In my earliest years as a pastor, I was just like Apollos. I could preach lots of great stuff about Jesus. *But I knew only the baptism of John.* Every sermon ended with a call to repentance: "Feel sorry for your sin, and try harder to do better." But I never went beyond that to talk about the power available in Christ to actually change.

It was while prepping for a sermon series on Galatians that I realized I was completely missing the point. As Paul suggests in that epistle, "try harder" is not good news at all. It's a non-gospel. I write extensively about my life-changing discovery in the book *Grace Immersion*.

Repentance is an important step: I realize my life is headed for disaster because of my self-centered, self-destructive behavior. But hope comes when I turn my life over to Jesus and let him empower me through his Spirit.

I love how Priscilla and Aquila take Apollos aside (they don't humiliate him in front of everyone else) and "explain the way of God more adequately." Then when Paul baptizes the people in the name of Jesus, they "receive the Holy Spirit." All that time they'd been trying to live the Christian life in their own power. Now they know they have something more—the same power that raised Jesus from the dead.

MAGIC JESUS

There's another group in this passage with a different, but still fuzzy, picture of Jesus—the "seven sons of Sceva." They see the name of Jesus as something magical, a code word that will give them victory over evil forces. As you've already seen, a belief in magic was very common in the first century. These men apparently think that if they pronounce "the name of Jesus" it will mystically imbue their prayers with power. They will be able to do whatever they want. But as they soon discover, life will beat you up if you cling to that idea.

Jesus is not a genie to be summoned whenever you want a wish to come true. Many believers even today hold a version of this magical view of Christ. They think that if they pray in Jesus' name, or learn some other secret, they're guaranteed power and prosperity.

The basic problem with that idea? It puts *you* in charge. You're still the one pulling the strings, the one invoking Jesus to do your bidding. It reduces the gospel to magic.

CLEANING THE PICTURE

But the gospel is not about some technique. It's not about learning formulas so you can pull God's strings. It's about you allowing God to pull your strings. You're yielding to him, not the other way around.

CLEARING UP THE PICTURE

Acts 19:8 says Paul taught in the synagogue at Ephesus for three months. Then he moves to "the lecture hall of Tyrannus" for the next two years, where he leads daily discussions. If Paul taught for just three hours a day, that means he gave the Ephesians about 3,100 hours of teaching. And you know what his teaching was about. He was clearing up their picture of Jesus.

Do you need someone to restore the picture for you?

The point of the gospel of Christ is not that you should feel bad about yourself and try hard to be better. The point is that you *can't* get all better, not in your own strength. You need God's free gift of salvation, where you find not only forgiveness of sin, but also the power to live a holy life.

Maybe you're in a cave right now. A cave of doubt or despair or disillusionment. Let me hold up a light for you and clear away some dirt on that wall. Do you see it? A restored picture of Jesus. That's what to focus on in this darkness.

> PRAYER FOR THE JOURNEY: *Lord, sometimes I feel like I'm in a dark cave, and the only picture I have of you is old and layered with years of neglect and confusion. Please peel off the layers of misunderstanding. I want to know you, the real you.*

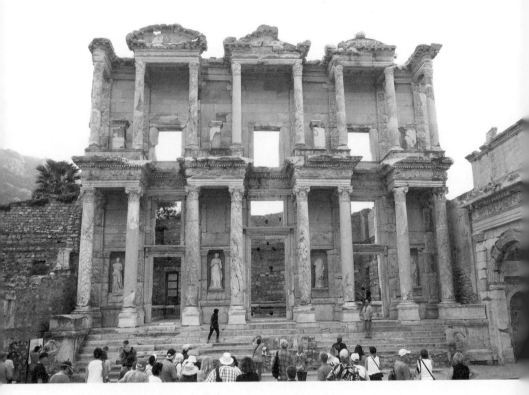

The Celsus Library at Ephesus.

THE SEVEN SLEEPERS

In a cliff above Ephesus you can see the alleged cavern of "The Seven Sleepers," characters in a very early Christian legend. The story: a group of young Christian men hide in a cave to escape brutal Roman persecution around 250 AD. Worried and upset, they eventually drift off to sleep. Upon awakening, they filter back into town to buy food… because, man, they are *super* hungry. But the merchants are confused when the young men try to use coins *over a hundred years old*. That's when the seven sleepers realize they've miraculously dozed through the entire persecution and have awakened a century later! In a development they could not have imagined, the Roman emperor is a believer, Christianity is now legal, and the threat to their lives is over. Cue Twilight Zone theme music.

Pure fairy tale, but there's a great moral to the story. Things change. Often in surprising ways. So when all seems darkest, don't give up. It's worth hanging in there just to see how it all turns out.

The ruins at Ephesus, painstakingly excavated by Austrian archaeologists, are among the most spectacular in Turkey.

ACTS ODYSSEY

PART SIX

ATTACKS & ASSASSINS

36
LOSING THEIR RELIGION

ACTS 19:23-41

Tulu was right.

She told us to wait until the afternoon to go see the rest of the ruins of Ephesus. Sure enough, by the time we get down to the city from Mount Bülbüldagh (say it again just for fun), the crowds have thinned, and by the time we leave, we're the only people remaining. I tell my wife and son, "I'm going to sit in the theater and wait until I don't see anyone here anymore, so I can be the very last person in Ephesus today."

I'm facing the ancient Roman road that once led straight from the theater to the city harbor. This is the road the Ephesian elders put Paul on after the city convulses in a riot over his teachings, just to get him safely out of town. It's a road that was hidden under silt for centuries, largely unchanged since Paul's time until it was unearthed a few decades ago. I want to have some time all to myself to walk slowly down this street and imagine the scene as Paul is hustled away.

I watch from the theater as the last group leaves. Then as the sun sets, I start walking.

TIME TRIPPING

It's eerie. Mist from the marshy valley ahead is beginning to snake around the ruins. I cannot hear any conversation, music, or footsteps. In fact, I can't even see the end of the street. I only see the old marble paving stones stretching from the massive theater behind me into the darkening landscape ahead. Faces of forgotten gods leer at me from toppled columns along the way. I imagine I'm about to step back into time, back to the pagan heyday of Ephesus.

Here's what I would have seen then: The road I'm on led to a busy port constantly servicing ships from all around the Empire. Today the harbor's completely silted up by debris from the river, and wears the perfect disguise of a wide flat valley. But in Bible times Egyptian, Greek, and Roman sailors streamed out of their boats by the thousands to experience the world's first all-marble city, gleaming and white and like nothing they'd ever seen before. The city was huge. At least 250,000 people lived here, making it the largest city in all Asia Minor. It was the capital of the province.

Among the luxuries of Ephesus in those days: Only this place and Rome had streetlights. The Ephesian library was one of the largest in the world. And the city had an amenity that has yet to be repeated in the modern world: public latrines, still visible today, with seats warmed by steam-filled lead pipes that ran under smooth white marble, and a stage with live performers to enjoy while you were... indisposed.

But none of that was the main attraction. There was a wonder of the world here that lured thousands of ancient tourists every year: the amazing Temple of Artemis.

ARTEMIS OF THE EPHESIANS

When I visit the temple today nothing remains except one wobbly-looking column topped by a stork's nest. But in its prime this was an amazing building. The Roman writer Pliny the Elder measured it as a mind-boggling 425 feet wide and 225 feet long. He counted 127 columns, 60 feet tall, supporting the roof. In comparison the famous Parthenon in Athens, itself a massive building, is only 230 feet long, 100 feet wide, with 58 columns. So the Temple of Artemis was more than twice the size of the Parthenon.

Tourists came to stare in awe at this massive structure and pick up a few keepsakes. In fact, tourism was a major engine of the local economy, supporting a cottage industry of silversmiths who made small replicas of the shrine to sell to visitors. The artisans even organized themselves into a guild, something like a forerunner to our modern labor unions.

And Paul gets in trouble with the union.

LOSING THEIR RELIGION

The miniature shrine manufacturers are incensed with Paul's teaching. What if people believe him? That might keep them from buying their merchandise. Demetrius, one of the silversmiths, sees his business in serious danger.

He has reason to be concerned. Several ancient writers describe the decline of the traditional Roman religions. In the Delphi Inscription, dated to 52 AD, the exact year of this passage in Acts, Emperor Claudius notes that the famous Temple of Apollo is "destitute of citizens."[1] A few decades later Pliny the Younger writes to the Emperor Trajan that the pagan temples had been "long neglected" and "almost deserted."[2]

The Roman world was tiring of the old gods. The brainy philosophies of Athens and mystery religions of Egypt and Persia were not really catching fire either. Many Romans were attracted to the monotheism of the Jews, but put off by the complicated religious law. Into this void stepped the Jesus movement.

Like many religious fundamentalists fearful of their own faith's decreasing relevance, Demetrius uses a combination of fear and fervor to start a riot against Paul. He fills the theater with an enraged mob chanting, "Great is Artemis of the Ephesians," as they demand to see Paul. The theater, still impressive today, could seat 25,000 people, so this is quite an intimidating crowd.

Paul, ever the opportunist, is eager to engage them all, thinking this an ideal opportunity. *Twenty-five thousand people, are you kidding me? Lemme at 'em!* But the Ephesian elders see it as a no-win situation, and hustle Paul out of town fast.

Fascinating fact: Luke points out that some of the highest

government officials, who were friends of Paul, also sent him a message, begging him not to venture into the theater. Luke uses the term "Asiarchs" to describe them. The Asiarchs were the leading men of the entire province of Asia Minor, members of the wealthiest and most prestigious families. They were also the group responsible for electing the high priest of the cult of Caesar every year, who always came from their ranks. It's remarkable that Paul had close friends from among this crowd.

And after wisely waiting for two hours to let the mob shout out some of their passion, the head city clerk (who would have been among those Asiarchs) gets up to calm everyone down further. He points out that Paul and his companions have done nothing worthy of arrest. He specifically says that they have not done any violence to the temple nor technically blasphemed Artemis. And if Demetrius thinks they have, then he should go through proper legal channels, and not create a mob scene.

It's a fascinating peek into how nuanced Paul's teaching must have been. Though he boldly proclaimed Christ, he did not, this Asiarch asserts, actually blaspheme or cause physical harm to the cult of Artemis.

DON'T CROSS THIS LINE

What an intense story. Just thinking about this mob as I walk alone down the ancient street to the silted-up port gives me the creeps. There's something about the still night air, the quiet of the ruins, the sense of history seeping out of the stones. My hair is standing on end as I imagine the bloodthirsty shouts of the crowd in the theater behind me and Paul being hustled away reluctantly on the road ahead of me, so I hightail it out of there too, back to the modern world.

I head toward the exit, turn a corner, and skid to a halt. I'm suddenly on a brightly lit street filled with tourists and one pop-up souvenir stand after another. And guess what? They're selling replicas of the shrine of Artemis. So little has changed.

But as I take my seat on a bus, I think back on what happened here all those years ago. And I see in this story a distinction Christians really need to stay aware of.

There are *necessarily* offensive things about our message. We shouldn't compromise those. God has to save us, because we are all sinners. That's kind of offensive to some people. But it's part of the gospel. And there are other core truths we can't dilute.

But there are ways Christians can be *unnecessarily* offensive. We can be insensitive to local customs. Speak rudely about other religions. Christians have even been violent in the past as they opposed perceived enemies to the faith. We need to steer clear of *unnecessary* offense.

Paul apparently does not cross that line here in Ephesus, which enables the town clerk to speak in Paul's defense. And note that Paul actually *made friends* with these Asiarchs, with whom he did not entirely agree. The takeaway: It's okay, and even strategically wise, to be friends with leaders in your society. Even the ones who believe some things you don't believe. That's a good role model for you and me as we learn to navigate an increasingly diverse culture.

> PRAYER FOR THE JOURNEY: *Lord, help me not to be unnecessarily offensive. Yet help me not compromise the necessarily offensive parts of the gospel. And give me wisdom to know the difference. Amen.*

The theater at Ephesus, where the riot against Paul took place in
Acts 19.

MY NAME IS LUCKY

There's an old joke about a handmade poster that reads, "Missing: One-legged dog, shriveled left ear, patches of baldness, one eye lost in fight. Answers to the name *Lucky*."

Reminds me of the strange little story Luke tells in Acts 20:7–12. Paul is speaking to the church meeting at Troas on a Sunday night, and because he intends to leave the next day, he keeps going, and going... until midnight! Then a fascinating detail: "There were many lamps in the upstairs room where we were meeting." (Acts 20:8) Ever been in a room with a lot of candles, a lot of people, upstairs, with heat rising? It gets very warm, and very stuffy. And here a young man named Eutychus drifts off to sleep while sitting in an open window and falls two stories to his death. Paul immediately goes down to the street, picks him up, and says, "Don't be alarmed; he's alive." The text suggests Paul healed him. Then (and I think this is another place Luke shows his amusement with his friend) instead of calling it a night, Paul goes right back upstairs and talks... until daylight. "Where were we before that guy fell asleep on me and died? Oh yes!"

Oh, and the name Eutychus? It means... *Lucky*.

37
ONE-ITEM BUCKET LIST

ACTS 20:1-38

Let me jet you back home for a day.

I'll lead you to a beautiful cemetery nestled close to the lovely Santa Cruz Mountains in the picturesque town of Los Gatos, California. Let's walk down this path to the spot where my mother and father are buried together, though their deaths were separated by five decades.

My dad discovered he had incurable cancer when he was just 36. He'd only been married five years, and had a baby girl, my sister Heidi, and a little boy, me.

Dad tried everything available in those days to find a cure. He explored all the medical options. Even faith healing. But he concluded that apparently, barring any last-minute miracle, God was going to allow this cancer to take his life.

Why go there in a study on Acts? It was in Acts 20 that Dad found his inspiration to face death.

APPOINTMENT WITH DEATH

In this passage, Paul believes he must go to Jerusalem to confront those trying to sabotage his ministry. Yet he's sure that violence awaits. And others think so too. As you'll see in the next chapter, the closer he travels to Jerusalem the more his friends who understand what is going on warn him to stay away from the radical element that has taken control there.

Both religiously and politically, Jerusalem was falling under the

227

sway of extremist fanatics. This is a picture entirely in keeping with what we know from other historical sources like Josephus, who says that nationalistic fervor was reaching a fever pitch as the century went on.

Paul weeps and embraces the Ephesian church elders after he tells them they will never see him alive again. He says he considers his life worth nothing (in other words, he's not afraid to die); all he wants is to be a witness of the gospel, in death or in life.

It's Paul's resolve here that my dad wrote about in the last letter he ever wrote, to his Young Adult Sunday School class:

> When the doctor revealed his diagnosis of lymphoma to me, I was at first shocked. He said I shouldn't expect to live a full life, perhaps only a few months.
>
> Immediately I thought of my young family; my wife, our 3½ year old boy, and the 15- month-old baby girl, and how their lives would be affected by an untimely death of their husband and father.
>
> The thoughts were unbearable and I quickly opened my Bible. The first verse I saw was Acts 20:24 — God's answer and encouragement for me:
>
> "But none of these things move me, neither count I my life dear unto myself, so that I might finish my course with joy, and the ministry which I have received of the Lord Jesus, to testify of the gospel of the grace of God." (Acts 20:24)
>
> In that moment I gave my life into the hands of my Lord, for Him to use according to His perfect will and to the glory of God — be it in sickness and death or in a miraculous healing. In that same moment an incomparable peace flooded my soul and has remained there ever since. I encourage everyone who hasn't done so to completely

dedicate his life to the Lord without reservation *and right now*, for we know not what tomorrow will bring.

I still meet people today who tell me, "Your dad's faith in the face of his death changed my life." Words from Acts 20:24 are even on my dad's gravestone.

MY ONLY AIM

As a newer Bible version translates it:

> I consider my life worth nothing to me; my only aim is to finish the race and complete the task the Lord Jesus has given me — the task of testifying to the good news of God's grace.

Paul's saying that when it comes down to it, he has just one thing on his bucket list. Be a witness of God's grace. That's what will matter most. Jesus gave his followers one command at the start of Acts, and that's it.

So how are we doing?

How are you doing individually? Are you staying on message or getting distracted? Are you a living example of someone confident he or she is unconditionally beloved of God, or are you still insecure, seeking approval, riddled with guilt?

How are we doing as a church? Are we witnesses of God's grace, or advocates for some other, lesser causes?

Paul is serene about the violence he faces in Jerusalem. But many of his friends will do their best to keep him from going there, as you'll see next.

> PRAYER FOR THE JOURNEY: *God, make my primary goal in life to be to testify to the good news of your grace. Help me see how everything else in life falls into place when I keep the main thing the main thing.*

AAA GUIDE TO THE EMPIRE

First-century travelers could purchase travel books and maps, known as *itinerarium*. Archaeologist Merilyn Hargis writes that publishers of such guides flourished in Rome. Among the most famous were Dorus and the Sosii brothers, sort of the Rick Steves of the ancient world. Their guides listed all the major roads, harbors, mountain ranges, temples, governor's residences, lighthouses, and more.[3]

The Peutinger Table is the only completely intact Roman road map to survive the centuries. A thirteenth-century copy of a map made during the reign of Augustus, it even has a rating system for lodging, using tower symbols much like our modern Michelin stars and AAA diamonds. One tower meant the hotel was basic, two towers meant it was a nice guest house, and four towers in a square indicated the best accommodations money could buy.

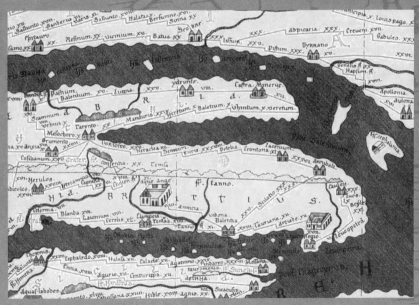

A portion of the Peutinger Table (Photo credit: Bibliotheca Augustana)

38
HOW TO DISAGREE

ACTS 21:1-26

Like Paul, I'm back in Jerusalem for my third visit after traveling through Turkey and Greece (and returning home to California for a while). I'm especially looking forward to another visit to the Church of the Holy Sepulcher.

Shafts of late afternoon light slant through the high windows. The sounds of the busy city are muffled by thick stone walls. The only people I see are priests padding softly down the halls.

And that means things may not stay calm for long.

Six ancient Christian denominations share stewardship of the enormous church and, as one journalist put it, "have been notoriously unable to keep themselves from throwing punches at the slightest perceived offense."[4]

During holidays, tensions are often particularly high, and have even erupted into priest-on-priest fistfights, which police have to break up. It took these denominations 17 years just to agree on a plan for painting the central dome. There's a ladder on a window ledge clearly visible from the street. No one has touched it since the early 1800s because everyone claims it's someone else's responsibility.

The Christian clergy here so distrust one another that they still hold to a peace agreement brokered in 1192 that gave a local Muslim family the keys to the church. The same Arab family has been locking and unlocking the church for all the subsequent centuries because none of the Christians will trust anyone else with the keys.

FAMILY FEUD

Disagreement between Christians does rise to comic (or tragic) levels at times. And it's always been a part of the Jesus movement. As Matthew Skinner puts it: "We in the church get caught pining for a golden age in church history that never existed when we conjure false memories of everyone in a Christian community getting along in perfect agreement."[5]

Of course there will be tensions. We're human! Luke never white-washes the character of these first Jesus-followers. Yes, there are those beautiful sentences at the end of Acts 2 and 4. But you also see the corruption of Ananias and Sapphira in Acts 5, the complaints about favoritism in Acts 6, the argument over John Mark in Acts 15. And here in chapter 21 there's another very real picture of devoted believers strongly disagreeing.

And this is a far more substantive disagreement than what color to paint the church dome. This one's life and death.

TRYING TO RESCUE PAUL

The bottom line here: Paul is travelling south to Jerusalem, knowing he's headed for trouble. And he just told the Ephesian elders in Acts 20 that he's fine with it. But when he gets to Tyre (a coastal city in modern Lebanon), the Christians there beg Paul not to go any further. It says they even urge him "through the Spirit," which implies they believe the Holy Spirit does not want Paul in Jerusalem. Then in the port city of Caesarea, a prophet named Agabus dramatically acts out how the Holy Spirit has told him Paul will be bound and handed over to Gentiles. Finally, even Luke begs him not to go.

And it all stands to reason: Everyone knows there's a radical religious element taking over in Jerusalem, brutally silencing any perceived blasphemy. And these believers know Paul will be accused of just that. And they all remember what Jesus told them: "You will be my witnesses in Jerusalem, Judea, Samaria, and the ends of the earth." Paul's going backwards.

But his mind is set. "Then Paul answered, 'Why are you weeping and breaking my heart? I am ready not only to be bound, but also to die in Jerusalem for the name of the Lord Jesus.'" (Acts 21:13)

So exactly one person, Paul, believes the Spirit is leading him to Jerusalem. Every other person mentioned here (the Ephesian leaders, the disciples at Tyre, the church at Caesarea, Paul's closest companions) all strongly believe the Spirit does not want him to go. What are they going to do?

What will *we* do when there's strong disagreement between believers who love each other and love the Lord?

AGREEING TO DISAGREE

This is really a story about agreeing to disagree. Even about something this major. When they see they can't dissuade him, the believers at Tyre kneel on the beach as Paul's about to get on his ship and pray with him. In a rare instance where Luke quotes himself, he says he simply gave up trying to argue with Paul and said, "The Lord's will be done."

The journey of faith is not only about navigating dangers. It's also about navigating relationships, about the stress that can come when on some crucial issue you just don't see eye to eye with your believing friends. You can have serious disagreements with those you love. Even if you all love Jesus very much.

But notice. No one is giving up on each other. On tactics they disagree sharply. But they still love one another, pray for each other. Those who disagree with Paul even accompany him on the journey. Quoting Skinner again, this is about how "a community of people, experiencing fundamental disagreement over how to respond faithfully to the Holy Spirit, stays in communion."[6]

You *will* have disagreements with fellow believers; sharp, deep, emotional, meaningful disagreements, as all these people had with Paul. You can interpret the Spirit's leading on even major issues completely differently. But... you can still live with each other and love each other. You don't have to get into fistfights over what color to paint the ceiling. Don't sacrifice the relationship. We're family.

So the tension is now thick. Many people in this chapter have been saying, like characters in a famous movie, "I have a very bad feeling about this." And then they walk into an environment seething with political and religious hatred.

> PRAYER FOR THE JOURNEY: *Lord, show me how to disagree without being disagreeable. Show me how to preserve relationships even when there is disagreement.*

THE RISE OF THE BOOK

At the birth of Christ most documents were still written on scrolls. But Christians preferred a newer technology — the book.

Romans began using personal notebooks and diaries around the turn of the first century, but books didn't pick up steam as replacements for scrolls until Christians began collecting their sacred writings.

The Christian preference for books was a distinctive feature of the movement. In the extensive library of a villa buried in the Pompeii eruption in 79 AD, all the Greek pagan literature is still written on scrolls. But all of the earliest Christian writings yet found are in book form.

The advantages of books (the scholarly word for an ancient handwritten book is "codex") are obvious. They're smaller, portable, sturdier. Most crucially, books decentralize knowledge because they're more economical than scrolls. They use both sides of a page, so they're less expensive to make.

The early Christians also "tended to write down almost everything," according to Hebrew University professor Doron Mendels.[7] In contrast to the pagan mystery religions that kept much knowledge of their faiths secret except to initiates, members of the Jesus movement wrote down details of every aspect of their beliefs for all to see. In many cases the movement spread through books even before missionaries paid personal visits.

39
MAJOR FIGHT IN THE CITY OF PEACE

ACTS 21:27–23:11

I'm eating in the pleasant restaurant at our Jerusalem hotel, the last place I'd ever expect to encounter any religious conflict, enjoying my hummus, when suddenly I hear a commotion. I look over to see a young, traditionally clothed orthodox rabbi loudly berating an older French woman.

One is yelling in Hebrew, the other in French, but as I see what the rabbi's pointing to, I need no translation. The woman has apparently smuggled in cream for her coffee. The problem? This is a "meat" meal where strict Jewish kosher law forbids dairy products. The restriction against mixing meat with dairy is an ancient application of the Levitical rule against "boiling a lamb in its mother's milk."

Neither of these two are backing down, and soon the entire restaurant is raptly observing their intensifying clash. Both Hebrew and French seem to be languages designed for passionate expression, so this is developing into quite a spectacle.

The coffee creamer debate is still raging as I slip out for a solo stroll down to the Old City. I'm happily half-jogging through an Arab neighborhood when I hear the sound of someone spitting. At me!

A very angry elderly shopkeeper is yelling at me in Arabic. "What in the world have I done to offend her?" I wonder. She points her shaking finger at a hand-written sign taped to the storefront: "No Danish!" At first I think she is just really against pastry. Then I remember the headlines from two days ago. A Danish cartoonist drew a political comic lampooning the prophet Mohammed. Insulting him was bad enough, but *any* display of human likeness is considered taboo in conservative Islam. I suppose that to her I must look European, and since some Europeans are Danish, and some Danish are indeed cartoonists, she spit at me, just to cover her bases.

CITY OF PEACE?

I'm experiencing a tiny bit of the religious and ethnic tension that has gripped this city for the better parts of two millennia. The suspicion and hatred that ran just beneath the surface during the New Testament era is captured well by the Jewish historian Josephus as he describes the run-up to the Roman destruction of Jerusalem in 70 AD:

> Great disputes and differences arose between the Sadducees and Pharisees; but the Sadducees were able to persuade none but the rich… while the Pharisees had the multitude on their side… and when they clashed, they did it by casting reproachful words against one another and throwing stones. And there was nobody to rebuke them; they acted with full license, as if there were no government over the city.[8]

He's describing the descent into chaos that sadly characterized late first-century Judea. A recap about the situation back then: Most Jews hated the Roman occupiers; only the aristocrats of the Sadducee class endured a working alliance with them—in part to protect their own positions of power. In turn, the Pharisees barely tolerated the Sadducees until arguments about the afterlife sprang up (Pharisees believed in a resurrection and life after death, while the Sadducees did not). Any of these tensions, theological or political, could suddenly erupt in name-calling and stone-throwing.

The word "Jerusalem" may mean "City of Peace," but it's often been a city of tension. As Paul is about to rediscover.

FLASHPOINT

Paul's return to Jerusalem goes pretty much the way everyone had been warning him it would go. It's a total disaster. The second day of his stay there, he's seized by an enraged crowd that thinks he's teaching against the Law of Moses.

As the mob attempts to beat him to death, Roman guards swoop in to rescue him. The crazed residents still want his blood. Paul's effort to calm them only infuriates them further. The soldiers decide, since they're not sure what to do, that they should probably torture him. Then the Roman tribune mistakes him for an Egyptian terrorist.

Paul is having a really bad day.

But just before the first Roman lash hits his back, Paul announces he's a Roman citizen — by birth. Now the nervous soldiers quickly untie him. They could get into huge trouble for mistreating a Roman; if he's really a born citizen, he outranks even them. The confused tribune decides to solve the problem by bringing Paul before his accusers. He gathers the leaders of the Pharisees and Sadducees into a big room and holds an investigation.

Paul kicks it off by saying that, from his perspective, he's on trial for his belief in the resurrection. As he surely anticipated, an argument about the afterlife instantly erupts between the Pharisees and Sadducees — and takes the focus off him. The Roman commander is so alarmed at the scene (I imagine loud shouting in Latin and Hebrew, not too different from the argument in French and Hebrew I heard that day in the hotel) he hustles Paul away for his own protection.

Then Jesus appears.

"Have courage!" he says in a vision to Paul that night. "For just as you have testified about me in Jerusalem, so you must also testify about me in Rome." (Acts 23:11, NET)

This statement seems incredible on the surface. Everything's falling apart for Paul. But Jesus says Paul will testify in the heart of the pagan world. This single vision must have inspired Paul many times in the bleak years ahead.

And God says the same thing to you and me: "Have courage." It's a version of the most common command in the Bible: "Do not fear." It's common because fear is underneath most of our troubles in life. We fear what people will say about us. We fear losing our spouse's love. We fear disapproval and rejection and failure. We fear the future. We fear death. We fear getting old.

What are you afraid of?

Jesus' words are reminders about some important truths.

1. YOU'RE NOT ALONE

Jesus is there. Think of how much this meant to Paul. Yes, he is isolated. Yes, he is in custody. But Jesus sees what he's going through and is with him every minute. And in many other verses in Scripture, we're told the same applies to you and me.

Do you suspect God has abandoned you to your circumstances or sickness or trial? The reality is, he is right there with you. *Right now.* Even if your situation is a result of injustice or foolishness.

2. THERE IS ALWAYS A PURPOSE

Jesus tells Paul that through this he will testify in Rome. Somehow this whole boondoggle will lead to that great result. God always has a purpose behind everything. I'm not saying God *causes* all our difficulties. I *am* saying he works through them all; he brings purpose to the worst absurdity.

Put it this way. You'd never read this story and get the impression Paul was doomed to failure, because you see the big picture. You're aware that you are reading a book of the Bible about the successful spread of the gospel. You already know God is somehow going to use this in mighty ways. But have you ever considered how Paul felt right in the thick of the story? Like it was all going from bad to worse.

You may feel like your life is one absurd calamity after another right now. You can't make any sense of it. It's okay to tell God all about those feelings. But know this. One day you'll see the big picture, just as you see it now in Paul's life when you read the New Testament. The only difference? *You are still in the middle of your own story.* There is much more to be written.

And God works even through our unwise moves. It could be argued Paul wasn't thinking straight when he went to Jerusalem. So many people had warned him not to go. But whether Paul was wise or unwise (and Luke doesn't comment either way, though he includes several warnings given to Paul, so I think he wondered about the choice himself), God still empowers Paul as a witness.

Just because you made decisions that may now seem unwise doesn't mean you are permanently disqualified from service to God, or his plan for you is derailed. And just because things don't seem to be working out for you doesn't mean God isn't still using you now! Maybe not, like Paul, in the way *you* dreamed. But he will still use you in ways *beyond* your dreams.

3. CONDUCT YOURSELF NOBLY

Even during an imprisonment which will last for several years, Paul always conducts himself nobly, as you will see. He treats others with respect. He even apologizes to the high priest for not recognizing him, and this after the high priest slaps him in the face. In fact, even when Paul is set free by a storm later in Acts, he refuses to walk away, perhaps thinking of the soldiers who would be killed if he escaped.

Your suffering is not an excuse for rudeness or self-centeredness. Like Paul, you'll find you can influence kings even while you remain in chains—if you stay centered on the gospel. Just keep telling your story. Remember your calling. *Be a witness.* That helps when you're suffering. Because the gospel is the story of the *ultimate* sufferer turning into the *ultimate* victor.

4. EXPECT SURPRISING CHAMPIONS

The most surprising part of this whole story for the largely Jewish members of the early Jesus movement would have been how the Romans are pivoting from being crucifiers of Jesus, and nearly torturers of Paul, to being his rescuers. More unlikely help could not have been imagined. And they're not helping Paul because they think he's a great guy. They just happen to be there, doing their job.

And the same thing will happen in your life too. Champions, supporters, helpers, will not always come from the ranks of your friends. Sometimes people who don't even share your faith will be of help at critical times. *Not everyone who seems like an outsider is an enemy.* Chin up. Eyes open. Keep a lookout for the amazing ways God will bring help from people around you.

Now that he is in Roman custody, Paul may have felt safely removed from the murderous mob. But forty assassins are lying in wait just down the road.

> PRAYER FOR THE JOURNEY: *Lord, help me to hear your voice saying to me, "Have courage!" I need it.*

40
HOW TO BE A HERO

ACTS 23:12-23:35

I'm far from Jerusalem, Judea, and Samaria. Two months after my trip through those Bible lands I visit one of the truly "uttermost ends of the earth."

It's taken several flights on progressively smaller aircraft and a very long journey by car to make it to the most remote corner of Zambia, in southern Africa. I'm here with a South African friend named Johan Combrinck to visit graduates of a Bible school our church supports. But it's a somber occasion. One of the grads, a young pastor named Crispin, was found hacked to death a few months ago, floating in a lake near the village where he led a new church. Occultists in that village had cursed and threatened him. They are suspected in his murder.

Now I'm at the service where a new pastor to that village will be commissioned. As we wait for the ceremony to start, I ask Pastor Rex, "How are you able to find the courage to go to the very village where Crispin was murdered?" I'll never forget his response.

"You cannot entertain fear."

Love that sentence. Fear may come. But don't *entertain* it. Don't coddle it. Don't let it into your house and serve it drinks and snacks. Don't give it a place to stay for the night. Do not *entertain* fear.

These Zambian pastors are on the edge of the frontier, just as Paul and his companions were in Acts. The rural areas they're reaching are as untouched by the gospel now as the far corners of the Roman Empire were then. And they're facing some of the same challenges.

They, and we, can gain a lot of inspiration from Paul's example. He will be thrown into one frightening situation after another in the next five chapters. *But he never entertains fear.* Instead, what does he do? He entertains *Jesus.* He invites him into his mind and shows him hospitality and makes him his constant companion.

THE PLOT THICKENS

First there's the riot and then the arrest and then the near-torture. And then... things *really* get bad for Paul. A band of over 40 assassins vow not to eat or drink until they have murdered him. I imagine they've heard of his daring escapes in Damascus and Ephesus and Thessalonica and they figure, this character's slippery. We need to get serious. We will fast until he's dead.

Well, those 40 guys must have starved to death, because things don't go the way they plan. Paul's nephew overhears them and reports their plot to the Roman commander. Under cover of night, 470 troops relocate Paul to Caesarea, the headquarters of Roman authority along the coast.

Some commentators cast doubt on the authenticity of this passage, claiming 470 soldiers must be an exaggeration. But here's what I think happened. Roman troops were organized into *legions*, which were themselves divided into *cohorts*. A cohort consisted of approximately 480 men, sometimes a little more, sometimes a little less. The Roman troops in Jerusalem regularly made the trek back to their headquarters in Caesarea after the Jewish feasts were over. So Paul's transfer was hidden in what appeared to be a standard cohort relocation.

GOD WORKS IN DIFFERENT WAYS

Paul could have been disappointed with the way things were working out for him. After all, previously in Acts, God miraculously freed Peter, John, Paul, and Silas on their very first night of various imprisonments. Chains fell off. Angels opened doors. Earthquakes shook shackles loose.

Not this time. Paul must have been wondering if he was instead about to share the fate of James and Stephen, who, you'll remember, were executed in Jerusalem earlier.

In fact, Paul does remain in chains for the remainder of the book. No miraculous release. For the rest of Acts, this great man will be shuttled around by bureaucrats and weather systems.

WHEN YOU DON'T GET THE MIRACLE

It's tough to watch others dramatically delivered from circumstances similar to yours—unemployment, cancer, loneliness, depression—while those same doors stay locked for you. And because those other folks have genuinely experienced amazing things, they'll try to encourage you with their stories, implying, "Just keep praying, it will happen for you too."

But sometimes God delivers his saints from their prisons. And sometimes he doesn't.

Don't consider someone else's experience with deliverance to be normative for you or anyone else. God answers prayer the way he knows is ultimately best. Miraculous agency or mundane bureaucracy, God works through both equally well in the Book of Acts.

And in your life too. God used Paul's extended stay in what must have seemed like red tape purgatory in great ways, eventually bringing him to Rome, all expenses paid by Caesar himself. Miracle or no miracle, God knows what he's doing.

Listen again to what Jesus says to Paul in that vision.

Take courage. Courage is a choice. It is possible to *take* it, to decide to focus your mind on faith and not fear.

As you have testified about me in Jerusalem... Jesus knows what Paul has done in the past there in Jerusalem. Even though it did not go well. At all. But he sees. He knows. He rewards. Same goes for you and me. You may feel that no one at all sees the sacrifices you make. Or like your best efforts have produced no results. But Jesus sees. He knows. And he will reward.

...so you must also testify in Rome. Even though Paul's life felt like it was on hold, and would be for another two years as he lingered in a Roman jail, God still had a purpose for him. You may feel like your best years are behind you, that you're stuck in a holding pattern. *But Jesus still has a purpose for you.* There is future ministry. Keep your eyes open and your spirit ready for it.

He is right there. Perhaps the most encouraging thing about the vision was the fact that Jesus' presence was right there with him. *And he is right there with you.* Just because the times are bad does not mean he's abandoned you.

PASSING THE BUCK

The Roman commander, Claudius Lysias, writes a letter exaggerating his own heroism and conveniently passes the buck to Felix, the Roman governor of the province.

They may both be recalling how the now-infamous Pontius Pilate lost his job. Pilate was ordered back to Rome after violently suppressing an uprising in Samaria about twenty years earlier. So these Romans tiptoe around Paul, not wanting to give him to the Sanhedrin lest they violently attack him, requiring an escalating Roman response. The Romans are trying to keep their jobs!

THE BALANCING ACT

And the universal human tendency to protect our own interests creates the longest-lasting hindrance yet to Paul's freedom. He has escaped mobs, assassins, and conspiracies. But here comes one of life's most formidable frustrations: plain vanilla government bureaucracy.

Sometimes I feel like I steadfastly endure the really tough times — grief, disease and other trials — only to be irritated beyond measure by the IRS or DMV or traffic jams or long lines. Do you relate? Then you'll resonate with Paul's next adventure.

> PRAYER FOR THE JOURNEY: *Father God, help me believe that, whether I receive a miraculous answer to prayer or not, you are still at work in my circumstances. And you are right here with me, telling me to take courage, because I still have a purpose.*

41
THE BARRIER OF BUREAUCRACY

ACTS 24:1-27

We are back in Caesarea, where Peter had that history-making encounter with the commander of the Italian Regiment, Cornelius. I'm glad to return; I always love visiting this seaside city, especially with visitors to Israel who've never been here before.

Imagine the scene. Your bus rolls into the nondescript parking lot with no hint of the beauty you're about to see. You walk through the admission turnstile and start to notice some ruins. There's a little Roman theater in front of you, so you walk in, under one of the arches. As you emerge from the stone tunnel you experience something like walking into an American baseball park and suddenly seeing the expanse of green grass. The gorgeous restored theater unveils itself all around you. Just beyond is the azure Mediterranean. Waves break on the promontory where a Roman palace crumbles. It's breathtaking, and a great introduction to this chapter of Acts.

If you were on a visit with me, we'd sit down right here in the theater. As you look out toward the ocean, with a Roman racetrack and ancient harbor off to your right, I'd describe the trial that took place, perhaps in this very theater or in the palace that once stood on the ocean cliffs.

THE TRIAL IN MINI-ROME
In Paul's day this was a spectacular settlement of over 125,000 residents — sort of a miniature Rome right on the coast of Judea,

showing off everything Romans could do with excellence. There were palaces and temples and theaters.

And a prison. Where Paul finds himself for more than three chapters of the Book of Acts.

The Imperial governors of Judea had one mission — to keep the peace in this volatile area. That meant the Romans didn't want people (like Paul) causing riots. On the other hand, previous governors (like Pilate) had gotten into trouble back home for suppressing rebellion too violently. In the mid-first century the Roman representatives here were under pressure from Caesar to keep the peace... *peacefully.* So for two years the governor Felix, hoping things calm down (and hoping for a bribe from someone) just keeps Paul in jail. Paul ends up living here, in this city, in prison, longer than he lives almost anywhere else.

You might feel like Luke's detailed description of Paul's long detention slows down the narrative. But I think it's meant to feel like that. Paul's relentless forward motion has now slowed to a standstill.

In fact, he's still in prison two years later, in 59 AD, when Felix' term as governor ends.

The next Roman governor, Festus, gets right to business when he hears about Paul. He's clearing his desk of the mess Felix left him. Festus wants to do the locals a favor so he says, "Paul, how'd you like to get some action on your case and start this trial? You can go to Jerusalem and resolve things there."

And Paul basically says. "No way. I cannot get a fair trial there. I'm a citizen of Rome, you are Rome's representative — so I appeal to Caesar." This was a legal right of any Roman citizen if they felt unjustly accused, sort of like appealing to the Supreme Court.

And Festus says, "Fine, to Caesar you shall go." He's likely thinking, at least I'll have you out of my hair.

But before he's shipped off, Paul has a chance to meet and share his faith with a relative of the man who helped kill Jesus. Note: On ice for two years, Paul has kept his mind sharp and his eyes open for opportunities to share his faith.

READY TO LOVE

Before we move on to his seafaring adventures, it's worth learning a couple lessons from this landlocked, dry-docked period for Paul. Because, let's face it. For most of us, life is not one adventure after another on the open ocean or facing riotous mobs. It's a grind. A slog. A red tape tangle. An irritating slow-motion sword fight with the dark legions of cubicle-dwelling functionaries, a dumb dance with the department of delays over at the government, the bank, the utilities, the cable company.

And this part of Paul's life makes him the patron saint of people who perceive they're on permanent pause.

The most amazing thing to me in this episode is how Paul stays sharp and polite. His amazingly respectful attitude toward these frustrating bureaucrats reminds me of Dale Carnegie's famous story of standing in line at the post office when an employee legendary for slowness and surliness was at the counter.

Everyone else scowls as they walk up to him, so angry about the delays he's forcing them to endure. But Dale looks for something affirming to say. Which is quite a challenge. But when he gets to the counter, he says, "You know, I just have to say, you have a really nice head of hair!"

The clerk blinks twice and responds, "Well, people used to tell me that when I was a child. Now... how can I help you?"[9] And he treats Dale like royalty.

Red tape producers may be frustrating your plans, but you can still remain calm and positive. And ready to love.

Life may have slowed you down. But stay alert for the chances to shine, even while in the chains of delay.

THE BARRIER OF BUREAUCRACY

PRAYER FOR THE JOURNEY: Lord, sometimes the drudgery of everyday life can dull my spiritual senses. Help me, like Paul, stay alert to opportunities that may surprise me.

42
THE BARRIER OF
BUREAUCRACY: PART 2

ACTS 25:1–26:32

I'm stuck. With one eye nervously on the time and one on the seemingly endless line of vehicles in front of me, I sit in one of the notorious traffic jams at the Allenby Bridge border crossing into Israel. We've spent several days enjoying a visit to Jordan, and are headed back to Tel Aviv to catch a plane home.

But the border guards here do not care about our schedule in the least. They have their own orders, and today they apparently include searching every single bus, taxi, motorcycle and car crossing into Israel, from top to bottom and front to back. All passengers need to disembark and go into the border control office where every passport is minutely scrutinized.

I'm calculating travel time, trying to figure out if we can still make our flight. It's tense. Frustrating. But at least I can take comfort that I'm keeping an ancient travel tradition alive.

THE CAESARS OF THE CUSTOMS OFFICE
Romans universally loathed the customs officers they too encountered during their travels. The system then sounds surprisingly similar to ours. Border agents demanded a written *professio*, a declaration of luggage contents. There was a list of duty-free items (including any personal belongings you brought with you from home). But anything purchased abroad was taxable. Luxury items fetched a fat 25 percent tariff. Ancient writer Plutarch complained,

THE BARRIER OF BUREAUCRACY: PART 2

"We object to customs officials when they feel they must finger everything in our bags... but they're really only doing their job."[10]

However accustomed to border bureaucrats people in the Roman world might have been, certainly Paul's situation was an extreme example. When we pick up the story, this active, entrepreneurial genius has been languishing in what amounts to the lost luggage office in Caesarea for two years.

HEARING BEFORE HEROD

Then Herod the Great's great grandson, King Agrippa the Second, comes to welcome the new Roman governor Festus to town.

Festus sees this visit as very fortuitous — because he can say now, "Well, you are the great-grandson of Herod the Great, the man who *built* the temple. This man Paul is accused of *defiling* the temple. What do *you* think of Paul?" Perfect opportunity to have someone else decide on Paul's case without involving the Roman government. He's trying to make Paul someone else's problem.

Unlike his great-grandfather and grandfather before him, Herod Agrippa had a pretty good reputation as a fairly reasonable guy. He was popular with both Romans and Jews. And he wisely says, "Let's hear what Paul has to say about himself."

And Paul is ready. The long time in life's waiting room has not dulled his intellect or readiness to share the good news. He assures this Jewish king his intent is not to overturn Judaism, that he is saying nothing beyond what Moses and the prophets already said. Then he gives his entire personal testimony. All about the road to Damascus and how Jesus, who was raised from the dead, changed his life. He then says this risen Messiah has a message not only for Jews but also for Gentiles.

And at that point, the Roman governor Festus roars, "Paul, you are out of your mind. Your great learning is driving you insane."

In a brilliantly witty rejoinder, Paul answers, "I assure you, Your Excellency, I am quite sane. This all really happened. I'm sure that King Agrippa has heard about these things. And I am sure he believes the prophets. Don't you, King? I know you do."

Aren't you amazed at Paul's witty, gracious way with these bureaucrats? Paul's modeling what he tells us all to do in Romans 12:18–21:

> If it is possible, as far as it depends on you, live at peace
> with everyone. Do not take revenge, my dear friends…
> Do not be overcome by evil, but overcome evil with good.

That wasn't just theory for Paul.

USE YOUR INDOOR VOICE

We used to tell our kids when they shouted at full volume in restaurants or in church, "Use your indoor voice!" I need to remind myself to do the same thing when frustrated by red tape, or even people deliberately being rude. What I *want* to do is shout at full volume about all my annoyances. What I *need* to do is calmly and quietly show respect and logic. An outdoor voice feels *great*. For a minute. Then it causes even more tension. My indoor voice may feel unnatural. But it's the only thing that works in the long run.

That's what Paul does. He uses terms like "Your Excellency" to refer to the very people who'd been treating him like a file folder in some forgotten drawer. And he is very tactful with Agrippa. After all, he could have said, "I know you know about Jesus, Agrippa, *because your relative helped sentence him to death!*" Instead he discretely says, "I am sure none of this escaped your notice."

Now every head swivels toward King Agrippa. And he realizes he is kind of trapped. If he says, "Yeah, I do know about these things, and I do believe the prophets," then Paul will say, "Then why not believe in Jesus?" But if he says, "I don't believe the prophets," then he'll lose the good will of the people.

So Agrippa gives a great political answer. "Paul, do you really think in such a short time you can convince me to be a Christian?" Like: *Look at the time. Sure wish we could chat longer. Gotta go.* Instead of engaging with Paul's arguments, he mildly pokes fun at him.

Probably got a laugh from the courtroom crowd. That's a tactic still used today by people who want to dodge serious discussion of the gospel.

I can see the smile on Paul's face when he says, "Well, yes, I *do* wish you could be exactly like me — except for these chains." And as they leave, Agrippa and Festus agree: Paul has actually done nothing against the law. If he hadn't appealed to Caesar, he could have been set free.

Again, Luke seems to be making a point of this. *Every reasonable authority figure in Acts believes Paul has broken no law.* It's a pattern, repeated again and again. I think it must be related to his purpose for this book. Are you starting to guess what that is?

And then Paul begins an amazing adventure across the sea.

GOD IS WORKING EVEN AT THE DMV
I love this story because it shows God working even through most aggravating, annoying, unjust, outrageous, grindingly slow government bureaucracy.

This case has everything in it that would make me tear my hair out and scream, "God, where are you? This is such a waste of time." There are lying lawyers and scheming conspirators and unjust imprisonment. Yet from our perspective as the readers, we can see God ultimately working through it all. Because of those very things, Paul gets an all-expense-paid trip to Rome courtesy of the Roman government. Once there he will influence people at the very pinnacle of power, even while in captivity. As a direct result of numbingly literal, by-the-book bureaucratic thinking ("He said he appealed to Caesar, so to Caesar he must go!"), Paul will help fulfill the quest given by Jesus. He will reach the "ends of the earth," the nerve center of the far-flung Empire.

Can you ask God to help you respond like Paul to the annoying slow-motion bureaucrats in your life? He didn't lose his cool. He kept his wits about him. Stayed focused on Christ. And God did amazing things that are still having impact today.

But as Paul sets to sea with his escort of soldiers, there was no way he could have known he was sailing right into one of the greatest ocean adventures of all time.

> PRAYER FOR THE JOURNEY: *Lord, I need your help. I want always to be ready to love even the bureaucrats in my life, or any who would try to intimidate or hassle me. I want to be respectful to them, like Paul. Work through me even in the mundane and repetitious details of life.*

SPEED UNDER SAIL

How fast was travel by sea for first-century Romans? A lot slower than our planes. A lot faster than their feet. Pliny the Elder described how long various sea voyages took if they were "fast runs," that is, if the wind was behind the ships and conditions were perfect:

Ostia (the harbor closest to Rome) to Africa: 2 days

Ostia to Spain: 2 days

Puteoli (near Naples) to Egypt: 9 days[11]

Of course under unfavorable conditions the nine-day trip to Egypt could stretch out to a month or longer. But those numbers were very tempting for travelers willing to gamble on the weather, since foot travel was much slower, and consequently more expensive when lodging and food were considered.

Historian William Ramsay tells of an imperial messenger squadron in the second century that took the land route from Rome to Egypt in *63 days*. And that's at an amazing pace of about 50 miles a day. Walking speed for a normal, fit person was about 18 miles per day (which is still pretty stunning for modern people to take in), or nearly six months for that trip from Rome to Egypt. No wonder Romans braved the open ocean and paid premium prices to ship owners. Like us, they valued speed.

ACTS ODYSSEY

PART SEVEN

SERPENTS & SHIPWRECKS

43
AGAINST THE WIND

The aging yet comfortable ship skims through the turquoise waters of the Aegean. We stop at some of the same islands Paul visited on his journeys.

I'm on board because I want to continue retracing the geography of Acts. But the experience I'm having could not be more different than what Paul and his companions went through on the open ocean, and I can't say I'm sad about that. I wonder what he'd think of our ship, with its restaurants, bars, casino, massage clinics, pools, and hummus.

"Hi, Paul. Can I interest you in a towel folding demonstration? How about a live concert, or a game of pick up basketball? Or a fruit carving class? We can design this watermelon to spell out the fruit of the Spirit."

Amazing amenities, but you know what I'm sure he'd envy most? Our propulsion. Giant diesel engines enable us to turn any way our captain wants, regardless of how the wind's blowing. That's the biggest luxury of modern sailing, though it's something most of us take for granted.

In Paul's era, triangular sails, which allow ships to tack against the wind, were not yet in wide use. Roman ships had square sails, which severely limited their ability to go anywhere but the direction the breeze was blowing. That's why they also often had dozens (sometimes hundreds) of oars for soldiers and slaves to help push against the wind.

AGAINST THE WIND

At first Paul's ship faces the wind, and makes very slow progress. Sometimes life is like that.

Have you ever been certain you were doing God's will only to feel you're constantly trying to sail into the wind? Like forward progress takes too much energy, and circumstances are constantly taking you in the wrong direction? Then you'll relate to Paul in this story. And you'll learn from this veteran of so many slowdowns and surprises how to stay flexible but focused when frustrated.

REALIZE TROUBLE IS NORMAL

When you're feeling impatient with your progress, it's natural to try to pinpoint the culprit: "Why is this happening to me? Is it something I did? Is God punishing me?"

But Paul's right in the center of God's will. Jesus even told him personally in a vision that he'd be going to Rome to testify. *But as we've seen throughout Acts, being in God's will doesn't mean everything goes smoothly.* You can be doing God's will, in God's way, in God's timing, and still have struggles. That's life. *Just because the wind is against you doesn't mean God is against you.* Paul knows this from vast personal experience. That's why he stays confident. He's seen God work through the worst difficulties again and again.

There was a bumper sticker a while back: "Life is hard. Then you die." A more biblical slogan would be, "Life is hard. And God works through it."

DECIDE WHO TO LISTEN TO

But here's an important decision to make in advance, before you hit that slowdown at sea. When times are tough, every decision becomes harder. You'll hear so many voices trying to give you advice. Who do you listen to? Tough question, because decisions made during hard times are often very important choices.

By the time he takes this trip Paul has already been in three shipwrecks, according to his letter to the Corinthians (2 Cor. 11:25).

He is experienced! So he's calm and knowledgeable as he tells the centurion that trying to sail in these conditions would be disastrous. It wasn't just some supernatural premonition. Luke says "sailing had already become dangerous because by now it was after the Day of Atonement" (Acts 27:9). In those days sailing between October and May was considered too dangerous because of winter storms, and they were already well within that window. This probably happened in the year 59 AD, when the Day of Atonement (more widely known as Yom Kippur) fell on October 5.

But the Roman soldier listens to the pilot and the owner of the ship instead of Paul, and sets sail anyway. Most of the people on ship are all for this. Luke says "the majority decided we should sail on," because the town of Fair Havens was "unsuitable" to winter in, and they would rather stay in Phoenix for the long cold months. They were probably motivated by their desire for pleasure and profit (a bigger port meant better diversions and more business opportunities to pick up extra passengers and cargo).

Sometimes the majority opinion is wrong! In 1950, a majority of Americans still thought smoking was healthy. Year after year, a majority of East Bay residents think the Raiders will win the Super Bowl.

You need to decide which voices you'll pay attention to when stressed. The voices of the majority—the cultural opinion makers—or the voices of wisdom. If you can't find clear direction in God's word, look for knowledgeable, godly people. Listen to them. Even if they disagree with your personal preferences.

WATCH OUT FOR YOUR OWN BIAS

Here's the problem. We humans are experts at finding opinions that justify our bad decisions. Researchers even have a name for it: "confirmation bias." That's why the ship captain found an excuse to sail even when common wisdom and the advice of Paul was against him.

AGAINST THE WIND

There will be times you want to do something unwise *so badly* that you will search and search until you find some article on the internet, or some loopy celebrity, or some podcast that confirms the decision you already want to make. Watch out for that tendency. Ask for wisdom to go with the truth, wherever it seems to point.

But what do you do when, despite the fact that you're doing God's will, despite doing your best to listen to wise counsel, through no fault of your own, you find yourself in a wild storm of life?

You'll find out next. Because when the storm of the century hits, Paul is at sea, chained to the ship.

> PRAYER FOR THE JOURNEY: *Lord, help me realize that just because the wind is against me, doesn't mean you are against me. And in times of trouble help me stay tuned to sources of wisdom, and not foolish counsel.*

ROMAN SHIP CULTURE

There's a lot of sailing in the Book of Acts. But it was much different than the cruising enjoyed on the Aegean today.

There were no pure passenger ships in the first century. Instead, freighters would take on paying travelers. In the typical first-century Aegean port about a dozen merchant ships came through each week. Departure lists were posted at the harbor, and travelers would negotiate rates directly with each shipmaster (the *magister navus* who was responsible for the commercial aspects of the voyage, often the owner of the ship).

There were of course no reliable weather forecasts in those pre-satellite days. So ship's captains (the *gubernatores*) were very sensitive to premonitions. They would delay departure if a passenger sneezed on the gangplank, or if a crew member reported a dream featuring a black goat, bull, or owl, all of which were considered omens of rough seas.[1]

Once on board passengers would be supplied with fresh water but were responsible for their own food and bedding. Often they'd bring tents with them, which they could pitch on deck each night to create temporary sleeping quarters. I imagine Paul, as a professional tentmaker, probably had some nice deck tents on his trips.

44
SURVIVING STORMS

ACTS 27:15-44

I've only been really seasick once, on a whale watching cruise in the Monterey Bay. It was a modern vessel, with powerful engines and weather radar. But the sea is still unpredictable. As we hit heavy, rolling swells, I didn't just feel sick. I felt like I wanted to die. Why, oh why, did I eat that extra helping of hummus and pita bread?

Experts say the real problem with seasickness is disorientation. With the horizon rocking, your inner ear desperately tries to get its bearings. But nothing works. There's no stability, no way to get oriented.

If you've ever been seasick, you can understand just a little of what the 276 passengers on this ship in Acts 27 must have been feeling. Their ship hits extremely bad weather and is driven uncontrollably by the winds. They're miserable to the marrow of their bones. They've completely given up hope.

Maybe you're in storms of life that have you feeling just as disoriented. Cancer. Divorce. Grief. Unemployment. Loneliness. Relationship trouble. Tensions at work. You're desperately trying to get your bearings. It feels like the storm will never end.

When you're in a crazy storm, ask yourself these three questions:

1. WHAT CAN I DO?
In most storms of life, no matter how intense, there are a few practical measures still in your control.

In the Acts story, these sailors realize that their lifeboat is not secure, so they hoist it aboard.

Then they protect the ship by wrapping thick ropes around the hull, sort of how you'd tie a roast. Ancient ships carried ropes for this purpose. Remember, this ship is only made of wooden planks.

Then they're being driven so fast by the wind that they're afraid of piling into "the sandbars of Syrtis" (which sounds like a line from a pirate movie, but these are real obstacles, a ship's graveyard of sandbars that extend 100 miles north of the coast of Libya). So they lower the sea anchor to try to scrub off some speed.

Do you see what's happening? In rapid succession, these men snap into action and do whatever they can.

When the storms hit, it's normal to first wonder, "Why? Why is this happening?" *But we rarely get an answer to that question.* A more productive question is, "What's *next*? What can I do right now?" Do the next, best thing.

2. WHAT CAN I DO WITHOUT?

Then the ship begins to take on water after a "violent battering from the storm." So the sailors throw all the cargo and tackle overboard.

You can only do so much without making sacrifices. Sometimes we have to *give up* in order to *go on.*

Use less salt. Give up red meat. Stop smoking. Go on a diet, set up a budget, sell a car, move to another location. *Often surviving a storm involves subtraction, not addition.* Moving ahead is as much about what we can *do without* as it is about what we can *do.*

3. WHERE CAN I PUT MY HOPE?

Luke says "...we finally gave up all hope of being saved." (Acts 27:20) Note he doesn't say *they* gave up hope. He says *we.* Even Luke admits he has no more hope than the Roman sailors. Everyone feels spent. Hopeless. Lost.

Why? Their bearings are gone. Luke says they had not seen the sun or stars for days. The ancient mariners navigated by the sun and stars. So these sailors quite literally had no clue where they were. Those sandbars of Syrtis could have been a hundred miles away — or a hundred yards.

When you lose your bearings, all sense of timing and direction, it's easy to feel hopeless. Many friends of mine who have fought cancer tell me the most hopeless they felt was in the days just *before* their diagnosis — because they had no idea what was wrong with them. Once they were diagnosed, and knew the odds, they felt oriented again. It was still a wearying journey. But they had direction.

So Paul gives them their new bearings. New data points for their internal GPS. Orientation for their souls. In the middle of the storm, Paul receives a message of hope from an angel for all the passengers and crew. Everyone will survive. *They* may not know the way. But the *Father* does.

Ultimately, that's the same encouragement you and I have from the Lord. The Father knows the way. You'll make it.

YOU'RE GOING TO MAKE IT

I hope you heard me. Especially if the seas are rough right now. *You're going to make it.* God will see you through. I mean, *all the way* through. You will be raised again.

Even if worse comes to worst, you'll be with the Lord, and ultimately resurrected. The promise of the resurrection is the ultimate reorientation. It puts all our struggles here on earth into perspective. You may even lose your life. But you will see the Lord, and your loved ones in the Lord, and you'll know joy and peace beyond anything you've ever even imagined.

You're going to make it. Really.

But all the other stuff? That sinks. Paul says all the cargo (most of which was already overboard anyway) and the ship will be lost.

You know what? Same with you and me, actually. The trophies, the awards, the cargo we drag along for the journey never makes it. It serves its purpose, then it's gone. And that's okay. One of the hardest lessons I've had to learn is not to waste my grief on inanimate objects. Enjoy it for what it is, for as long as you have it. But eventually it all sinks. That's just reality.

PREPARE FOR THE STORM

Every winter, meteorologists warn their viewers to "be prepared for winter storms." Clean the gutters, have flashlights and extra food and water, keep a generator handy if possible. Same thing applies to the storms of life. *Your preparation before tragedy strikes is essential.* Paul was not only experienced with shipwrecks, he was experienced at looking to God when things went haywire. He knew the Bible well. He prayed regularly. Because of this prep, he was able to stay confident when the storm struck.

This is one of the most important reasons for your own times of daily prayer and Bible reading. It's not just for *that* day. It's laying a firm foundation for the day the storm hits.

Ultimately, you don't have faith in God *so that* things will go well in your life. You have faith in God *because* things will *not* go well. You will have storms. You will experience grief and illness, or get fired, or lose valuable stuff. Not because you're bad. But because that's life. No one has sunny weather all the time. Storms strike. So set a foundation of faith for the rough times to come.

RIDING THE SURF

Back to our story. The ship's run aground and pummeled into pieces by the surf, and the single-minded guards plan to kill the prisoners to prevent their escape (this was normal Roman procedure, since the penalty for losing prisoners was death). Luke and Paul had to be thinking, *We made it through two weeks of this storm and now the soldiers are going to kill us anyway? Really?!*

Things do not look good for Paul. Again! But he has won the respect of Julius the centurion, and to save Paul's life, Julius orders the soldiers to stand down. (Note: Another example of a Roman authority making a reasonable decision to spare Paul's life.) Those who can swim are ordered to strike out for the island, and the others cling to planks and wash ashore through the surf. Every single person survives.

When things seem to be going wrong, sometimes all you can do is surf the surge. You can't control the weather (or most things in life). In the words of that great religious thinker Dory the fish, "Just keep swimming." That's what Paul and his companions do here.

When Paul washes onto the beach, he surely thinks the worst of his troubles are behind him. And that's when he notices the viper on his hand.

> PRAYER FOR THE JOURNEY: *Father, help me prepare for the storms by laying a foundation of biblical thinking and godly habits. Then when I am in the storm, help me ask, "What's next?" instead of obsessing on "Why?" And when I'm seasick and disoriented, help me regain my bearings by focusing on your promises. Amen.*

ANCIENT STORMS

Sailing directly between Greece to Asia Minor was faster than walking all the way around the Aegean coastline, but it was dangerous and shipwrecks were common.

The poet Ovid described a storm that gripped his ship in 8 AD. If you have a tendency toward seasickness, just envisioning this might put you over the edge:

> Look how the billows huge as mountains move;
> Each one, you think, will touch the stars above.
>
> Look how the valleys deep beneath them sink.
> Each one might reach to Hell's profoundest brink.[2]

An ancient Greek aristocrat named Synesius recounted the scene on his ship when a sudden gale hit. His description helps fill out the picture from Acts:

> The men groaned, the women shrieked, everybody called upon their God, cried aloud, remembered their dear ones… Then someone called out that anyone who had any gold should hang it around their neck. This is a time-honored practice: The body of a drowned person must have money on it, so that anyone who finds it won't mind providing a decent funeral. When we touched land we embraced the soil like a long-lost mother![3]

45
SNAKE ATTACK

ACTS 28:1-10

I'm enjoying an afternoon run when suddenly, across my path, I see a slithering snake. I could win a long jump competition with the leap I manage over that serpent. Then it happens again — another snake sunbathing on the same path. So I jump over this one too. Now I'm so shaken that, just as a precaution, I'm bounding down the path like a gazelle. I'm sure I'm amusing any observing picnickers.

Then toward the end of the same run I spot a massive snake resting length-wise right down the middle of the sidewalk. What is it with the snakes today? I wait and wait for it to leave. Finally I timidly approach... to find I've been delayed ten minutes by a rope.

The thing with snakes is, once you've seen a couple, you start seeing them everywhere. Even where they're not.

That's how it is with tough times too. You get clobbered once. Twice. Pretty soon you're shy about risking any new venture.

Think of all that Paul's been through on his journeys. One riot after another. Slander. Jail. Earthquake. Jail. Murder attempt. Jail. Shipwreck. Snake. *And he's just trying to do the right thing.* I'd be looking up and asking, "Why, Lord?" Paul just looks around and goes, "What's next?" He's up for it.

A GOD MAN?

After surviving the shipwreck Paul is helping gather fuel for the fire when a poisonous viper whips out of his pile of brushwood and fastens itself on his hand.

Paul's composure amazes me. As I write this, I'm still shaking. Because I had yet another encounter with snakes.

This afternoon I was all alone in the ruins of Laodicea, another biblical city in Asia Minor. Our group had taken the last tour of the day, and I slipped back inside the city gates for a few final photographs. And nearly stepped right into a nest of serpents.

As I chased a lizard under a rock, several snakes suddenly slithered and hissed, writhing like Medusa's hair—and my own hair must have stood straight on end! I backed away quickly. But then, realizing what a great story this would make for the book, I tiptoed back and snapped a picture of the snake nest. Then I hightailed it out of the ruins and ran right to the Turkish security guards. I think my voice was two octaves higher than normal as I explained through trembling hand motions and iPhone photographs just what I saw.

The nest of snakes I almost stepped in while in the ruins of Laodicea.

SNAKE ATTACK

Paul is a much cooler customer than I was. He calmly shakes off the snake. The watching villagers first assume Paul is some guilty criminal because the Fates have clearly not allowed him to live. But after he doesn't swell up, keel over, and die, they change their minds and assume he's a god!

The Greeks of the first century kept their eyes out for people they referred to as *theios aner*, literally "god-men" or divine men, individuals who looked normal but were demigods, humans with godlike powers. They believed such demigods walked among us from time to time.

Greek stories are filled with examples. The famous mathematician and philosopher Pythagoras, who lived centuries before Paul, was considered to have been a *theios aner* specifically because he overcame a poisonous snake. In some versions of the story Pythagoras bites the snake to death. In others he drives the snake and all its kind out of a village. I suspect this well-known story was in the minds of the people proclaiming Paul to be divine.

I don't know about you, but if I'd been Paul, after all the deprivations I'd been through the previous two years, I'd have been tempted to say, "Yes. Yes, I am a god. Now serve me some food and peel me some grapes. And these Roman soldiers guarding me? Lock 'em up and throw away the key."

STAY FOCUSED

But Paul always stays focused on his objective. He won't allow these people to put him on this pedestal, because it would distract from the message.

No matter what happens to you, good or bad, can you pray that God will help you react the same way? Stay focused on the gospel. That is your one objective. So many distractions will try to dig into your mind like the snake in this story. You've felt their fangs fastening, even today. Worries about news headlines. Outrage about the latest political controversy. Some family drama. It can all become like so many slithering, distracting serpents. Shake it off. Stay focused.

And at times people may even try to glorify you like the people here tried to worship Paul. You'll feel your ego puffing up. That's more fatal than swelling from a snake bite. So shake that off too. You don't have to offend the people who are impressed by what God is doing through you. Serve them.

Oh, and in this story there's another clue about the reason Luke wrote this book. Did you see it? Stay tuned for more.

> PRAYER FOR THE JOURNEY: *Lord, no matter what nest of snakes I step into, help me shake them off and stay on message.*

SNAKE DETECTIVE

What kind of snake bit the Apostle Paul? It's a simple question that may clear up another mystery in the text: Where was this island? The actual Greek name of the island is "Melita," but most translations modernize it to read Malta.

The large island we associate with the name Malta today, south of Sicily and just 176 miles from the Tunisian peninsula of North Africa, would have been spectacularly off course, although it is possible Paul's ship was blown this far.

But there is another option.

There are no poisonous snakes on modern Malta, nor is there fossil evidence of any in the island's past. The traditional explanation given by Malta residents is that Paul miraculously drained the venom from all the island's snakes when he was bitten, although nowhere in the Bible is this even implied.

However, the most dangerous true viper species in all of Europe does still live on an island in the Adriatic, the island known to Romans as Melita. Today it's known as Meleda or Mljet, the southernmost island off the coast of modern Croatia, across the Adriatic from Italy. Until recently this island was so heavily infested with the horned viper *Vipera ammodytes* that a predatory mongoose was introduced in 1910 to control these snakes.

According to local biology expert Stephan Mifsud, the symptoms of a bite by this viper match exactly what the islanders in Acts expected to see from Paul: immediate swelling, fainting, followed by circulatory shock, then pulmonary congestion and internal bleeding, all of which would lead to death if not treated properly.[4]

This also helps explain a puzzle in the text. Acts 27:27 says the ship was in the Adriatic Sea. But the modern island of Malta is not. Interpreters have tried to come up with other explanations, but it may be that the island in Acts named "Melita" was not modern Malta but the snake-infested Melita, which is indeed in the Adriatic. Remains of a substantial palace from the Roman era have been discovered there, indicating the presence of a wealthy official, as we see in this story.

Not all experts agree, but this solution may also explain why the shipwreck survivors have to be told the name of the island. The place we refer to as Malta is a large island that was very well known, with a long-established Roman presence. Melita, on the other hand, is a tiny island of about 100 square miles, with a sparse population, both then and now.

The horned viper that infested the island of Melita. (Photo credit: Elena Terkel, 2008)

46
ROME AT LAST

I spent some time in Naples, Italy, one summer with my stepfather Jet, who retired after 20 years in the Navy to run a ministry to sailors there. His full name was Jet Turner (One of my friends saw his Navy name tag and thought that was his job — a jet turner!). By the time he came into our lives, Jet was a stateside pastor. Visiting Naples with him and reliving his days as a sailor and then as a minister to sailors gave me a sense of what maritime life in this ancient harbor must have been like.

Paul and the soldiers guarding him disembark in Puteoli, a harbor on the beautiful Bay of Naples, a sweeping semi-circular section of coastline that reminds me of Monterey Bay. After all they'd been through, this bunch was probably eager to get out of the boat and continue the journey on land.

Jet told me how, after long and arduous deployments at sea, Navy sailors would pour into Naples looking for fun and fellowship. Often they'd find it in salacious diversions just as available today as they would have been to sailors in Paul's time (the ruins of nearby Pompeii infamously preserve a large house of prostitution, complete with lurid painted advertisements on its walls).

But not all sailors wanted to go there. Some sought more uplifting (and less dangerous) amusement. Recognizing that need from his own days aboard ship, my stepdad rented second-story space at the large Naples shopping mall near the docks and started a service-man's center complete with food, games, music, sports tournaments,

275

and more. Contrary to the stereotype of sailors in port behaving badly, it was often packed.

And that tradition of Christians in Naples showing hospitality to visiting sailors begins right here in Acts. Whether or not they were looking for uplifting company, the sailors with Paul get it. You share a sense of amazement with Luke as he describes how they stumble across a group of Christians here. The Roman centurion Julius agrees to a week-long stay with these local believers, which must have been a welcome respite for this exhausted band. They're all ready for some down time.

GATEWAY TO THE ENDS OF THE EARTH

Then as they approach Rome, Paul and his companions get another pleasant surprise. Some Roman Christians come out to greet them.

The first place that some Christians from Rome meet Paul, *Forum Appii* in Latin, was a post office and tavern on the Appian Way about 43 miles southeast of Rome. The Roman writer Horace mentions it as the usual overnight stop when travelers were one day's journey from Rome. He describes it colorfully as full of boatmen and cheating innkeepers. The boatmen were there because it was the starting point of a canal that ran parallel to the road. Travelers often used the comfortable canal ferries instead of the busy thoroughfare.

Even more Roman Christians meet Paul's growing group at the Three Taverns, which is about 30 miles from Rome, the last major rest stop before the city. Ancient writers describe it as having three shops, plus a blacksmith, a general store, and a restaurant.

Why do these Roman believers come out this far, a long day's journey from home? It was traditional for Romans to greet visiting dignitaries exactly this way. They would escort VIPs for the final day's trip from Three Taverns into the sprawling megalopolis. What a blessing it must have been for Paul to be honored like this after all he'd endured on the journey. This also reveals that Paul was already respected as a leader of the faith, even in his lifetime.

ROME AT LAST

And as he arrives, Paul sees Rome, a place like nothing that had ever before existed (see the next page for more details). This was the heart of an empire that stretched from Africa to England and governed over 50 million people. Paul knows that if the Jesus movement catches fire here, it will spread through merchants and statesmen to ports of call everywhere — to *the very ends of the earth*. And he's exactly right.

It's clear now that the prophecy of Jesus in Acts 1:8 will be fulfilled. Maybe that's why Luke ends his narrative so suddenly, with Paul under house arrest in Rome, teaching everyone who comes for an audience with him. It's as if he's saying, "And the rest is history."

LOOKING FOR FRIENDS

As I left my home in California for the trip I describe in these pages, the U.S. State Department issued a travel warning advising American travelers to Turkey and Israel to be constantly vigilant, keeping their eyes open for threats from enemies. I can't fault their logic, especially with the rise in international terrorism. In fact, less than a month after we returned home, two places we had visited were bombed. As Paul and his companions traveled in Acts, they had to keep their eyes open for enemies too.

But I see another dynamic at work here. Also keep your eyes open for *friends*. Wherever you go in the world, look for friendly faces and warm hearts. You may meet fellow believers. Like Paul did on his way to Rome. Or you might interact with sympathetic souls who are not yet followers of Christ, but help you on your journey. Like some of the kind Romans in Acts.

The pattern we see in Acts is true for your life and mine. Yes, there are surprise enemies. But there are also surprise friends. Travel advisory: Expect them both.

> PRAYER FOR THE JOURNEY: *Lord, open my eyes to see surprise friends around me today, not just the unpleasant surprises I face. Help me remember I'm not meant to be a loner. Help me see how others can assist me, and how I can assist them.*

THE CITY

My memories of Rome start in childhood, when I traveled there from Switzerland. All those early impressions, whether they're of the Forum or the Vatican or the modern city, are filled with the sensation of crowds: constant sound and motion, honking cars, squealing trains, zooming taxis, burping mopeds, burbling fountains, babbling foreigners.

I could almost be describing the Rome of Paul's day.

By the end of the first century, the city of Rome's population reached one million, the first time in history a city ever reached that mark.

And what a city. The Circus Maximus stadium could hold an amazing 250,000 people for world-famous chariot races held 240 days a year. A survey taken in the fourth century, when Rome was actually smaller than in the first, counted 46,602 apartment buildings, some of which reached ten stories in height. There were 290 warehouses in the business district, 1,352 swimming pools, and 12 massive public restroom complexes, the largest of which was as big as Notre Dame cathedral. Rome was referred to by its proud residents simply as *Urbs*, Latin for "The City."[5]

One common complaint about Rome in those days adds a humanizing perspective to the numbers: all the noise, noise, noise, noise. Juvenal wrote in 100 AD, "The thunder of wagons in those twisting streets, the oaths of the draymen caught in a traffic jam, would shatter the sleep of a deaf man."[6]

And in Acts 28, Paul is finally in The City. He arrives in a way he never expected, as a guest of the Roman judicial system. But he's finally here, in the center of the known world. This is the moment to which the Book of Acts has been pointing since chapter 1. Rome is the gateway to the "ends of the earth."

Ruins of the Roman Forum, the center of the city in Paul's time. (Photo credit: Marco Verch, 2015)

47
SPEAK TO THOSE WHO LISTEN
ACTS 28:17-18

I speak publicly several times a week, and have discovered no two audiences are the same. I know I'm not always riveting. But I can give the same speech to two different groups, and one will seem absorbed, while the other is bored out of their skulls. Every speaker, if they're honest, will tell you they've experienced the same thing.

Can't you hear Paul's frustration as he (once again) encounters this very dynamic? He's just received a warm response to his message on the pagan island of Melita. Even Julius, the Roman commander guarding him, now seems kind and sympathetic. But apparently his own peers, the Jewish synagogue leaders in Rome, are cold to his message about Christ.

So he quotes verses from the Jewish prophet Isaiah where God tells the prophet, basically, I'm calling you to preach to Jerusalem, but no one's gonna listen:

> "Go to this people and say,
> 'You will be ever hearing but never understanding;
>   you will be ever seeing but never perceiving.'
>
> For this people's heart has become calloused;
>   they hardly hear with their ears,
>   and they have closed their eyes.
>
> Otherwise they might see with their eyes,
>   hear with their ears,
>   understand with their hearts

and turn, and I would heal them." (Acts 28:26–27 quoting Isaiah 6:9–10 from the Septuagint)

Paul's point? Even the (temporary, not permanent, Paul explains in Romans 11) reluctance of his own countrymen to receive Jesus as their Messiah is no surprise to God. It was prophesied hundreds of years before.

REJECTED PROPHETS: A LONG TRADITION

This very same passage from Isaiah is also quoted in Matthew, Mark, Luke, John, and paraphrased in Romans. Stephen makes a similar point in his speech in Acts 7. Paul did too, in his first sermon in Acts 13. So obviously this concept had huge meaning for the early Christians. They're reminding themselves that even the message of the revered prophet Isaiah was controversial in his own time. And they're bolstering their confidence that their own belief in the *arrival* of the Messiah will one day become just as accepted as Isaiah's *prophecies* of the Messiah.

Then Paul declares he's going to focus on the Gentiles in Rome. This is not an anti-Jewish statement (remember Paul is Jewish himself). It's simply a repetition of the same strategy he's kept throughout Acts. Paul always goes to the local synagogue first, if there is one. If he receives a warm reception (like in Berea), he stays, and invites Gentiles to join Jews as he preaches. If not, he goes to a Gentile venue, where he continues to share his message, still with Jew and Gentile alike.

SPEAK TO THOSE WHO LISTEN

The principle, as Paul models, is to share Christ with everyone. But recognize it's okay to spend your time where the message is bearing the most fruit. You don't have to expend your energies equally on every opportunity. Use your time wisely. Go where the door is open.

And the quote from Isaiah reminds us that not everyone will receive every message warmly, even if it's true, free, logical, and liberating. You can share honestly and respectfully regarding your own experience with Jesus. But some will mock you. That doesn't mean you're "not doing it right." Some will hear the gospel with enthusiasm. That doesn't mean you suddenly discovered the secret key to witnessing. Some may reject the message now. That doesn't mean they won't accept it later.

Again, you can only control the content of your own message. You can't control the response to it. Don't stress over that. But like Paul, do focus your energies on the people who are responsive, on the fields that are ripe for harvest. Because that window of opportunity will not last forever.

> PRAYER FOR THE JOURNEY: *Lord, help me let go of the temptation to try to control the responses of other people. Help me see where my efforts are likely to bear the most fruit, and focus my time there.*

THE LOST AND FOUND TOMB OF LUKE

In 1998, archaeologists pried open the lid of an ancient tomb with centuries-old seals. Then an international team of over 30 experts — including specialists in ancient coins, metals, chemistry, and writing ancient scripts — undertook an investigation of human remains purported to be those of Luke, the author of Acts. After nearly a decade, the results were announced in a *New York Times* article headlined, "Body of St. Luke Gains Credibility."[7]

Orthodox tradition holds that Luke died at age 84 and was buried in Thebes, Greece. Indeed, there is a 1900-year-old tomb in Thebes with a narrow slot alleged to have once contained Luke's coffin. But Constantine transferred the casket from there to Constantinople in 357 AD. During riots in the eighth century a monk named Urio supposedly fled with Luke's casket to the town of Padua, Italy, where it was reburied under a chapel. That's the casket that was excavated a few years ago. Are these really the remains of Luke?

DNA samples extracted from a tooth in the skull showed the remains were from the right time period and location. Other evidence was equally positive. The clincher — the measurements of the casket precisely fit the slot in the ancient tomb in Thebes. Though many relics turn out to be forgeries, the body in Padua seems likely to be what it is claimed to be — the body of Luke.[8]

48
NEVER ENDING STORY

ACTS 28:30-31

So the Book of Acts ends here, with Paul in semi-freedom. He's living in his own rented house, freely teaching about Jesus, and yet he is still technically under house arrest, watched over by a Roman guard.

Is there a note of sadness in these two verses? Or is it confidence? With just a hint of a smile?

I vote the latter.

I used to get so frustrated with the ending of Acts. Why doesn't it have a standard "happily-ever-after" conclusion? But I've grown to love it. I now think that, after all the ups and downs and perils and predicaments of Paul and the others in Acts, this is the best ending possible. It's pure literature, almost a humorous wink from Luke, a sense of... "Here we go again!"

Will Paul be rescued from his house arrest? It doesn't really matter. The scene in Acts fades to black with Paul finally in Rome, at the expense of Nero himself, happily teaching, even though technically under arrest. If you've read all through Acts to this point, you have to smile, knowing that God's will is going to be accomplished in amazing, effective ways. Even if Paul is never out of his chains.

That's because in the pages of Acts, again and again, you've seen God blast through every barrier between him and the people he loves. So you have a supremely confident expectation that it's going to happen here, somehow, in some way. And it did, of course. Paul was released and went on at least one other journey, though he was eventually imprisoned in Rome again and executed by Nero. Many of Paul's letters that became books of the Bible were written during his various incarcerations.

I like the way Acts ends. After all, how's your life going to end? Ultimately most of us will be in chains of some sort as we enter life's final stage. Chains of sickness. Chains of physical or mental limitation. Chains of financial limits.

And won't you encounter chains before then? Surprising obstacles, seeming dead-ends, bureaucratic snarls, unthinking mobs enforcing their version of political correctness. You've seen it all in Acts.

And God worked through every barrier, every time. Not always by changing the circumstances. But by changing peoples' hearts. And He'll work that way in your life too.

To use a baseball analogy: The score may seem lopsided. *But God always bats last.*

The Book of Acts shows that making a difference for God, fulfilling your purpose in life, always remains a possibility for you. Even in prison. Even when shipwrecked. Even if threatened by a mob. Even as you're murdered.

But don't miss the point. This is not a story of the "indomitable spirit of faith heroes" like Peter or Paul or Stephen. The hero of the story is God. This is all about how the Holy Spirit works through these people no matter what crazy circumstance they're in.

And isn't that more exciting, and more inspiring, and more like real life than a pep talk about your potential, or a health-and-wealth promise that you'll never be sick or in trouble?

Your situation now may not be what you always envisioned. And God may change it. Or not. But this is for sure: He *will* work through it. In ways that will continue the story *He* is still writing. It's a story where you now take your place with Paul and Peter and Lydia and Tabitha and Stephen and Priscilla and Aquila and all the rest. You could say we live in Acts chapter 29. God is still breaking down barriers. And still changing the world.

> PRAYER FOR THE JOURNEY: *Father, help me realize that no matter what circumstances I'm in, I am part of the story you are still writing.*

EXPLORING FURTHER

TOMB OF PAUL

On December 11, 2006, *National Geographic* reported that Vatican archaeologists had unearthed what was apparently Paul's tomb in Rome. The sarcophagus was uncovered in Rome's Basilica of St. Paul's Outside-the-Walls, named for its location beyond the ancient walls of the city. In 2000, experts began their research to determine the truth behind centuries of tradition that Paul was buried beneath the church's altar. They found a Roman-era casket under the Latin words *Paulo Apostlo Mart* ("Paul, Apostle, Martyr").

According to early Christian writers, Paul was beheaded by Nero in 65 AD and buried in the family tomb of a Roman Christian noblewoman, Matrona Lucilla. A small chapel was built over the spot of his grave. In 390 AD, Emperor Theodosius encased Paul's remains in a larger sarcophagus and enlarged the church. Lead archaeologist Giorgio Filippi told reporters, "We know for sure it's the same object because the stone coffin is embedded in the layer of the Theodosian basilica."[9] The first scientific tests on the remains in 2009 seemed to give credence to the tradition that the casket contained the body of Paul.[10]

49
IT CAN HAPPEN AGAIN

Luke may have ended his story with Paul under house arrest because this is where Paul was living at the time he writes. And that brings me to my theory about why Luke wrote this book.

Since Acts ends abruptly with the imprisonment of Paul in Rome, Luke may have been writing on Paul's behalf to an official of the Roman court, perhaps even Paul's lawyer. The person Luke addresses Acts to, Theophilus, Greek for *"god-lover,"* may have been an influential monotheist sympathetic to Judaism. And back in Luke 1:3 he's referred to with a title that means "Your Excellency," which implies an imperial connection.

It's intriguing how often Luke goes out of his way to show how reasonable Roman officials were to Paul. Have you been noting all the clues?

- In Acts 13:12, Sergius Paulus, the governor of Cyprus, becomes a Christian.

- In Acts 18:12, the Roman governor of Achaia, Gallio, finds no fault in Paul.

- In Acts 19:36, the Ephesian city clerk rebukes the crowd trying to lynch Paul.

And you probably noticed many more examples. Of course, Luke is not blindly pro-Roman. He definitely also shows Romans acting hastily. But he seems to be making a case that, when Paul was on trial before intelligent leaders who took the time to look at all the evidence, they found his message at least *tolerable*, and sometimes even persuasive. It all points to the possibility that Luke wrote Acts as a sort of "friend of the court brief," perhaps as background for a Roman lawyer defending Paul.

Here's what we know for sure. Luke wrote this for one person. Theophilus. But then his words were collected and preserved by the very earliest Christians. They knew these stories would inspire Christians for years to come.

Are you a "God-lover"? Then these words are for you too!

And I saw the relevance of Acts in one more amazing way during my own involuntarily lengthened stay in Athens.

HIS MESSAGE FOR YOU
Back to the beginning. I started this book in Athens. I was stranded by slow bureaucracy for a few days after my passport was stolen.

Let me take you back to that church service where I'd been asked to share. At the very end of the service, two young people from Kurdistan, new believers, were baptized. And as they posed for a photograph with their family at the front of the church, they beckoned enthusiastically to someone in the congregation to join them for the snapshot. I remember thinking they must have a shy friend, because they kept shouting, "Come, come! You are family."

I looked around to see the shy one. Then I realized they were gesturing to *me*.

"Me?" I ask. "Yes," they insist. "You are part of us now. We're all Christians, and we're all stuck in Greece."

And I run up and put my arms around family.

Remember the verse from Acts I shared with that church? *Do not be afraid. Many people in this city belong to me.*

And as I wrap up our trip through Acts, I believe these are God's words for you too. Wherever you are.

Life can get tough. It can seem like the circumstances you face are too hard. Especially if you take seriously the commission from Jesus to be his witness everywhere you go. Sometimes it feels like the barriers are just too high.

God says, Do not be afraid. Don't give up. Keep being a witness. You are not alone. I am with you. And I have many people in your city.

Can't you use those words right now?

See, that's the truly supernatural thing about the Bible. I'm sure you've felt it on our journey. Words written two millennia ago — the very same words — still speak to you and me today.

IT CAN HAPPEN AGAIN

That's because the same Spirit who inspired those words *still empowers you today.*

All the stories of how people survived shipwrecks and dodged conspiracies and endured maddening red tape and met influential God-seekers and found unexpected friends and received mighty spiritual power to do amazing things — *they can all happen again.*

So go be his witness. To the very ends of the earth.

May the odyssey continue.

> PRAYER FOR THE JOURNEY: *Lord, my prayer is simple: May it happen again. Through me!*

ENDNOTES

PART ONE: THE PROMISE AND THE POWER

1. Tony Perrottet, *Pagan Holiday: On The Trail of Ancient Roman Tourists* (New York: Random House, 2003), 141.

2. Max Lucado, *Outlive Your Life* (Nashville: Thomas Nelson, 2010), 12.

3. William Barclay, *The Acts of the Apostles* (Philadelphia: Westminster Press, 1976), 15.

4. Perrottet, 141.

5. Merilyn Hargis, "On The Road: The Inns and Outs of Travel in First-Century Palestine," *Christian History* 59, accessed at www.christianitytoday.com/history/issues/issue-59/on-road.html

6. Perrottet, 141.

7. Ibid.

8. Paul Zacharia, "The Surprisingly Early History of Christianity in India," *Smithsonian Journals Quarterly*, Feb 19, 2016, accessed July 8, 2016, http://www.smithsonianmag.com/travel/how-christianity-came-to-india-kerala-180958117/?no-ist

9. This outline adapted with great appreciation from a sermon I once read by Ray Stedman.

10. Lionel Casson, *Ships and Seamanship in the Ancient World* (Princeton: Princeton University Press, 1971), 108.

11. Ibid.

12. Lucado, 5.

13. Clement, "First Epistle of Clement to the Corinthians," *Early Christian Writings*, accessed June 25, 2016, www.oneonta.edu/faculty/farberas/arth/arth212/early_christian_texts.html

PART TWO: NEW FRIENDS AND NEW ENEMIES

1. *Jesus and the Gospels: Online Museum*, accessed at http://gospelsmuseum.div.ed.ac.uk/exhibits/show/caiaphas-ossuary/discovery-and-preservation

2. Josephus, *Jewish Antiquities* 18:95.

3. John Ortberg, *When the Game Is Over, It All Goes Back in the Box* (Grand Rapids: Zondervan, 2009), 14.

4. Josephus, *War*, 6.5.4 312–315.

5. Library of Congress exhibit accessed July 8, 2016 at: https://www.loc.gov/exhibits/americancolony/amcolony-aid.html

6. Ibid.

7. Ibid.

8. Warren Wiersbe, *Wiersbe's Expository Outlines on the New Testament* (Colorado Springs, CO: David C. Cook, 1992), 83.

9. I first learned the descriptive vs. prescriptive distinction from *How to Read the Bible for All Its Worth* by Fee and Stuart

10. N.T. Wright, *Acts for Everyone, Vol. 1* (Louisville, Kentucky: Westminster John Knox Press), 2008, 85.

11. D. A. Carson, *Love in Hard Places* (Wheaton, Ill.: Crossway, 2002), 61.

12. Rudolph P. Boshoff, "First Century ossuaries reveals Biblical names," *The American Journal of Archaeology* (Oct.–Dec., 1947, LI.4, pp. 351ff.), accessed June 27, 2016, http://rabtessera.blogspot.com/2013/09/first-century-ossuaries-reveals.html

13. Wayne Jackson, "Another Voice from the Tomb," *Christian-Courier.com*, accessed June 18, 2016, https://www.christian-courier.com/articles/588-another-voice-from-the-tomb

PART THREE: SWORD AND SORCERY

1. "Tomb of Apostle Philip Found," *Bible History Daily* (October 16, 2015), accessed at http://www.biblicalarchaeology.org/

ENDNOTES

daily/biblical-sites-places/biblical-archaeology-sites/tomb-of-apostle-philip-found/

2. Matthew L. Skinner, *Intrusive God, Disruptive Gospel: Encountering the Divine in the Book of Acts* (Grand Rapids: Brazos, 2015), 61.

3. Hargis.

4. Strabo, *Geography*, 14.5.13.

5. Acts of Thecla 3, cited in William Ramsay and Mark Wilson, *St. Paul: The Traveler and Roman Citizen* (Grand Rapids: Kregel), 46.

6. Ibid.

7. Wright, 170.

8. Lucado, 144–145.

9. Josephus, *War*, 2.17.2, 408–410.

PART FOUR: GOING GLOBAL

1. Wright, 177.

2. *Life of Josephus*, (31) 150.

3. Perrottet, 4.

4. Ibid., 5.

5. Tony Perrottet, "Jupiter's Panorama," *Route 66 A.D.: On the Trail of Ancient Roman Tourists*, accessed June 17, 2016, http://www.worldcat.org/wcpa/servlet/DCARead?standardNo=037550432X&standardNoType=1&excerpt=true

6. Jim Collins quoted in Max Lucado, *You'll Get Through This*, (Nashville: Thomas Nelson, 2015), 149–150.

7. Thomas Cahill, *Sailing the Wine-Dark Sea: Why The Greeks Matter* (New York: Doubleday, 2003), 238.

8. Ibid., 252–253.

9. Daniel Berrigan, "Advent Credo," *Journey with Jesus*, accessed

July 9, 2016, http://www.journeywithjesus.net/PoemsAnd-Prayers/Daniel_Berrigan_Advent_Credo.shtml

10. N.T. Wright, *Acts for Everyone, Part 2* (Louisville, Kentucky: Westminster John Knox Press, 2008), 29.

11. Amanda Foreman, "Hotels From Ur to Us," *Wall Street Journal*, May 7–8, 2016, C12.

12. John Ortberg, *The Life You've Always Wanted: Spiritual Disciplines for Ordinary People* (Grand Rapids: Zondervan, 2002), 33–34.

13. Ben Witherington, *The Acts of the Apostles: A Socio-Rhetorical Commentary*, (Grand Rapids: Eerdman's, 1998), 464.

14. F.F. Bruce quoted in Witherington, *The Acts of the Apostles*, 464.

15. PGM XII.14–95, cited in Witherington, *The Acts of the Apostles*, 464.

16. R. M. Ogilvie quoted in Witherington, *The Acts of the Apostles* 464.

17. 20th Homily of Chrysostom, quoted Witherington, *The Acts of the Apostles*, 463.

PART FIVE: RIOTS AND REVELATIONS

1. See Rodney Stark, *The Rise of Christianity: How the Obscure, Marginal Jesus Movement Became the Dominant Religious Force in the Western World in a Few Centuries* (San Francisco: HarperSanFrancisco, 1997).

2. Catherine Kroeger, "The Neglected Role of Women in the Early Church," *Christian History* (17:1988), accessed at http://www.christianitytoday.com/history/issues/issue-17/neglected-history-of-women-in-early-church.html

3. *NOVA: Secrets of the Parthenon*, aired January 28, 2009, PBS

4. An idea adapted from Paul Copan and Kenneth D. Litwak, *The Gospel in the Marketplace of Ideas: Paul's Mars Hill Experience for Our Pluralistic World* (Downer's Grove: IVP Academic, 2014), 93.

5. Quarles, Charles L., *Illustrated Life of Paul,* Nashville, B&H, 2014), 113.

6. N.T. Wright, "Jesus and the Identity of God," *Ex Auditu* 14 (1998): 44, as quoted in Copan, 97. See also Diogenes Laertius, *Vit.* 10.131.

7. Copan, 34.

8. Quarles, 115.

9. These descriptions adapted from Quarles, 119.

10. Ibid., 120.

PART SIX: ATTACKS AND ASSASSINS

1. Norman Geisler and Joseph M. Holden, *The Popular Handbook of Archaeology and the Bible* (Eugene: Harvest House, 2013), 357.

2. Pliny, *Letters,* 10.96–97.

3. Hargis.

4. Nina Strochlic, "Christian Monks Square Off at One of Jerusalem's Holiest Sites," *The Daily Beast* (July 4, 2013), accessed May 10, 2016 at http://www.thedailybeast.com/articles/2013/07/04/christian-monks-square-off-at-one-of-jeru-salem-s-holiest-sites.html

5. Skinner, 153.

6. Ibid., 158.

7. Doron Mendels, "Why Paul Went West: The Differences Between the Jewish Diasporas," *Biblical Archaeology Review,* 37 Vol. 1, January/February 2011, 53.

8. Josephus, *Antiquities* 13.10.7 and 20.8.8 180–181.

9. Adapted from Dale Carnegie, *How to Win Friends and Influence People* (New York: Simon & Schuster; Rev Sub edition, 1981), 94.

10. Perrottet, 207.

11. Lionel Casson, "Speed Under Sail of Ancient Ships," *Transactions*

of the American Philological Association Vol. 82 (1951), 136–148 accessed July 9, 2016, http://penelope.uchicago.edu/ Thayer/E/Journals/TAPA/82/Speed_under_Sail_of_Ancient_ Ships*.html

PART SEVEN: SERPENTS AND SHIPWRECKS

1. Perrottet, 191.

2. Descriptions of ancient shipping from Perrottet, 190–195.

3. Ibid., 208–9.

4. Stephan Mifsud, "Which viper bit St. Paul in Malta?" *Times of Malta*, accessed July 9, 2016, http://www.timesofmalta.com/ articles/view/20140219/opinion/Which-viper-bit-St-Paul-in-Malta-.507396

5. Perrottet, 40.

6. Ibid., 42.

7. Nicholas Wade, "'Body of St. Luke' Gains Credibility," in *The New York Times* (October 16, 2001), accessed June 25, 2016, http://www.nytimes.com/2001/10/16/world/body-of-st-luke-gains-credibility.html

8. Brian Janeway, *Associates for Biblical Research* (May 27, 2015), accessed June 25, 2016, http://www.biblearchaeol-ogy.org/post/2015/05/27/The-Tomb-of-Luke-the-Evangelist. aspx#Article

9. Maria Cristina Valsecchi, "St. Paul's Tomb Unearthed in Rome," *National Geographic News* (December 11, 2006), accessed June 15, 2016 http://news.nationalgeographic.com/ news/2006/12/061211-saint-paul.html

10. "Pope Says Tests 'Seem to Conclude' Bones Are the Apostle Paul's," *The New York Times* (June 28, 2009), accessed June 15, 2016, http://www.nytimes.com/2009/06/29/science/29vatican. html

RESOURCES

Many books and sermons and conversations provided invaluable insights into the history and context of Acts, including, but not limited to, the ones I've listed here. Especially useful were the books below by N. T. Wright, John Stott, Ben Witherington III, and travel writer Tony Perrottet. Their writings are heavily quoted and referenced in these pages. I was also greatly helped by online sermons from Ray Stedman and Mark Driscoll, particularly for the videos we filmed on site. Stedman's sermons were so influential in my understanding of the Bible. I have paraphrased him a lot in these pages because his insights need to be heard by a new generation. Long on-the-road discussions with Tulu Gokkadar, our Turkish guide and archaeologist, also provided helpful background. If I didn't reference a fact in the text, that's probably because it found its way into my travel diary courtesy of Tulu or another local expert along the way.

Barclay, William B., *The Acts of the Apostles,* Louisville, Kentucky: Westminster John Knox Press, 1973.

Bruce, F.F., *The Book of Acts*, Grand Rapids: Eerdmans, 1988.

Breaking Down Barriers: Journeys of the Apostle Paul, Goshen College Communication Department, Distributed by Vision Video, Worcester, PA.

Cahill, Thomas, *Sailing the Wine-Dark Sea: Why The Greeks Matter,* New York: Doubleday, 2003.

Casson, Lionel, *Ships and Seamanship in the Ancient World*, Princeton: Princeton University Press, 1971.

Cimok, Fatih, *Journeys of Paul*, Istanbul: Mumhane Caddesi Mangir Sokak, 2004.

Copan, Paul and Litwak, Kenneth D., *The Gospel in the Marketplace of Ideas: Paul's Mars Hill Experience for Our Pluralistic World*, Downer's Grove: IVP Academic, 2014.

Drane, John, *Paul*, New York: Harper & Row, 1976.

Fairchild, Mark R., "Why Perga: Paul's Perilous Passage Through Pisidia," *Biblical Archaeology Review* 39 6, Nov–Dec 2013: 52–59.

Fant, Gerald E., and Reddish, Mitchell G., *A Guide to Biblical Sites in Turkey and Greece*, Oxford: Oxford University Press, 2003.

Foreman, Amanda, "Hotels From Ur to Us," *Wall Street Journal*, May 7–8, 2016, C12.

Gallagher, Robert L., and Hertig, Paul, ed., *Mission in Acts: Ancient Narratives in Contemporary Context*, Maryknoll, New York: Orbis, 2007.

Geisler, Norman, and Holden, Joseph M., *The Popular Handbook of Archaeology and the Bible*, Eugene: Harvest House, 2013, 357.

Hargis, Merilyn, "On The Road: The Inns and Outs of Travel in First-Century Palestine," *Christian History*, Issue 59, accessed at http://www.christianitytoday.com/history/issues/issue-59/on-road.html

Hemer, Colin, *The Book of Acts in the Setting of Hellenistic History*, Tuebingen: J. C. B. Mohr, 1989.

Hurtado, Larry W., *The Earliest Christian Artifacts: Manuscripts and Christian Origins*, Grand Rapids: Eerdmans, 2006.

Lucado, Max, *Acts*, Nashville: Thomas Nelson, 2006.

Lucado, Max, *Out Live Your Life*, Nashville: Thomas Nelson, 2010.

Mendels, Doron, "Why Paul Went West: The Differences Between the Jewish Diasporas," *Biblical Archaeology Review*, Vol. 37, No. 1, January/February 2011, 53.

Ortberg, John, *When the Game Is Over, It All Goes Back in the Box*, Grand Rapids: Zondervan, 2009.

Perrottet, Tony, *Pagan Holiday*, New York: Random House, 2003.

RESOURCES

Quarles, Charles L., *Illustrated Life of Paul,* Nashville, B&H, 2014.

Ramsay, William M., and Wilson, Mark, ed., *St. Paul: The Traveler and Roman Citizen,* Grand Rapids: Kregel, 2001.

Sanneh, Lamin, *Whose Religion Is Christianity? The Gospel Beyond the West,* Grand Rapids: Eerdmans, 2003.

Skinner, Matthew L., *Intrusive God, Disruptive Gospel: Encountering the Divine in the Book of Acts,* Grand Rapids: Brazos, 2015.

Stott, John, *Acts: Seeing the Spirit at Work,* Downer's Grove: InterVarsity, 1998.

Stott, John, *The Spirit The Church and the World: The Message of Acts,* Downer's Grove: InterVarsity, 1990.

Vermes, Geza, "From Jewish to Gentile: How the Jesus Movement Became Christianity," *Biblical Archaeology Review* 38 6, Nov–Dec 2012: 53–58, 76.

Walker, Peter, *In The Steps of Saint Paul: An Illustrated Guide to Paul's Journeys,* Oxford: Lion Books, 2008.

Wilson, Mark, *Biblical Turkey: A Guide to the Jewish and Christian Sites of Asia Minor,* Third ed., Istanbul: Ege Yayinlari, 2014.

Witherington III, Ben, *The Acts of the Apostles: A Socio-Rhetorical Commentary,* Grand Rapids: Eerdmans, 1998.

Wright, N.T., *Acts for Everyone, Parts 1 & 2,* Louisville, Kentucky: Westminster John Knox Press, 2008.

Zacharia, Paul, "The Surprisingly Early History of Christianity in India," *Smithsonian Journals Quarterly,* Feb 19, 2016, accessed July 8, 2016 at http://www.smithsonianmag.com/travel/how-christianity-came-to-india-kerala-180958117/?no-ist

ACTS ODYSSEY

GROUP DISCUSSION
RESOURCES

PRINCIPLES FOR STUDYING ACTS

When studying a "narrative" part of the Bible like Acts (narrative just means that it reads like a story instead of a letter or list of rules) there are some basic common-sense guidelines:

THE FIRST STEP
Read Acts like you'd read a book or novel, all the way through, or at least one long section at a time instead of just one verse at a time. That way you get a big-picture sense of where the story is going.

THE SECOND STEP
Ask if there is a principle for Christian living being modeled or taught here.

Remember the descriptive/prescriptive distinction: If you think you see principles for living *described* in the story you're studying, ask if that principle is also explicitly *prescribed* in other Bible passages.

For example, in Acts 18:9, Jesus tells Paul in a vision, "Do not be afraid, for I am with you." In Acts 23:11, Jesus tells him in another vision, "Take courage!" In Acts 27:24, Paul describes another vision where Jesus told him, "Do not be afraid." Those verses seem to teach a principle: You should be courageous and not afraid, because Jesus is with you!

But how do you know this doesn't just *describe* what was true for Paul? How do you know it applies to you too? Because that principle is taught *prescriptively* in many places in the Bible, in places like Matthew 10:28, where Jesus tells his disciples not to fear people—even those who have the power to kill. Or Hebrews 13:6: "We can confidently say, 'The Lord is my helper, I will not be afraid. What can man do to me?'"

PRINCIPLES FOR STUDYING ACTS

THE THIRD STEP

Ask if there is a repeatable pattern in this story. Stories in Acts can have illustrative and "pattern value," even if that particular point may not have been Luke's primary purpose in that story, and even if it's not a command for every Christian.

In other words, you don't have to argue all Christians *must* do this or they're disobeying God's Word. But you can say that it's *possible* for Christians to do this, because, even if it's not *prescribed*, at least there is *precedent*. You don't have to conclude, "We *must* do this," but you can say, "We *may* do this." I know some would disagree with me, but I would argue that speaking in tongues falls into this category in Acts. Nowhere does Luke say this *must* happen to every believer. But apparently it did happen to some. So it is something that is possible but not required. And there is *prescriptive* teaching about speaking in tongues in 1 Corinthians 14, where Paul gives instructions on how and where and when it can happen.

THE FOURTH STEP

Go back to the big picture. What is this story in Acts to show? The big picture of the whole Book of Acts is the spread of the gospel across the world against overwhelming odds through the power of the Holy Spirit.

Luke seems to me to be suggesting that this same vigor and courage and power can be part of the readers' lives too. Certainly Christ's *prescriptive* commission to the disciples applies to all believers: Be his witnesses, everywhere you go, empowered by the Spirit. Then Luke *describes* ways that happened.

So ask how that applies to you: What discouraging or challenging situations are you facing? God can use them and work through you to spread the gospel in ways that may long outlive you, with impact beyond your wildest dreams. Just as he does on every page of Acts!

VIDEO GROUP DISCUSSION QUESTIONS

You can find these videos we filmed on location at our website: www.tlc.org/acts. They are designed to enhance your personal or group study of Acts Odyssey.

WEEK 1
JERUSALEM

TOUCH BASE

Take some time to go around the room and briefly introduce yourselves. What are you hoping to gain from studying the Book of Acts and the early church?

TAKE IT IN

- Watch Video #1: *Jerusalem*
- Read Acts 1:1–12 and Acts 2:1–8; 14–41

As you watch the video, take notes on the elements of Peter's speech.

He talks about:

Two_____ (the crucifixion and the resurrection)

Two_____ (the prophets and the apostles)

Two_____ (forgiveness and the Spirit)

Two_____ (believe and be baptized)

The first church is a...

_____ church

_____ church

_____ church

_____ church

_____ church

JERUSALEM

TALK IT OUT

1. What do you think this "speaking in tongues" miracle is really all about? In other words: Why do you think it's significant that the first public miracle in the history of Christianity (after Christ) was this amazing moment when the international pilgrims to Jerusalem all hear the disciples speaking in their own languages? What could God be showing through this about his heart for all these people?

2. Look at the elements of Peter's speech. In your own personal experience with churches in your life, which (if any) teachings were under-emphasized?

   ❏ The crucifixion

   ❏ The resurrection

   ❏ The prophets (the Old Testament, or Hebrew Scriptures, especially prophecies about Jesus)

   ❏ The apostles (The New Testament, especially the epistles from apostles like Peter, John, and Paul that contain their teaching)

   ❏ Forgiveness

   ❏ The Holy Spirit

   ❏ Personal belief in Christ and repentance

   ❏ Baptism

3. What can churches do to make sure those aspects are not left out?

4. What is attractive to you in the descriptions of the early believers in Acts 2:42–47?

5. Look at the five characteristics of the early church on the next page. In your own personal experience with churches in your life, which if any do you think has been under-emphasized?

305

6. What practical steps can churches take to try and encourage all these characteristics:

- A learning church:

  "They devoted themselves to the apostles' teaching…"

- A loving church:

  "…and to fellowship… all the believers were together and had everything in common. They sold property and possessions to give to anyone who had need."

- A worshipping church:

  "Everyone was filled with awe… They continued to meet together in the temple courts… praising God…"

- A joyful church:

  "They broke bread in their homes and ate together with glad and sincere hearts…"

- A growing church:

  "And the Lord added to their number daily those who were being saved…"

TAKE IT WITH YOU

Speaking honestly, does anything about these descriptions of the early church make you feel uncomfortable? What is it? Though it makes you uncomfortable, are you open to God working in that way in your life? Or at least open to praying for God to work in your life however he pleases?

For next week, come prepared to briefly share your own spiritual journey, in 4 minutes or less. How did you become a believer in Jesus? Did someone share Christ with you? Did it happen suddenly or slowly? What was the biggest thing that caught your attention and drew you in to Christianity? If you would not yet identify as a

Christian, consider sharing with the group your spiritual journey so far.

TALK TO GOD

Take some time to share prayer requests with each other. Have someone close in prayer, asking God to give you all the courage to read Acts with fresh eyes, open to what God wants to say to you and how he wants to grow you.

WEEK 2
DAMASCUS ROAD

TOUCH BASE

What impacted or encouraged you this week from the daily devotions? Share one highlight from your week.

TAKE IT IN

- Watch Video #2: *Damascus Road*
- Read Acts 7:58b–8:3 and 9:1–15

TALK IT OUT

1. Prior to his conversion, how does the Bible describe Saul? (See Acts 7:58b–8:3)

2. What do you think was it was about Saul's background that would make him particularly effective as a spokesman for Christ?

   ❑ He was a Type-A person

   ❑ He was a religious person

   ❑ He was an observant Jew

   ❑ He spoke several languages

   ❑ He was well-educated

   ❑ He was a Roman citizen

   ❑ Other:

3. How have you seen God use something in your background in a way that has surprised you?

4. Talk about light bulb moments: The light literally dawns on

Paul when he has this encounter in Acts 9. Describe your own faith journey. Was there a "light bulb moment" on your road to faith or in your spiritual growth? Did it happen suddenly or slowly? At home, at church, or somewhere else? What was the biggest thing that caught your attention and drew you into (or back into) Christianity?

If you would not yet identify as a Christian, share your spiritual journey so far. What brought you to this study?

5. Saul was so certain he knew all about God—yet when God appears to him in the vision, Saul doesn't even know him. He is totally surprised by what God is really like. Did anything surprise you about what God is like the more you drew near to faith in Christ? Or perhaps you, like Saul, were a religious person who discovered something surprising and delightful about God as you grew in your faith. What was it?

6. In most of his sermons in Acts, Paul refers in some way to this personal experience: The risen Lord has touched his life in a powerful way! Why do *personal* stories of faith have so much impact?

7. How have you "witnessed" God working lately?

TAKE IT WITH YOU

In the video, René said, "You can spend your days worrying that something is going to get you. Or you can live knowing God has already got you." What is worrying you these days? Share it with the group and ask for prayer that you would have serenity even in the face of this.

TALK TO GOD

Take some time to pray about the worries that you have shared with each other. Ask God to give each of you the peace and serenity that comes from knowing that God is with you and will never leave you.

WEEK 3
CAESAREA

TOUCH BASE
What impacted or encouraged you this week in the daily devotions? Share one high point from your week.

TAKE IT IN
- Watch Video #3: *Caesarea*
- Read Acts 10:1–48

TALK IT OUT
1. Peter was a religiously observant Jew, keeping all the kosher food laws as best he could. That meant no shellfish, no eels, no pork, and many other dietary restrictions. Then he has this vision in which God declares that all food is clean. This recalls a couple verses in the Bible:

   - Read Genesis 9:3. Here God gives Noah everything to eat.

   - Read Matthew 15:10–20. Here Jesus declares that the rigorous enforcement of kosher laws by the Pharisees misses the point. It's not what goes into your stomach that defiles you, but what comes out of your heart.

     What does this mean? Why do you think this was so difficult for Peter (and the other early Christians) to accept?

2. How do you see God preparing both Peter and Cornelius in this passage? How are you encouraged by their faith? How did Peter's vision change his view of God and the church?

3. Acts 10:34–42 contains the essential Christian message that has

remained unchanged for 2,000 years. The truly revolutionary part of this message is that God shows no favoritism; he treats all people equally, and invites all to come to him through faith in Christ. How do you struggle with living this out? Have you ever felt separated because of racial or cultural differences?

4. How can a lack of unity be harmful to the church? What are some practical ways you can be part of bringing unity in your church?

5. Racial tension continues to harm society today. Is there a step you can take in your neighborhood, church, or even your small group to reach out to people from a different racial or ethnic background? What are the obstacles to bridging these gaps? What are the benefits?

TAKE IT WITH YOU

Take an honest inventory — what prejudices are you holding on to? Maybe you're prejudice towards people who are a different race than you, or people who are more conservative than you, or more liberal than you, or poor, or rich, the list of ways we judge people is way too long! How can you move towards Peter's "aha moment" where he says, "I now realize how true it is that God does not show favoritism..."?

TALK TO GOD

Take some time to share prayer requests with each other. Have someone close in prayer, asking God to help you each embrace and live out the truth of God's wide and gracious love.

WEEK 4
THESSALONICA

TOUCH BASE

What impacted or encouraged you this week in the daily devotions? Who have been two of the most influential women in your life and why?

TAKE IT IN

- Watch Video #4: *Thessalonica*
- Read Acts 17:1–15

Video Notes:

Four Truths:

God's will is not always _____

God's purpose is more important than _____

There will always be opportunities so _____ !

Judge everything by the _____

TALK IT OUT

1. Thessalonica was a wealthy trading city on a major road. How was Paul received there? What accusations did Paul encounter?

2. What cultural barriers were being broken down in Thessalonica?

3. Who are the early adopters of Paul's message? Why do you think it was so appealing to them?

4. What are some things that hold people back today from

accepting the Gospel? What can you do to break down barriers with the true message of the Gospel?

5. Paul is charged with turning the world upside down. In what ways is he really helping to set it right?

TAKE IT WITH YOU
The Gospel has the power to break down all barriers. What barrier in your town needs to be broken by Jesus Christ's power? How about in your life? How can you move towards barrier-breaking this week?

God was working through Paul and Silas to turn the world right-side up again. But when you yourself are upside-down, right-side up appears to be upside-down! What area in your life needs to be turned right-side up by God?

TALK TO GOD
Take some time to share prayer requests with each other. Have someone close in prayer, asking God to turn what is upside-down right-side up in your lives.

WEEK 5
ATHENS

TOUCH BASE
What impacted or encouraged you this week in the daily devotions?

If Paul were addressing your friends and neighbors today, how would he start? What positive aspect of the culture would he first highlight as a bridge to the Gospel? Complete this sentence:

"People of (my town/community), I see in every way you are very _____."

TAKE IT IN
- Watch Video #5: *Athens*
- Read Acts 17:16–34

TALK IT OUT
1. What was the city of Athens like in those days? How is the cultural environment we live in today similar or different? What impresses you about Paul's experience in Athens?

2. What was Paul's reaction when he saw the multitude of gods and idols in Athens? What distresses you about your town and would it line up with what distressed Paul? What action did Paul take (vv. 16–17)? What does this tell you about the kind of person Paul has become versus what he was like before his encounter with Christ?

3. How did the Athenians react when they heard Paul speaking in the marketplace (vv. 18–21)? Do you see a similar reaction as you share and live out your faith?

4. How did Paul compare/contrast the "unknown god" to the one true God? What does Paul say about God (vv. 24–29)?

5. How does God respond to man's pursuit of substitute gods and idols (vv. 30–31)? Once the Gospel is heard, what is the hearer's responsibility (v. 30)? How did the Athenians respond to Paul's message of the Gospel (vv. 32–34)?

6. How can you follow Paul's example in the way he approached the Athenians with the Gospel? Are there any opportunities in the course of your daily activities you might have to share the Gospel with others in this way?

TAKE IT WITH YOU

What "unknown gods" (idols) are you tempted to "worship"? Think about things in which you seek self worth, status, fulfillment, comfort, stress-relief, happiness, satisfaction, etc. Any thing (or person!) you rely on, or seek your value in, can become an object of worship.

TALK TO GOD

Take some time to share prayer requests with each other. Have someone close in prayer, asking God to help each one of you turn towards God this week and worship him above all else. Pray for the boldness of Paul to share the Gospel this week.

WEEK 6
CORINTH

TOUCH BASE

What impacted or encouraged you this week in the daily devotions? Have you ever moved or visited a new city and felt lost? How did you settle in or find your way in that situation?

TAKE IT IN

- Watch Video #6: *Corinth*
- Read Acts 18:1–28

TALK IT OUT

1. What kind of people did Paul surround himself with? How do you think serving alongside others encouraged and strengthened Paul's ministry?

2. Paul began his work, as usual, in the synagogue. What verbs are found in verses 5 and 6 that show Paul's passion for the gospel?

3. How does God encourage Paul in verses 9–10? Why do you suppose God timed it after "many of the Corinthians who heard Paul believed and were baptized" (vs. 8)?

4. Have you ever felt, when things are going well in your life, that there might be something bad just around the corner? Why do you suppose we tend towards this fear?

5. Someone once said, "Trust Sovereignty when there is no clarity." What does this mean to you? How does the Book of Acts demonstrate this truth?

6. In this story, Paul's freedom to preach is affirmed by a surprising source: the pagan Roman governor. How have you seen God work through non-believers or secular authorities to advance the Gospel? How does that encourage you?

7. In what ways have you seen God working in your city, community, or neighborhood to set people free?

TAKE IT WITH YOU

No doubt Priscilla and Aquila were a tremendous encouragement and support to Paul in his ministry. Who in your life needs you to come alongside them for a season to support and to encourage them? How will you do that this week?

TALK TO GOD

Take some time to share prayer requests with each other. Have someone close in prayer, thanking God for the Priscillas and Aquilas in your lives and asking God to open your eyes to see how you can be an encouragement and support to people around you this week.

WEEK 7
CAESAREA MARITIME

TOUCH BASE

What impacted or encouraged you this week in the daily devotions? Think of someone you know that has withstood extreme hardship or pressure well. What did you learn from watching them stay strong?

TAKE IT IN

• Watch Video #7 *Caesarea Maritime*
• Read Acts 22:1–29

TALK IT OUT

1. What is Paul accused of in Acts 21:27-29? What is Paul guilty of? Have your intentions ever been misunderstood? How did you respond?

2. Look at Paul's defense in Acts 22:1–29:

   • vv. 1–3: How does Paul open his testimony? How would you describe his tone?

   • vv. 4–5: How does Paul describe his past religious actions?

   • vv. 8–11: What is most striking to you about Paul's encounter with God?

   • vv. 12–16: Who came to see Paul? Why do you think God chose him to visit Paul?

   • v. 21: What does God commission Paul to do?

   • vv. 22–24: How did the crowd respond to Paul's defense? Why do you think they responded this way?

   • vv. 27–29: What does Paul reveal about himself in these verses and why does it matter? Why do you think he waited to reveal this?

3. In what ways are you like or unlike Paul in your response when falsely accused?

4. After reading Paul's testimony in this passage and learning about him throughout the Book of Acts, what do you see in his life that you'd like to imitate?

5. (If your group plans to meet next week for a series-ending celebration save this question for next week. If this is your last week, take a moment to think and share your answer now.)

As we wrap up our study of the Book of Acts what resonated most with you? (Some options: The many examples of perseverance through trial, an anticipation that God will work in great ways, the work of the Holy Spirit, the kindness of the Christians — especially Paul — towards those who were persecuting them, how the early church impacted all of church history, how diverse the church was — Jews, Gentiles, men, women, slave, free, etc.)

TAKE IT WITH YOU
"But I have had God's help to this very day…" (Acts 26:22a)

The history of the first church and its beginning depicts bitter persecution and miraculous triumph! But the courage of the early Christians to stand firm despite suffering testifies to the power of the Gospel and faith in God that is available to us all. The same Spirit who empowered the early believers empowers you today!

How have you seen "God's help to this very day" in your life recently?

TALK TO GOD
For the final time, take some time to share prayer requests with each other. Have someone close in prayer, thanking God for the opportunity to study his word together. Pray that God will use each one of you as he continues to write the story of his bride, the church.

THANKS

First of all, thanks to my wonderful wife Laurie for her editorial suggestions and encouragement.

I'm so grateful to our absolutely amazing book and video production team: Jamie Rom, Valerie Webb, Kevin Deutsch, Kéla Toback, Martin Olander, Karen O'Connor, David Schlaepfer, and many more. Mark Spurlock's great insights into Paul's shipwreck were very useful in chapters 43 and 44. Thanks also to Jennifer Andrew, Kim Breuninger, Jim Josselyn and Jane Romberger for their help in writing the small group discussion questions.

Finally, special thanks to Levent Oral of Tutku Tours for arranging wonderful visits to Turkey and Greece. While we had many great guides on various trips to the places in the Book of Acts, Tulu Gökkadar in Turkey and Kenny Garon in Israel stand out as exceptional.